D1368484

Picture Yourself Making Creative Movies with Corel® VideoStudio Pro® X5

Marc Bech

Course Technology PTR
A part of Cengage Learning

COURSE TECHNOLOGY
CENGAGE Learning™

Australia • Brazil • Japan • Korea • Mexico • Singapore • Spain • United Kingdom • United States

COURSE TECHNOLOGY
CENGAGE Learning™

Picture Yourself Making Creative Movies with Corel® VideoStudio Pro® X5

Marc Bech

Publisher and General Manager, Course Technology PTR:
Stacy L. Hiquet

Associate Director of Marketing:
Sarah Panella

Manager of Editorial Services:
Heather Talbot

Senior Marketing Manager:
Mark Hughes

Acquisitions Editor: Heather Hurley

Project Editor/Proofreader:
Karen A. Gill

Technical Reviewer:
Jason Harrison

Copy Editor: Sara Gullion

Interior Layout Tech:
Judy Littlefield

Cover Designer: Mike Tanamachi

Indexer: Larry Sweazy

For product information and technology assistance, contact us at
Cengage Learning Customer & Sales Support, 1-800-354-9706.

For permission to use material from this text or product, submit all requests online at **cengage.com/permissions.**

Further permissions questions can be e-mailed to
permissionrequest@cengage.com.

Corel KPT Texture Explorer, Painter, PaintShop Photo Pro, VideoStudio Pro, and WinZip are trademarks or registered trademarks of Corel Corporation and/or its subsidiaries in Canada, the United States, and/or other countries.

All other trademarks are the property of their respective owners.

All images © Cengage Learning unless otherwise noted.

Library of Congress Control Number: 2012936598

ISBN-13: 978-1-285-07901-1

ISBN-10: 1-285-07901-9

Course Technology, a part of Cengage Learning
20 Channel Center Street
Boston, MA 02210
USA

Cengage Learning is a leading provider of customized learning solutions with office locations around the globe, including Singapore, the United Kingdom, Australia, Mexico, Brazil, and Japan. Locate your local office at: **international.cengage.com/region.**

Cengage Learning products are represented in Canada by Nelson Education, Ltd.

For your lifelong learning solutions, visit **courseptr.com.**

Visit our corporate Web site at **cengage.com.**

Printed in the United States of America
1 2 3 4 5 6 7 14 13 12

To my daughter Jacqueline,
who has brought meaning to my life.
I love you more every day.

Acknowledgments

My name may be on the cover, but there is a small army of people behind the scenes who got this book into your hands or on your computer. My project editor Karen Gill has the patience of the Dalai Lama, the sense of humor of Seinfeld, and more detail than a quad core processor. I would also like to thank Heather Hurley, my acquisitions editor, for helping to keep this project on track with an equal amount of concern and patience.

Jason Harrison, technical editor, made me look good by checking and rechecking that all the lessons and files worked as written and that terms were correctly and logically explained. Thank you to Corel for comarketing this book with me and for giving me access to Jan Piros, senior strategic product manager, and Greg Wood, digital media product marketing manager.

There are also many layout and quality assurance folks too numerous to mention. I have a newfound respect for the publishing industry.

About the Author

Marc Bech started his digital career at Macromedia (before the company coined the term *multimedia*) and now has more than 20 years of experience in multimedia, graphics, and e-learning software sales, sales engineering, product marketing, business development, and training.

At first, Marc joined a start-up called Paracomp, which merged with MacroMind and Authorware, to create Macromedia. Over 12 years and at least a dozen acquisitions and mergers later, Marc was a consistent top salesperson, Macromedia's first sales engineer, sales engineer manager, and technical evangelist, entertaining global audiences with the exciting possibilities of desktop and Internet multimedia software.

Marc was then recruited by Adobe Systems as a web business development manager. Further opportunities took him to Corel as a field market specialist and then back to Adobe as an Acrobat specialist. From there, it was onto custom e-learning developer, Enspire Learning, in a business development role. From there he went back to Corel, which is how this book turned from an idea and a need into reality. (How many times can you say that you've returned to two employers twice?) Marc recently became the product marketing manager for WinZip.

Born in France and raised in Hawaii, Marc is now based in Austin, Texas.

Table of Contents

Introduction

MY, HOW THE WORLD of video and video editing has changed over the years. Video has evolved as fast and as far as the automobile in about the same number of years. The first automobile was introduced in the same decade and just a few years after a team of inventors at Thomas Edison's lab created a motion picture camera called the kinetograph. In just over a century since then, cars have gotten faster, easier to use, and more complex, not unlike the digital camcorders of today. Now you can hold a high-definition video camera in the palm of your hand and purchase very capable video editing software for under $100 that just about anyone can use and many can master. Prices continue to drop, and features continue to evolve.

Whether you're in this for fun, a serious hobby, or for your business, I will show you how to create digital videos that you'll be proud to share with family, friends, customers, and colleagues by following the easy-to-use steps included in this book. I'll show you how to share them on the web, upload them to portable devices, and burn CDs and DVDs with custom menus and labels.

You'll learn how to add your own animated titles and audio clips, as well as create premade and custom video, title, and audio effects. Using the downloadable working files means you'll learn by doing and can experiment on your own to build digital videos that are uniquely yours.

What You'll Need

Since you have purchased this book, I'm going to assume you have also purchased the Corel VideoStudio Pro software. And although it is not a requirement, it is highly recommended for obvious reasons that you have the version of VideoStudio Pro that's covered in this book, version X5 (15). You also should know the basics of using a computer, such as how to open, save, and close files, as well as use a mouse to access menus, select commands, and move objects around the screen. You should also make sure that your computer meets at least the minimum system requirements of running VideoStudio Pro X5. (The requirements are written on the software package and mentioned on Corel's website.) Please remember that using HD (high-definition) clips requires more computer "horse-power" than using SD (standard definition) clips.

How This Book Is Organized

This book has 18 chapters. You'll start out with some video basics and then learn the basics of getting the software up and running. Following that, you'll capture, edit, and share video using VideoStudio Pro X5 through step-by-step instructions with actual video clips that you can download from this book's companion website. Tips and notes are interspersed throughout the book.

While I highly recommend going through the chapters in order because many of the projects progress through multiple chapters, you can jump around by using the already completed projects from previous chapters that you can find on the companion website.

This book also has two appendixes: one is a table of keyboard shortcuts, and the other lists some useful websites you can visit for more information. The links appendix is also on the companion website as a PDF that offers clickable links so you can go right to the websites.

The companion website also has many of the chapter start lessons. Read the next section for information about how to access the companion website downloads.

Companion Website Downloads

This book has a companion website offering additional content related to this book. You can download files from www.courseptr.com/downloads. Please note that you will be redirected to the Cengage Learning Online Companion Website. Simply enter this book's title, ISBN, or the author's name in the Companion Search field at the top and click on the Search button. You'll be taken to the book's companion page, where you can download the related files.

Videography

Basics

C AN I REALLY SHOOT decent videos and edit them myself? Odds are, you've asked yourself this very question at some point during your video-taking adventures. Most likely, you've already taken hundreds, or even thousands, of photos; maybe you've taken hundreds of videos over the years and are deciding to advance to the next step of editing and sharing them with family, friends, colleagues, and customers.

Perhaps, you're already sharing some of your videos. You might share a lot more, though, if they weren't turned on their side, jittery, or too long or too large to email or post on a website.

On average, over 50 percent of you manage and edit your photos, but only about 5 percent do so with videos. Fifty percent of folks do most of their photo *and* video shooting with pocket-sized point-and-shoot cameras, while only 30 percent use a digital camcorder to shoot video (see Figure 1.1). As you can see, digital video shooting (and more so with digital video editing) is still in its infancy. Video sharing lags behind photo sharing by half. Backing up media is another issue altogether!

If you're in these lower percentage categories, again you may wonder, can I really edit and customize my own videos? Yes, you can! Follow the lessons in this book, and you will not only impress your family and friends, but have fun doing it. With VideoStudio Pro X5 (VSX5), it's much easier than you think. Let's start learning with some basics on the basics.

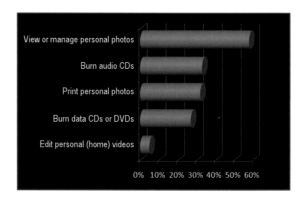

Figure 1.1
How people work with their photos and videos.

What Kind of Video Camera Is Good Enough?

YOU WILL GET A DIFFERENT answer to this question from everyone you ask. But the questions you may be asked in return are these: What do you want to accomplish? And what is your budget? I guess my first recommendation is to not purchase a camera beyond your means to take advantage of its features; you'd be wasting your hard-earned money, and you might become so intimidated by what you have that you set the camera aside altogether.

Instead, purchase a camera that meets your immediate and short-term goals. But, you might say, "I may want to make the next Avatar sequel." Don't worry; cameras are getting better and less expensive all the time. Buy one that meets your needs now and maybe with just a few new bells and whistles you may want to try out. Important features to consider are the following:

▶ **Standard Definition (SD) vs. High Definition (HD):** High-definition cameras are already rapidly dropping in price and size. They're almost becoming the standard in consumer digital video equipment. If you want to shoot in HD, now is as good a time as any to make that move, especially if you already have or plan to purchase an HD TV soon. A simple buying guide resource can be found here: www.pcworld.com/article/125646/how_to_buy_a_digital_camcorder.html.

▶ **Standard Width vs. Wide Screen:** HD and some newer SD cameras allow you to shoot in both standard width (a ratio of 4:3, width to height) and wide screen (a ratio of 16:9). If you're shooting in HD, you'll also want to shoot in wide screen. Be sure to enable or disable the Widescreen (16:9) option in the VideoStudio Settings menu *before* you edit your video.

▶ **Image Stabilization:** Unless you'll be carrying around a tripod everywhere you go, I think image stabilization is an important feature to consider that will help reduce the effects of camera movement while you're shooting. VideoStudio also has an image stabilization filter for use during editing, but it tends to slightly crop border areas.

▶ **Zoom (Optical vs. Digital):** With a point-and-shoot camera, you're lucky to get more than a 3X zoom. Point-and-shoot cameras in between pocket-sized and DSLRs (digital single-lens reflex) can reach up to 10X and higher. Digital camcorders, on the other hand, can reach up to 10-70X and more. Digital camcorder zoom can reach over 3000X. A note of caution, though: Optical zoom is real, while digital zoom is interpreted. Therefore, digital zoom may adversely affect the quality of your video. Digital zoom can vary between cameras and brands, so make sure you understand which zoom figure they're advertising: optical or digital.

▶ **Point-and-Shoot Camera with Video Capabilities vs. a Digital Camcorder with Photo Capabilities:** Both are getting much stronger at their secondary capabilities. I recently purchased a Canon Elph that I can hide in the palms of my hands that does amazing 1080i HD video. Digital camcorders are also getting much better at photo capabilities with anywhere from 8 to 10+ MP (megapixel) resolutions. These secondary options may lack many features beyond the basics, but at least the higher resolutions are there. You can always edit the photos later in an image editing application, such as Corel's PaintShop Pro.

▶ **Night Vision:** Night vision is a great feature to consider for events like birthday parties (blowing out the candles!), sneaking up on people in their sleep, and the newly popular activity, ghost hunting! It usually adds a good chunk to the selling price, though.

▶ **External Light:** Probably more useful than night vision is having a spotlight attached to the front of your video camera. This, again, adds to the price somewhat and drains your battery much more quickly. It's also good for night situations, but without the surprise attack!

▶ **LCD Screen:** The LCD screen refers to the hinged panel that swings out from the camera's base containing a viewing screen that allows you to see your shot without having to look through a tiny viewfinder. The benefit is that you can glance around your viewing area at the same time, making adjustments as necessary. I recommend getting a camcorder that has both, as the LCD screen can be very difficult to view in bright outdoor conditions. Be aware that some camcorders may only have a black-and-white viewfinder, even if they have a full-color LCD screen.

▶ **Battery Life:** What good is having all this storage space to record if the battery is constantly dead? Good camcorders will have a long battery life. Most cameras, however, don't ship with a large-capacity battery. Make sure you include the cost of an extra battery in your budget and take that extra battery with you when you travel.

But wait! There is something else to consider that's equally as important, and maybe even more so. Shooting video takes up *huge* amounts of hard drive space on both your camera and your computer. HD video takes up even more—lots more!

Memory is commonly referred to as RAM (random access memory), or the system memory that designates how many applications and files you can have open and use at the same time. These are long, narrow chips that are installed side by side inside your computer. The contents of RAM change constantly, depending on what applications are open and running. RAM is accessed several hundred times faster than hard drive memory and is very important to the function and speed of your computer during video editing. The more RAM (again, it's cheap and getting cheaper) your computer has, the faster and smoother your computer will perform. Don't scrimp on it. Serious video editing loves at least 3+ gigabytes (GB). One gigabyte of RAM can be had for about $50.

Hard drive space refers to the "library" of space that permanently holds *all* of your applications, files, photos, videos, and more. It's what you hear spinning off and on inside your computer. It can also be connected as a separate external device, either for extra space or as a backup device. It, like RAM, is cheap and getting cheaper; 500 GB is a great start for basic video editing and can be had for under $100. You might even consider doubling that to a 1-terabyte (1T) hard drive instead.

While photos can take up space in the range of a few hundred kilobytes (KB) to 25–50 megabytes (MB) each, videos can take up space in the order of hundreds of megabytes to multiple gigabytes. High-definition video can take up to four times the size of standard-definition video. So, you can see how space (both RAM and hard drive space) is *really* important when considering not only the camera you'll be shooting with, but the medium you'll be using to capture and store your videos to.

Camcorder Storage Options

Let's take a look at the capture and/or storage options inside your digital camcorder. I say "and/or" because, while most folks will download their video and erase what's on the camera's memory in order to reuse it, some folks use these devices to store their content and then purchase additional camcorder storage media for new content. The following list discusses the most popular choices (at the time of this writing) down to your lesser choices.

▶ **Internal Hard Drives:** Hard drives have rapidly become the most popular storage medium on digital camcorders for their reliability, convenience, and rapidly increasing capacity. Hard drive space can range from 30 GB to 220 GB and more. Obviously, the more space you get, the less often you'll have to transfer your video from your camera to your computer, CD, or DVD. Just don't neglect to do that, or you'll probably find yourself out of space *and* away from your computer at just the wrong time!

▶ **Internal Flash Memory Cards:** Memory cards (see Figure 1.2), a type of removable memory that has no moving parts (as opposed to hard drives), are especially handy. When you run out of room, you can just insert a new memory card. The most common types of memory cards found in camcorders are SD cards or Memory Sticks. Memory cards also make it easy to transfer video to your computer; just pop it into a memory card reader or card slot on your computer. However, the downside to memory cards is their limited capacity compared to internal hard drives.

▶ **Digital Video (DV) Tapes:** DV tapes (similar to mini-cassette tapes) come in many sizes. Most are pocket-sized and inexpensive. Tape is known for its long-lasting durability and reusability. The current sizes, in order of popularity, include S-size or MiniDV, M-size or medium, L-size or large cassettes, and XL-size or (as you guessed it) extra large size. Any cassette size may be used for either SD or HD video and may be recorded over multiple times. Although you can purchase tapes that record for varying lengths of time, the different physical sizes are manufactured more for the requirements to fit the different DV cameras (see Figure 1.3).

Figure 1.2
Various multimedia cards.

Figure 1.3
Digital video tape.

Flash memory is a nonvolatile computer storage type that can be electrically erased and reprogrammed. Since flash memory is nonvolatile, no power is needed to maintain the information stored on the chip.

▶ **Optical Discs:** Optical discs, like CDs and DVDs, were popular DV recording media, but they are rapidly waning due to their short recording time and relative inconvenience. There are two physical sizes of optical discs: 12-cm discs are your typical audio CD and DVD size, whereas the 8-cm discs are referred to as *mini-CD* and *mini-DVD*. Capacities can range from 1.5 GB up to 100 GB for dual-layered Blu-ray discs. Data are added to optical discs using lasers (see Figure 1.4). Although the media is long-lasting, it is not as durable as tape due to its propensity to scratches. Discs also include many recording types. Regarding recording time, if you want to record the highest HD quality, an average optical disc may only record 10–15 minutes of video before you must finalize it, eject it, insert a new one, and prep it for recording. In that time, your child could've recited the Gettysburg Address at the school play and you would've missed it.

Figure 1.4
The laser mechanism of a CD/DVD player.

Use the settings in your camcorder to designate how much video each storage device (mini-CDs, Multimedia Cards, and hard drives) will save or store in terms of length and quality. Lower settings will allow your camcorder to store more video, but at a lower quality. Since storage is inexpensive, try to find the setting that will provide the quality you desire and just make sure you have enough extra storage devices.

Video file size can vary depending on the features and quality settings you choose (e.g., resolution and frame rate). As a result of these settings, SD video can take up anywhere from 11 GB to 22 GB per hour of video on your hard drive. HD video can take up anywhere from 145 GB to over 400 GB per hour of video. Keep these figures in mind when choosing storage space on both your camcorder and your computer.

Check your manual *before* you purchase any internal camera storage to see what media your camcorder supports. For consumer cameras, only one type of card can be used, while a few of the top-of-the-line professional DSLR cameras might allow for using both Compact and SM cards at the same time.

What Kind of Media and Features Can I Include in My Movies?

THIS MAY SEEM LIKE a question with a very obvious answer, and you're partially right. You can obviously include videos in your movie projects. But did you know that you can also include photographs? There's a reason that most camcorders these days also have the ability to shoot and store high-quality photographs. Beyond the obvious convenience of not having to carry two devices with you on vacation, camcorder manufacturers know that most video editing applications have the ability to intersperse images in between video clips, along with separate audio clips (and VideoStudio Pro X5 is no exception).

VideoStudio Pro X5 also allows you to add, create, and customize titles that can stand alone or be overlaid on top of your images and video clips.

Music and voiceovers, video and audio filters, as well as special effects between scenes, can also be incorporated into your production.

One of the coolest and most unique features of VideoStudio Pro X5 is the Painting Creator (see Figure 1.5). The Painting Creator allows you to record animated painting, drawing, or writing strokes to use as an overlay effect.

Other visual and audio features you can add to make your video projects unique include special video effects, fancy transitions between scenes, picture-in-picture, animated picture frames, and more. So what kind of media can you include in your movies? The answer: A LOT!

Figure 1.5
Painting Creator.

How to Get the Best Results *Before* You Edit

I'M SURE YOU'RE AWARE of the adage "garbage in, garbage out." This applies to many things, including shooting video. Your editing results in VideoStudio will only be as good as the movies you've imported into it. True, many of the best shots happen when quickly grabbing your camera and shooting when the opportunity presents itself. Sometimes you plan to shoot one thing but end up getting something completely unexpected. This is the YouTube generation, after all.

But there are many ways to get the most from your videos. Knowledge and a little planning can go a long way. You can pretty much narrow down best video shooting practices to just a few items:

▶ **Learn Your Camcorder:** The last thing you want to do, as you pick up your camcorder to record a shot, is to reach for the manual to learn how to do something. It's often too late at that point. Whether it's to set auto or manual focus options or to set the quality of the video, knowing how to quickly set these choices will let you focus more on the shot itself. Take time to read through the manual, and at least play-test the top half dozen or so features you think you'll be using. Remember, we're now in the age of digital video. You can erase and reshoot at will. Take a few minutes before each event to familiarize yourself again with your favorite features, and maybe add a new feature or two to your arsenal each time.

▶ **Hold Your Camera Steady:** Even if your camcorder has image stabilization, do your best to hold your camera steady. Okay, it may have worked for *The Blair Witch Project* and *Cloverfield* (actually, I almost got ill watching the latter), but the last thing you really want is to give your viewers motion sickness. Videos of UFOs really lose credibility when camera shake makes the object look like a Frisbee or a flare. Use a tripod or lean your camera on the roof of your car, a fence rail, a chair, a window sill, a friend's or stranger's shoulder, as long as you ask them nicely.

▶ **Lighting:** Shooting outside in the daytime usually doesn't present a problem. If you're indoors, make sure to turn on enough lights or turn on your camcorder's light. Use the night vision option (if you have it) if you're in candlelit or dark rooms.

▶ **Know What's in the Background:** Although what's going on in the background could be crucial or otherwise add to what's happening in the foreground, make sure it doesn't do the opposite and distract from your main subject. Zoom in to concentrate on the important stuff or zoom out to include what might get your point across even better. Sometimes you might want to do both!

▶ **Sound:** Another distraction can be background sounds. Unless it's desired (like a sporting event, a concert, pounding surf, or a babbling brook), do your best to minimize background noise. Camcorders are sensitive to sounds, as they try to make sure all sounds are represented equally in your movie. For this same reason, try to make sure your subject is speaking clearly and loud enough, especially if having to drown out background noise. Consider a microphone to isolate what sound you want recorded.

▶ **Avoid Really Short Shots:** Again, this is not a hard, fast rule. But it takes a good 5 to 10 seconds for the viewer to comprehend what's going on and recognize all the elements in your shot. Shooting for longer periods of time will also give you more room for trimming and editing afterward. Plus recording is inexpensive and can easily be written over the next time. Don't be shy about it, but make sure to turn off the camcorder when you're done so you don't shoot the ground like my dad does....

All these rules are just guidelines. These days, pretty much anything goes when it comes to the quest for the ultimate video. Consider these basic rules, but don't let them sway you if you want to create something unique. Videos, after all, are an expression of you. Have fun!

Getting Your Video Clips onto Your Computer

OKAY, NOW THAT YOU'VE SHOT your Hollywood-worthy photos and videos, what's next? There are typically two ways to get your camera content onto your computer for editing. One way is to use the transfer cables that should've been included with your camera.

Connect your camera directly to your computer and then download the material either into an application provided with your camcorder purchase or by capturing directly into VideoStudio Pro X5. If your camcorder uses a hard drive or mini-DV tapes to capture and store video, then physically connecting your camera is the only method to get your content onto your computer. The differences between capturing and downloading are explained in further detail in Chapter 4, but basically, capturing involves downloading plus converting to a compatible file format for your computer.

If cables were not included, refer to your camera's user guide. Most cameras will require modified USB cables—usually one with a mini-USB connection on one end and a regular USB connection on the other (see Figure 1.6). But there are different mini-USB ends. Again, refer to your manual (or a blue shirt at Best Buy) for the correct cable. The mini end will connect to your camera's USB slot, and the regular end will connect to your computer's USB slot. For capturing video from a tape-based camcorder, you will need to have a high-speed transfer FireWire (IEEE 1394) cable. (This is discussed further in Chapter 18.)

The other method for transferring your video to your computer is to take the storage media out of your camcorder and either plug it directly into your computer's card slot, use an external MMC (MultiMedia Card) reader, or use the CD/DVD tray for camcorders that save to mini-discs. You can purchase small MMC readers that will fit your specific memory card or a reader that can fit several sizes for several different devices. MMC readers are usually small enough (even with the USB cable connector) to fit in your pocket and are inexpensive, in the range of $15 to $30.

Tip

Placing your mini-CDs/DVDs into a computer tray will not work on a Mac computer. Apple uses a slot that you slide CDs and DVDs into, instead of a pull-out tray that PCs use. Do NOT slide a mini-disc into an Apple computer slot because it will get stuck and not eject.

Figure 1.6
Regular to mini-USB cable.

Backing Up Your Video Clips

YOU'VE HEARD THE PHRASE OFTEN: "Save your work!" Well, here's another one: "BACK UP YOUR PICTURES AND VIDEOS!" Does it seem like I'm yelling? That's because I AM! Hard drive space and blank CDs and DVDs are *so* cheap these days. Would you believe you can purchase a 1-terabyte external drive (that's 1,000 GB!) for between $100 and $150? You can also get a 100-pack of blank DVDs for $20 or $30. This will also alleviate the possibility of running out of room on, or accidentally deleting content from, your camera.

You would be surprised at how many people are actually afraid to take the video clips and photos off their cameras! Are you one of these? Take a look at Figure 1.7. Only 35% of users back up their photos to CDs and DVDs. Thankfully, roughly 70% back up their video clips. What happens to the other 30%? These folks must keep buying more MMCs, DV tapes, and mini-CDs to shoot and save their videos and photos with. That has to get expensive! Inadvertently deleting content is probably the biggest fear involved in transferring content from your camera. Do NOT be afraid. Your content will not be deleted when copying it to your computer. Video is only deleted if you erase your media card/disc in a completely separate operation.

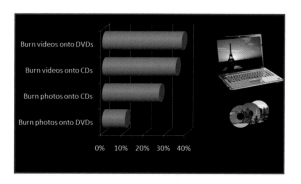

Figure 1.7
Backup is critical.

One of the topics in this book will be to show you how to use VideoStudio Pro X5 to back up your content. The Backup feature is located in several places within VideoStudio, as if it's acting as a constant reminder to do so.

Comparing Video File Formats

ALTHOUGH VSX5 (VideoStudio Pro X5) allows you to output to many formats without having to know the particulars about them, I thought I would provide a brief (very brief) explanation of what these formats are and what main purpose(s) they were created for.

Most of the following file formats were designed specifically with the end result in mind (for example, SD vs. HD, DVD vs. web, Mac vs. PC, social networking sites, or mobile/portable devices). VSX5 offers the following choices:

- ▶ Video files (e.g., QuickTime, AVI, WMV, MPEG, and so on)

- ▶ Sound files (e.g., WAV, WMA, MP4, and OGG)

- ▶ DVD (e.g., AVCHD, Blu-ray)

- ▶ Recording back out to your camera, such as putting your finished movie back onto recordable tape or disc

- ▶ Mobile devices (e.g., iPod, iPhone, Android, Blackberry, HTC)

To make things even more confusing is the major crossover between all these formats, which is why I'm only explaining the basics. This is merely an overview of what you'll encounter in VSX5.

Out of over 225 different video file formats that exist, here is a brief explanation of the major video output formats pertaining to VSX5:

- ▶ **MPEG:** Short for Moving Picture Experts Group, this group sets the standards for the digital encoding of movies and sound. The format includes, but is not limited to, the following:

  - ▶ *MPEG-1* (*.mpg*): Early format used for audio and video compression, output to the web, and video CDs.

  - ▶ *MPEG-2* (*.mpg*): Subset of MPEG-1 used in media, such as DVDs.

  - ▶ *MPEG-4* (*.mp4*): A highly compressed format used for videos on portable devices (like the iPod) and the Internet (YouTube). This format creates very small files.

- ▶ **AVI (.avi):** Short for Audio Video Interleave and used specifically for playback on Microsoft Windows. AVI files are larger because there is less compression, and thus, may not be suitable for the Internet or email. It is also the container many software applications wrap around raw video to make it playable on PCs. A "container" can be described as a bucket. A bucket can contain different types of content, such as sand, water, etc. A container in the video file world can contain different types of video and audio content.

▶ **WMV (.wmv):** A video compression format similar to AVI but used mainly for downloading to PCs. WMV was developed by Microsoft and used originally for Internet streaming applications and as a competitor to RealVideo.

▶ **QuickTime (.mov):** A format originally developed to display video on the Macintosh, it is also viewable on PCs and other operating systems using Apple's QuickTime player.

▶ **3GP, 3G2:** Multimedia formats used on 3G mobile phones and on some 2G and 4G phones.

▶ **AVCHD:** Short for Advanced Video Codec High Definition and based on the MPEG-4 format, it was specifically designed for HD camcorder use. It uses a disc structure designed for Blu-ray disc/high-definition compatibility, but it can also be used on standard DVDs. If you have an HD camcorder that does *not* record in Blu-ray, it records in AVCHD instead; in fact, there's a good chance you'll see the letters AVCHD imprinted on your camcorder.

▶ **H.264:** The latest HD format that provides powerful compression technology while delivering a superior video experience at a low bit rate. H.264 is what YouTube now uses to convert uploaded HD clips for playback on its website, which is a relatively new feature. Similar to AVI, H.264 is a container for the MP4 audio and video format.

▶ **Blu-ray:** Sometimes known as BD or BDMV, this format uses a new blue-violet (hence the name), smaller wavelength laser for HD video, allowing for more capacity on DVDs. It provides the best video and audio quality of any home-based media... so far.

▶ **Flash Video:** Developed by San Diego–based FutureWave Software. Originally called FutureSplash Animator, it was first acquired by Macromedia, which turned into the Flash we know today. Macromedia was recently acquired by Adobe Systems. Flash powers a great portion of video we now see on the Internet. There are two different video file formats defined by Adobe Systems and supported in the Adobe Flash Player: FLV and F4V. Flash video content may also be embedded within SWF files. Flash video, although small in file size, is also known for its processor-intensive requirements and sometimes buggy nature. A recent choice and growing in popularity is HTML5.

▶ **HTML5:** The fifth version of the HTML authoring standard for the Internet and still under development, it aims to vastly improve the Internet multimedia experience, while maintaining readability and compatibility with all browsers. HTML5 video is an element of HTML5 and aims to become the new standard way to show video online. VSX5 will now output to HTML5 code as an option.

▶ **WebM:** Another video format specifically for Internet playback, the WebM project is dedicated to developing a high-quality, open video format for the web that is freely available to everyone.

RAW video formats usually have the DV or DIF extensions. *RAW* files are those that have not been touched by any file conversion or compression while still in your camera. Many advanced users prefer this format for photo editing. Most camcorders automatically "wrap" RAW files in the AVI or MOV format, so video editing software will be able to recognize and work with them. After editing the clip, you can either save it back in the AVI or MOV format (which will replace the RAW DV or DIF formats), or you can save in one of many other formats.

Now, let me see if can summarize these formats for desired playback devices. Again, these are just generalities and are not meant to be steadfast rules:

▶ **Windows Computers:** WMV, AVI, MOV, MPG, MP4, Flash

▶ **Macintosh Computers:** MOV, MPG, MP4, Flash (although the QuickTime player and those of third parties can play most Windows video formats)

▶ **Websites:** MPG, MP4, MOV, Flash, HTML5, WebM

▶ **Portable Devices:** MP4

▶ **Social Sharing Sites:** MP4, H.264, Flash

▶ **Standard-definition DVDs:** MPEG2

▶ **High-definition DVDs:** H.264, AVCHD, Blu-ray

Quick Quiz

This first chapter has hopefully given you the knowledge and confidence to move on to Chapter 2. Even if you don't yet feel comfortable, future chapters and VSX5 itself will help guide you. Don't be afraid. Let's see if you know these answers. If not, feel free to thumb back through the pages of Chapter 1 to review. Don't worry; you won't be graded!

1. What are at least three items to consider when choosing a video camera? (See "What Kind of Video Camera Is Good Enough?")

2. Name three types of media that can be used to capture video on a camcorder. (See "Camcorder Storage Options.")

3. What are the two most common HD formats? (See "Comparing Video File Formats.")

4. Name at least two video file formats that are cross-platform for both the Mac and PC. (See "Comparing Video File Formats.")

5. Name at least three destinations where you can display your final video. (See "Comparing Video File Formats.")

6. Bonus: What's the easiest way to prevent losing your work? (See "Backing Up Your Video Clips.")

Getting

Started

S O NOW YOU KNOW A LITTLE about the technical aspects of video formats, ideas to consider when getting the right video camcorder, getting the most out of shooting your videos, and the common methods for saving your shots and turning them into memories you'll have for generations.

This chapter will introduce you to the VSX5 package, as well as this book and how you can get the most out of it. I'll cover a little product history on VideoStudio Pro, acquiring the files to use with this book, and, if you haven't done so already, installing VSX5. I'll give you a quick tour of the application, as well as where to get assistance if you run into problems—not that you'll need it with *my* expert guidance! I'll also show you how to download additional free content that Corel provides right in VSX5.

Ready? Set? Go!

The History of VideoStudio

YOU MAY OR MAY NOT KNOW that Corel has been around for over 20 years, celebrating its twentieth anniversary in 2009. The CorelDraw Graphics Suite was the first "blend" of graphics software applications on the market, even before any of the Adobe Suites.

VideoStudio, originally from a company called Ulead in Taipei, Taiwan, started a groundbreaking history of its own. Back in the early 1980s, Taiwan decided that the IT and PC industries were a good bet for future fortune and created the Science Park in Hsinchu, about an hour outside of Taipei.

At about that time, three really smart guys were working on image editing software at the Institute for Information Industry (III), Taiwan's hotbed for developing software technology. When the interest in the Taiwan computer industry turned to building scanners to help get existing content onto computers, bells went off. The three smart guys joined forces with Microtek to create Ulead (named in Chinese for the idea of "strength through friendship"). Their first product was a little number for scanners called iPhoto Plus—yes, that IS where the Apple product name came from. The next thing they made was a retail product called PhotoStyler.

After scanners, video looked like the next big thing for Taiwan's computer industry, and display card makers started ramping up products to take advantage of Microsoft's new Video for Windows technology. Ulead was there with a simple video editor it called VideoStudio—just right for the new crop of video capture cards. As a result, VideoStudio versions 1 and 2 were designed as OEM (see Note) products that would only work with these new video display cards.

OEM stands for *original equipment manufacturer*. It's a term used by companies, such as Ulead, that include their products in a larger solution, making it a more attractive and useful "all-in-one" offering. This is also where the term "value-added" comes from. An example is when you purchase a computer that has a host of other solutions, such as Internet browser software or Corel's Painter Essentials.

In the late 1990s, consumers started asking for products they could purchase separately from the video cards and computers. As a result, Ulead launched its first standalone VideoStudio as version 3 in 1998 in the U.S., Germany, and Japan. It was built around the core technology of Ulead MediaStudio Pro, a multi-award winning video editing program designed for the professional market. Would you believe it was priced roughly the same as VideoStudio is today at $99? And it allowed users even then to share video via the web, through email, and on CD-ROM. Amazing!

The next big thing was Motion JPEG (M-JPEG) technology that allowed a user to plug in an analog (nondigital) VHS (Hi-8) tape and convert (encode) it to digital in real time. Modern non-linear (being able to jump to any frame at any time) video editing for home users was born. This ability was added to the next version of VideoStudio.

VideoStudio 4 (1999) added support for DV (digital video) camcorders and the ability to utilize high-speed IEEE 1394 (FireWire/i.LINK) to transfer data at high speeds in real time along with the ability to control the video camcorder. The quality of 1394 support propelled VideoStudio to the number-one spot in the important Japan market, a position the product enjoys to this day! Version 4 also added MPEG-2 and MP3 format compatibilities.

VideoStudio version 5 (2001) added the ability to author and burn VCDs (Video CDs) (MPEG-1) and DVDs (MPEG-2). Unique Ulead technology called "Smart Rendering" eliminated *generational loss* (quality loss resulting from repeated renderings) when editing. If a clip in the timeline is not edited, it will not be rerendered. Rendering, in videography terms, refers to the process of finalizing all your edits and effects into a single file for playback.

Also added in version 5 was the consumer request to improve the interface and make it more user-friendly, which at that time (and much like other applications of that period) had a similar interface to Microsoft Office. Talking to consumers and professionals, Ulead created a GUI (graphical user interface) for VideoStudio and one for Photo Express (the company's consumer photo editing application) in order to create a smoother and more direct workflow.

Version 6 (2002) continued to improve the GUI and video editing features. Version 6 introduced separate DVD authoring workflows, the DVD MovieFactory application, video filters, transitions, text effects, voiceover, real-time preview, and multiple export options. Version 7 (2003) added more Timeline tracks for video overlay, as well as titles and audio, while still maintaining its $99.99 price. Version 7 also became a CNET Editor's Choice Award winner, with increased speed, dual-processor compatibility, support for DVD-VR and DVD+RW video recording formats, as well as "on-disc" editing capabilities.

Version 8 (2004) introduced the idea of shorter paths to get the basics accomplished more quickly with the Movie Wizard and DV-to-DVD Wizard, support for MPEG-4 and 3GPP (a mobile broadband standard), and Dolby Digital audio mixing, all while receiving seven additional Editor's Choice Awards.

Version 9 (2005) added still more powerful video editing tools, including Chroma Keying (blue/green screen effects), Flash Animation overlays, Pan and Zoom on video, and more video and audio filters. Also new was the DV Quick Scan feature in the DV-to-DVD Wizard. The Movie Wizard offered over 20 movie templates to choose from. Version 9 also included Smart Pan and Zoom (which automatically detected faces in photos), the unique ability to reshape overlaid video clips so they could appear at an angle, and a new Movie Screensaver feature.

VideoStudio 10 (2006) brought the first HDV capabilities. HDV was the first high-definition video (HDV) capability that's captured via digital tape, introduced by Sony through FireWire and the MPEG-2 file format. Also added were multiple video overlay tracks and Smart Proxy, the ability to play back and render large video files (especially HD) in smaller files as proxies and then render the larger ones at the end. Version 10 also upgraded the Dolby Digital support to version 5.1.

Version 11 (2007) brought Advanced Video Codec-High Definition (AVCHD) compatibility, the MPEG Optimizer, more advanced DVD templates and improvements, as well as enhancements to many other areas.

VideoStudio 12 (2008) added the Painting Creator, the ability to upload video to YouTube, Blu-ray support and output, NewBlue Film Effects, iPhone/iTouch, H.264, FLV (Flash video), Intel Quad Core Technology support, a resizable interface, Auto Pan and Zoom, Auto video transition and audio cross-fades, and faster encoding and rendering times.

VideoStudio X3 (version 13 - 2009) added a big jump in editing and rendering speed along with direct compatibility with Intel's Core I7 technology. Also added were advanced third-party FX filters from NewBlue and Corel's KPT Collection, royalty-free editable/mixable music from SmartSound, and more templates for movies and DVD menus. You could also create advanced Blu-ray menus and then actually burn Blu-ray discs (requires a Blu-ray burner) and save HD files or movies for YouTube and other Internet sites using the H.264 standard.

Finally, VideoStudio X4 (2011) continued to provide groundbreaking new features with Stop Motion Animation, Time-Lapse Photography, adjustable workspaces, 3D output, as well as continued improvements with speed, performance, instant projects, HD authoring, DVD burning, and more.

Starting with version X4, Corel also began offering an Ultimate version. The Ultimate version includes all the functionality of the Pro version but adds a bunch of free video and titling effects from NeBlue, Boris, and proDAD.

Wait until you see what version X5 offers!

Getting the Book's Lesson Files

THIS BOOK IS DESIGNED to get you involved in the video editing process and help you to try out most everything I discuss. The book's lesson files include video and audio clips, as well as photographs. Although you'll have access to all the files needed for use in the book, there will be some cases where you can use your own. I will point out these options as we get to them. On the other hand, many of the book's companion files are designed to show specific features, so be sure to keep them handy.

Although high-definition (HD) files would be lovely to work with and produce beautiful quality projects, their RAW file size would be prohibitive to download. (RAW HD AVI files are much larger than their compressed finished DVD cousins.) You'll be using mostly standard-definition (SD) clips instead, although there is one HD project you'll use. I will point out where HD-specific features exist and how you can use them if you have HD video you want to try out.

To download the lesson files, go to www.courseptr.com/downloads, which will take you to the Cengage Learning Online Companion website. Simply enter this book's title, ISBN, or the author's name in the Companion Search field at the top and click on the Search button. You'll be taken to the book's companion page, where you can download the related files. Be sure to put it someplace that you'll remember, such as in My Documents or the Desktop, and then make a copy of the entire folder. You will be using some files more than once, and sometimes you'll want to go back to the original versions.

Rules to Live By

THIS BOOK SHOULD BE easy to follow without any upfront instructions; but just in case, and since every learning book operates a little differently, here are a few rules that will make your experience smoother.

▶ In addition to the step-by-step instructions, you can use the many screenshots to help you locate a button, a menu item, or a tool to use. They will be labeled for easy identification.

▶ Although VSX5 has very few menu commands that you'll need to access at the top of the application window, you'll occasionally see the following instructional format: File > Insert Media File to Timeline > Insert Video. This describes the menu path to a command. In this case, you would go to the File menu, click on Export, and choose DV Recording from the submenu. Another example might be this: Edit step > *icon*. In this case, select the Edit tab (called a *step* in VSX5) at the top of the application window, and then click on the described icon in the newly appearing interface.

▶ To access files that you'll need to use with the lessons, I'll assume you remember where you put the folder that you downloaded from the Cengage Learning website (www.courseptr.com/downloads). I will start each path to a file with that folder's name. The rest of the path will be similar to getting to a menu item, for example, VSX5_book_files > Videos > Balloon Trip > File name.

▶ When I ask you to select or highlight something, such as a clip in the Timeline, a library item, or an icon or tool, I mean to click it only once. If I need you to double-click an item, I will specifically ask you to double-click that item. Double-clicking an item will often bring up different tools or options than merely selecting that item once.

▶ There are several naming conventions for VideoStudio Pro X5. You might hear it referred to as VideoStudio, VideoStudio Pro X5, VSPro, or VSX5. I will try my best to limit references to one or two of these, but if I slip in any of these names, just know that they all refer to this application.

Once you're using VSX5, your screens will look the same; however, my screenshots of anything outside the application may look a little different from yours, since I'm using Windows 7. Paths to any files, though, will remain the same.

If you'd like to jump through the chapters of this book in random order, go for it. There's a folder of already completed chapter lesson files on this book's companion website (www.courseptr.com/downloads), enabling you to open a lesson file that's been completed up to that chapter.

Tip

Since I'll point out where you can use your own content during the lessons, it would be helpful if you already have some photos and videos you want to use organized in easy-to-find locations.

Although this book has a lot of good stuff to learn about, sometimes you may want to dispense with all my words of wisdom and just get down to business, especially if you're going through the book a second time. Therefore, the steps to accomplish all the tasks will be in numbered lists that will be easy to locate and refer to.

Installing VideoStudio Pro X5

I REALIZE THAT IF YOU HAVE read the book this far, you probably already have the VSX5 software. If you've already downloaded and installed it, you can proceed to the next topic. If you have yet to purchase VSX5 and would like to try it out on a trial basis, you can do that, too. Corel offers a free download of a 30-day, fully functional, save-enabled version. Go here to get it: www.corel.com > Free Trials tab at the top > VideoStudio Pro X5 Download Trial button.

Whether you've downloaded the trial or purchased the full version, double-click the installer icon to open it and follow all the installation instructions. More detailed instructions are included in this section.

If you're downloading and installing the 30-day trial version, a window will display with a choice to enter a serial number or to run the app in the trial mode. If you've purchased the software, you'll get a different window asking you to enter your serial number before you can install the software. In this situation, you will not be able to continue installation without having a valid serial number.

Let the installer place VideoStudio in its default location. If you purchased the boxed version, insert the DVD. It will auto-start once inserted into your DVD drive. Again, follow the onscreen instructions.

If you have purchased VideoStudio Pro X5, you will also need to register the product either by creating a Corel account or by logging into your existing account. Doing so will get you additional templates and video content, update notifications, and other important notices. It's a good thing. You can opt out of any newsletters if you like. I usually opt in and wait to see if they get annoying before making my decision to opt out or not.

If you've launched VSX5 recently, you should be able to see it in the main section of your Windows Start menu, as a recently launched application. If not, you can click on the Windows Start button > All Programs > Corel VideoStudio Pro X5 or click on the shortcut that you may have allowed the installer to put on your Desktop.

Tip

I usually don't like having a bunch of application shortcuts littering my desktop, but in this situation, since you'll frequently be using VideoStudio over the course of using this book, I recommend leaving it on your Desktop for now.

In this book, I will be using and showing the Ultimate version of VSX5. You will be using either the Pro version or the Pro Ultimate version like I'm using. Although I highly recommend spending the extra few dollars to get/upgrade to the Ultimate version, with its multitude of extra content, you'll still be able to use all the features described herein with just the Pro version.

Launching VideoStudio Pro X5

AFTER YOU'VE EITHER acquired the trial version or purchased the full version of VSX5 Pro or Ultimate, you will encounter a different situation when you first launch the application. Following are instructions on how to launch and proceed with either one.

Launching the Trial Version of VSX5

1. Double-click the VideoStudio Pro X5 application icon you downloaded from the Corel website.

2. In the window that appears, if you have a serial number, click either of the two Activate now buttons to register the software (see Figure 2.1). If you do so, this window will no longer appear in the future. Follow the activation instructions to register and launch VSX5.

3. If you have yet to purchase the software and would like to continue with the 30-day trial period, click the Activate later button in the lower right corner. This will launch VSX5. You will see this window each time you launch the trial version of VSX5 over the next 30 days, or until you activate it with a serial number.

Launching the Purchased Version of VSX5

1. Double-click the VideoStudio Pro X5 application icon. Your first stop will be the Corel Guide displayed atop the main VSX5 interface. See Figure 2.2. As you can see, there's another good reason you'll want to register your copy of VSX5. Corel restricts access to the Corel Guide, including the Help file, any software updates, and free content, until you do. Pretty smart move, if you ask me.

Time left on your
30-day trial

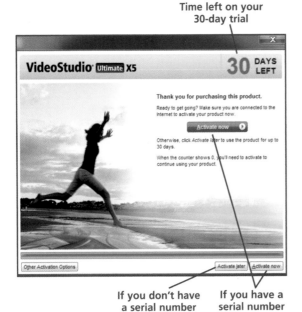

If you don't have
a serial number

If you have a
serial number

Figure 2.1
The VideoStudio Trial Version Splash Screen.

CAUTION

Only electronically obtained serial numbers (from the Corel website) will register a downloaded trial version. If you were using a trial version and then purchased a boxed version of VSX5, you need to uninstall the trial version and then reinstall VSX5 using the disc that came in the boxed version.

Figure 2.2
The VideoStudio Register now window.

2. To begin the registration process, click the green Register now button in the center of the Corel Guide window. Another window then will pop up.

3. Unlike the entry I made in Figure 2.3, enter a valid email address to receive all the valuable information and click Register. You will next receive a confirmation email to the address you entered, and VSX5 will launch into the application itself.

Figure 2.3
The VideoStudio Registration window.

Help, The Corel Guide, Additional Content

SOFTWARE DEVELOPERS INVEST a lot of effort in their application's Help system. It's there for you to use. I'm amazed at how many users fail to consider it when they hit a roadblock in an application. As a sales engineer (technical sales) at several software companies, nine times out of ten, I would answer a user's email questions by referring him to a specific, easy-to-find item, found right in the Help file.

You can access Help in VSX5 by pressing the F1 key or clicking the small round icon in the upper-right corner of the main screen.

▶ Pressing the F1 key will bring up VideoStudio's Help file in a browser-based window. This online access method is more commonplace these days (instead of, say, downloading or installing a PDF version with the application) because the remote version can easily be updated by the software developer to remain current. This helps you get the latest and best methods to learn features and get around difficult situations.

▶ The second choice to access Help is by clicking the same icon you can use to access the Corel Guide and get the free downloadable content (the same window you see when first launching VSX5). This icon is located in the upper-right corner of your screen, just to the left of the minimize (-) icon. It looks like a down arrow in a circle of dots. It might be orange at first. More on this later. See Figure 2.4.

This will bring access to the Help file via the Learn tab in the Corel Guide. To launch Help again, click the Launch Help button.

Figure 2.4
Access icon for the Corel Guide, Help,
and Product Information.

Tip

In various locations around VSX5, you
may see that same arrow surrounded by
dots icon appear in orange. This indicates
that new content is available, either for
free or at a nominal cost, in the Do More
tab of the Corel Guide. Check it to see if
there's something you like!

Back in the Corel Guide, notice there are four tabs
at the top of the Corel Guide. The Guide starts in
the Home tab first. The Help link is located in the
Learn tab. There is also access to a number of video
tutorials in this tab. I encourage you to view them
at your convenience. They will play in this Corel
Guide window and are great for reviews of what I'll
teach you throughout this book, and maybe even
give you some new ideas. Keep checking back for
new ones!

Next, click the Do More tab (see Figure 2.5). This
provides a collection of downloadable extras, such
as titles, filters, audio clips, special effects, and
more via several categories, many of which are free.
Grab 'em! Some of the free content will be used
in this book. The download and install process is
quick and easy. Available content can change at
any time.

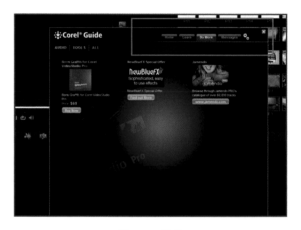

Figure 2.5
Accessing extras for VideoStudio.

So to wrap up, use Help whenever you need to,
both when you want to learn more than this book
will provide (which won't be much!) and when you
get stuck and want to learn more about a feature
or task. Using Help along with its Index and Search
features will get you answers quickly!

Visit the Learn and Do More tabs frequently for the
latest video tutorials and downloads.

Tip

Another excellent resource that will avoid the long line at tech support is the Corel online forum. This forum is almost constantly manned by experts in video and VideoStudio. One assistant is in Australia! It's also likely that you'll get multiple responses from other contributors. Go to http://forum.corel.com and choose the appropriate product from the main page. You will have to create a free account to ask questions, but you can also choose to get an email every time there's a response to your question.

Additional Product Information

Click on the small icon that looks like two blue gears meshing together (shown in Figure 2.6). This provides additional choices to communicate with Corel with items such as version number, Messages, Preferences, registering, or product updates.

Figure 2.6
Other Corel Guide communication options.

Quick Quiz

1. What company owned VideoStudio before Corel acquired it? (See "The History of VideoStudio.")

2. Name at least one benefit of registering your copy of VideoStudio. (See "Launching the Purchased Version of VSX5.")

3. Where should your first destination be if you have a question regarding a feature or task in VideoStudio? (See "Help, The Corel Guide, Additional Content.")

4. Before calling/emailing friends/family/Corel tech support, what is the best resource already in VSX5 to answer questions you may have on features and processes? (See "Help, The Corel Guide, Additional Content.")

Introduction to

VideoStudio Pro X5

WELCOME TO THE HEART of this book! Now it's time to start creating and editing videos!

Of course, this is still just the introductory chapter. Just remember, baby steps. There is a lot to learn in VSX5 as a whole, so I'll use this particular chapter to give you a tour and get you comfortable with how the interface is laid out, where the tools are, and where your video, graphics, and sound assets will be stored. You'll learn the steps necessary for creating an actual video in VideoStudio, as well as the three main work areas where you'll make this happen. I'll also show you how to add basic content into a multitrack Timeline so that you can begin assembling a video project.

VideoStudio Moviemaking Terminology

BEFORE YOU START CREATING a video, it's important to understand what terms I'll be using and what they refer to throughout the video-making process.

▶ **Title:** In the movie business, the term *title* refers to the final output—a completed movie or a finished DVD. However, for the purposes of this book, any reference to a *title* means a text title, such as "Our Vacation," "Chapter 1," "Chapter 2," and so on, not the finished product.

▶ **Clip:** Video and sound assets you'll be importing will be referred to as *clips*. Still graphics you'll be adding will be referred to as graphics, photos, backgrounds or the like, depending on what's appropriate for the discussion.

▶ **Project:** This is the VSX5 file created when you do a File > Save. It does not contain

any content, but rather contains instructions on how to assemble the content, what clips (or portions of clips) to use, where to place clips in the Timeline, what filters to apply, and so on. It contains instructions for creating the sequence of events for your movie. It's often referred to as an Edit Decision List (EDL). Projects and how they're saved are explained further in the "Saving Your Movie" section at the end of this chapter.

▶ **Movie:** A movie is your exported project, made up of multiple clips of videos, stills, sounds, and titles. This could be a QuickTime movie, a Flash movie for YouTube, or a DVD movie.

▶ **Scene:** When placed on the Timeline, a scene is a combination of individual, layered clips (e.g., video with an overlaid title and background audio).

Touring the VSX5 Workspace

IT'S TIME TO BECOME FAMILIAR with navigating the VSX5 interface, finding where the important tools reside and what the workflow is. For what might be the first time, you'll be working with a *multitrack Timeline*—a Timeline with separate but concurrent tracks for video, audio, graphics, and titles.

In VSX5, the Timeline takes up half of your workspace, and rightly so. It's where you'll spend most of your time creating your movie with, if necessary, frame accuracy. A Preview window and galleries of items you can use in your videos will take up the rest of your screen. Instead of working through a sequence of tasks in a sequence of windows (similar to Microsoft PowerPoint), in VSX5, almost all your work will be accomplished in one main screen, using the different panels for various tasks.

One of my favorite features of VSX5 is that necessary tools automatically become visible, depending on which asset you select. For instance, when you double-click an audio clip in the audio track of the Timeline, audio tools for editing will pop up. The same thing occurs with video clips, transitions, and special effects or video filters.

Although there is a lot to know about creating videos in VSX5, the general path to getting there is the same: import your media, place and arrange it on the Timeline, and then export it in the desired format. Let's take that tour.

If the Corel Guide is still visible on top of VSX5, close that window. Or relaunch VSX5, if necessary, by clicking on the Desktop shortcut (see Figure 3.1) or through the Windows Start menu. VSX5 will open in its default view, showing the multitrack Timeline (but currently in Storyboard view), Content Libraries, and Preview panel (see Figure 3.2). The three main work areas are explained in the following list (with more detailed explanations following later in the chapter).

Figure 3.1
VSX5 launch icon.

Menus · Authoring steps · Preview panel · Content libraries

Timeline · Library Navigation panel

Figure 3.2
Default VSX5 interface.

▶ **Preview panel:** Preview any photo, video, or audio clip that resides either in the collection of libraries to the right or in the Timeline below. All you need to do is select the asset in its respective location to view and play it in the Preview panel.

▶ **Library Navigation panel:** Use this list to select different types of libraries to be displayed. You can also create new sub-libraries (I call them galleries) for the first Media library, such as those for specific projects, to help you stay organized.

▶ **Content libraries:** Includes all your media, the samples that came included with VSX5, free content you downloaded from the Corel Guide, imported content used in movies, movies you exported in VSX5, and customized content you saved from the Timeline. Content libraries will not contain assets that you import directly into the Timeline (thus bypassing the library), although these assets can be placed in the library afterward.

► **Timeline panel:** Organizes your content for playback using either sequential clips (Storyboard view) or multiple, concurrently displayed layers along with sequentially playing clips (Timeline view). The Timeline includes views called Storyboard, Timeline, and Audio. The default view when you first launch VSX5 is the Storyboard view, which only allows and displays video and still clips that will be used in the Timeline view's background layer. Afterward, VSX5 will display whichever Timeline view you were using the last time you quit the application.

► **Menus:** At the top left of your screen are four menus: File, Edit, Tools, and Settings. These contain functions common to many applications (e.g., Save, Export, and Exit), as well as functions that are unique to VSX5. You'll notice the menus are not that long. Most of the tools you'll be using are context-sensitive. They will become available when an asset is selected in the main window.

► **Capture, Edit, and Share steps:** These are actually tabs (to the right of the menus) that represent the three main processes (steps) in authoring videos in VSX5 (and most videography software).

Tip

Click once on an asset in a library or the Timeline to view and play it in the Preview panel. Click a clip twice in the Timeline to open the clip's editing tools in the Options panel.

Customizing Your Workspace

THERE ARE A FEW FEATURES in VSX5 that allow workspace customizations. So that your views will match the book's screen shots, I'll stick with the default view in the end. Afterward, though, you can use any of the other views you like.

VideoStudio version X4 forced its view to fill your entire screen. There was no ability to adjust the actual screen size any smaller than your screen, at least not on a single monitor system anyway. With VSX5, there is now a maximize and restore icon in the far upper right of your screen, adjacent to the close window "x". VSX5 no longer requires a minimum screen area of 1024×768 pixels. It can now be adjusted to any size.

Resizing the Workspace

In the default workspace, there are several ways to resize and reposition each of the three (Preview, Library, and Timeline) panels. Resizing any of them will cause the others to resize accordingly so that they all still fit into your overall screen space.

To resize any of the three panels, do the following:

1. Place your cursor in the narrow area between each of the panels until your cursor changes to a double-sided arrow. See Figure 3.3.

Figure 3.4
Possible workspace arrangement.

Figure 3.3
How to resize workspace.

2. Hold down the left mouse button and drag right and left, or up and down to adjust the relative sizes of the panels to your liking. Let go of the mouse when you've resized the panels to the desired positions. One way to rearrange your workspace panels might be similar to that shown in Figure 3.4.

Undocking the Workspace Panels

A feature in VSX5 is the ability to actually unlock/undock any of the three panels and freely place them anywhere you choose on the screen, even on top of other panels. To move the panels in your workspace, follow these steps.

1. Click and hold the top bar of the Preview panel, and then pull the panel away from its current docked location (see Figure 3.5). As you do so, a blue transparent rectangle will appear attached to your cursor. This represents the panel you're moving. Moving the blue rectangle near other panels, you will see blue arrows appear at their sides.

Figure 3.5
Undocking a panel.

Figure 3.7
New panels view.

2. Move your cursor directly over the blue arrow on the far right of the Libraries panel (see Figure 3.6); then release your mouse. The blue rectangle will snap into place to indicate where you will be placing the panel. The remaining panels will move out of the way accordingly, and your workspace will be updated with the new view (see Figure 3.7).

3. From its new position, click and drag the Preview panel away from its new location and drop it anywhere in the center of the window, but not on any of the blue arrows (see Figure 3.8). You should now see a view very similar to Figure 3.9. Loose panels can also be resized by grabbing any corner or side.

Figure 3.6
Repositioning a panel.

Figure 3.8
Undocking the Preview panel.

Figure 3.9
Undocked panel placement.

Figure 3.10
Saving a custom layout.

4. Take a couple minutes to try placing this panel and others in different locations. Don't get freaked out when the arrangements look a tad bizarre. It may take a few tries to get the panels where you expect them to go. That's the learning process. It really does all make sense.

5. If you find a panel combination that you might like to use in the future, you can save the arrangement as a custom setting. To save your new view, go to Settings > Layout Settings > Save to > and choose Custom #1. (See Figure 3.10.) As you can see, you can create up to three custom views.

   You'll need to return to the default view so your screen will reflect what you see in the book's screen shots.

6. Return to Settings > Layout Settings > Switch to and choose Default.

Tip

If you change the interface layout and restart VSX5, it will continue to display your last layout settings, whether you saved it to a custom setting or not. You can still return to the default layout through the Settings menu.

Another new feature of VSX5 is its ability to expand the interface across multiple monitors. This has been a highly requested feature.

In the past this has just stretched the Timeline and content libraries to the other monitor, creating extra long panels. With the new custom layout features, panels can be placed anywhere and in any size on your second monitor as well.

Steps 1, 2, and 3: Capture, Edit, and Share

CAPTURE, EDIT, AND SHARE. These three steps are pretty much the order of creating videos, not only in VideoStudio, but also in other video authoring/editing applications. I mean, it makes sense, right? You first need to acquire the material to make your video (capture). Then you need to have the tools to edit your clips, making your video in that special way you would like to express your experience and style (edit).

Finally, you want to output or export your video into a useable format so you can share your favorite moments with your friends and colleagues, making sure they can see your movies in the most ubiquitous, accessible methods possible (share).

As the title of this section suggests, these three tasks are the main steps in the video creation process. I'll show you how VSX5 distinguishes these tasks when it comes to the work area. The tabs at the top (collectively called the Step panel) of the VSX5 screen are identified to represent these most common sequential steps in the movie making process: 1 Capture, 2 Edit, and 3 Share. These will be referred to as the Capture step, Edit step, and Share step.

▶ **Capture step:** This tab, although the logical first step in any video project, is only required for certain media and devices. You may already have uploaded or downloaded your clips onto your computer, in which case, they're already captured and converted. If your content is already accessible, you can import it into VSX5 via the Edit tab, either directly into the Timeline or into the appropriate content library.

Even though the end result is the same, there is a difference between the terms *capture* and *import*. There is also a difference between importing and merely opening files.

Importing media is the simple act of bringing already digitally compatible files into VSX5. These imported files are already compatible with the software and do not need to be converted in order to be used.

Video that needs to be converted, on the other hand, needs to be *captured* first. Even if the files are already in some digital format (e.g., digital TV or DV tape), they still need to be "wrapped" in a format that VideoStudio can understand and work with, usually AVI or Mpeg. The default capture option is usually Mpeg, the default project settings are Mpeg, and the most popular formats are all based off the Mpeg standard (mts, m2ts, mp4, dvd, vcd, etc.).

The Capture tab, though, specializes in making it easy for you to acquire initially incompatible digital media from various methods by first choosing your source (see Figure 3.11). Once the source is chosen, VSX5 knows how to communicate with the selected device, where to find the video files, and how to convert them into a format that VSX5 can use. In most instances, you can actually take control of your external device in VSX5 when capturing.

Click here...   ...to get here

Figure 3.11
The Capture step.

When returning to the Edit step from the Capture step, your Timeline will probably change to the Multitrack view, from the Storyboard view. Nothing to worry about.

▶ **Edit step:** This is the tab that VSX5 defaults to when launched and where you'll be spending the vast majority of your time in the rest of the book's lessons (see Figure 3.12). As its name implies, the Edit step is where all the fun editing stuff takes place: the movie assembly process, adding text, special effect filters, scene transitions, picture-in-a-picture, narration, and so much more. (You'll learn about these features throughout this chapter and the rest of the book.)

▶ **Share step:** This final step in the video production process is done in the Share tab. It is really just a pop-up panel that appears in the center of the Edit area (see Figure 3.13), asking you to select your choice of output methods. Is your movie destined for one of the many video file formats, a DVD, or a mobile device? Do you want to upload it to the web for a social site like Facebook, a website like YouTube, or maybe your own website? The Share Step is where you'll begin this process.

Notice that the choices don't specify any particular file format, but instead, a destination. You will be able to choose a specific file format along with options within those formats after you first choose a destination.

Figure 3.12
The Edit step.

Figure 3.13
The Share step.

Content Libraries

THIS SECTION WILL COVER the Edit step in further detail, starting with the content libraries. I mentioned earlier that you can bypass the content libraries and import content directly onto the Timeline. You can also take any item from the Timeline and drag it to the appropriate content library for reuse.

However, using the content libraries, instead of importing directly to the Timeline, provides many advantages. Content libraries allow you to store and organize your assets into various media categories, such as video, audio, titles, stills, and more. Importing into and storing assets in the libraries allows for unlimited reuse in your current video and any subsequent videos you create. These assets will stay there until you delete them. Each clip is represented by a thumbnail, or small photo representation. Movies you output via the Share step are also stored in the libraries after VSX5 creates them so you can easily preview them without leaving VSX5.

Deleting a thumbnail in a library will not delete the original file or affect the clip if it's already in the Timeline.

The visual method to access the various content libraries and galleries is through the Library Navigation panel in the center of your screen, between the Preview panel and content libraries (see Figure 3.14). In order, from the top down, are Media, Instant Project, Transition, Title, Graphic (solid background color chips), and Filter (special effects).

Figure 3.14
Various media libraries.

The following explains how the media libraries are laid out and organized.

▶ From the Edit step, click the Media icon at the top of the Library Navigation panel (see Figure 3.15). It should be highlighted yellow. The media library contains video clips, still graphics (photos and backgrounds), and audio clips (music, narration, and so on). Any videos you render out (or shared) will also be added here.

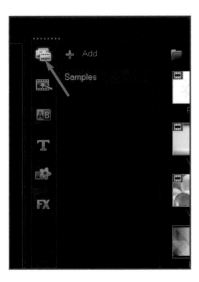

Figure 3.15
Selecting the Media library.

Figure 3.16
Media library view options.

▶ The Samples category represents all the media elements included with VSX5 and that you downloaded after installing VSX5. Using Figure 3.16 as a guide, click each of the three icons (Hide Videos, Hide Photos, and Hide Audio Files) to narrow the library collections to specific media types. When finished, turn them all back on (yellow) so all the samples clips are visible.

Access to Instant Projects has been moved from just above the Timeline in the last version to the Library area. This is the next category listed in the Navigation panel below the Media library (see Figure 3.17). Instant Projects are movie and slideshow templates that already include placement holders for videos/images, titles, and music. All you have to do is swap out the placeholders with your own content. There are even shortcuts to do this.

Instant movie templates are also a great way to learn about several VSX5 features, including how Timeline tracks interact with each other. They're categorized into suggested areas they're to be used within a movie such as the beginning, middle, or end.

Figure 3.17
Instant Projects library.

▶ Click on the Transition icon to preview the selection of available transitions (see Figure 3.18). Transitions are special effects that will stylize the change from one clip or scene to another. Transitions are placed on the Timeline between any two video clips or still graphics in any of the video or overlay tracks.

Figure 3.18
Transition library.

You may notice that only three transitions are displayed. Click on the down arrow next to My Favorites to see a list of Transition categories (see Figure 3.19). You can choose any one of the options or click All to see all of the 125+ transitions.

Figure 3.19
Transition categories.

Tip

Transitions can easily be added to the My Favorites list. Select any transition in any of the categories (except My Favorites).

At the top, the icon with the star and plus (+) will become active. Click that icon to add your currently selected transition to the My Favorites category. To verify the addition, go to the My Favorites list to make sure it's been added.

▶ Select the T icon to open the Title library. It includes a couple of dozen customizable, animated text titles (especially if you downloaded the free content) that you can drag and drop into a title track on the Timeline and edit in the Preview panel. This collection also includes a My Favorites category. Once you've edited a title, you can also place it back into the library as a new custom choice.

In versions previous to VideoStudio X4, titles could only be displayed in title tracks, and thus only on top of all other elements in a video. In VSX5, you can now use them in overlay tracks too, so you can create some cool layering effects with your titles. I'll cover this feature in Chapter 9.

▶ Colors are used as backgrounds or "blank" clips in video tracks. An example of this might be at the start of a movie where you only want a title to show on the screen. You could place the title on top of a video clip or use a blank colored background chip and put your title on top of that instead. They make for useful fillers, because you cannot have a blank spot in the main video track.

▶ Select the Graphic icon to open the Graphic library (see Figure 3.20). This includes four galleries: Color, Object (decorations), Frame (similar to picture frames), and Flash Animation.

CAUTION

You cannot leave a blank space at the start or between any two clips in the background video track. It must be filled with a video, still, or color clip. You may, though, leave blank areas in other tracks.

Graphics libraries   Graphics categories

Figure 3.20
Graphic library.

▶ Objects in this category are decorations and meant to be used in overlay tracks where you can place them anywhere on the stage. They can be resized.

Any object placed in the background video track will only occupy the entire movie screen. Objects added into any of the overlay tracks can take up the entire screen or any portion of it.

- ► Frames make for a great effect that mimics a video playing in a picture frame. You can also use them to frame still images.

- ► Flash animations are relatively new to VSX5. These include both frames and decorations. The advantage of using Flash animations is that they are, well, animated. Flash objects also have the unique characteristic of being re-sizable without losing quality. They also have a very small file size.

- ► Select the FX icon. This is the Filter library (sometimes called an *Effects* library), and it includes numerous special effects that you can apply directly onto video clips, and in many cases titles, in the Timeline. These effects will

actually distort the video according to the customizable settings in each filter. Effects can include color corrections, weather effects, warping effects, painting effects, and many more. Many of these effects are also customizable over time through a process called *tweening*. Filters will be covered in more detail in Chapters 7 and 8.

All objects used from the Media library can only be placed into the video or overlay tracks.

The Preview Panel

THE PREVIEW PANEL (see Figure 3.21), in the upper left of your screen, is exactly what its name implies. It allows you to preview content from your libraries, from content placed in the Timeline, or even audio. If you preview content from your Timeline, you can preview all the content at any point in time or just one clip from a specific track.

For example, if at 35 seconds into your movie, you have a video clip with an overlaid video or graphic on top of that, with a text title, and a music track, you can play all of it at the same time. It also allows you to preview your entire movie. If you select just one clip in one of the tracks, the panel will only play that clip. In this section, I'll show you how to control which content and what part of that content plays.

Figure 3.21
The Preview panel and its controls.

Controls in the Preview panel are explained in the following list (see Figure 3.21). These controls will be used extensively in the next chapter.

A. **Play/Stop button:** Allows you to control playback of any video or animation.

B. **Home/Step Back/Step Forward/End controls:** Controls (from left to right) for rewind to start of clip or project, step back one frame, step forward one frame, and fast forward to end of clip or project.

C. **Repeat:** When the clip gets to the end, it immediately loops and restarts to play again. This can be toggled on or off.

D. **System volume:** Toggles audio playback on and off.

E. **Scrubber track:** The horizontal lines represent the entire clip's, or project's, length that will play if placed in the Timeline (it can be shortened). Use the white slider to move (scrub) the clip to quickly locate a particular location or frame.

You can manually move the orange end points (select a library item first) to adjust the start and end points of the clip that will actually play when placed on the Timeline. The horizontal line will represent that length of time. Trimming a clip this way will not alter the original clip. It will only designate what part of that clip will be used in the Timeline.

Figure 3.22
Scrubber controls.

F. Timecode: This stopwatch-like viewer will display the exact frame (called a timecode) that your clip is currently displaying. From left to right, the figures displayed represent hours:minutes:seconds:frames. For example, 1:25:48:15 means the clip is displaying the frame at precisely 1 hour, 25 minutes, 48 seconds, and 15 frames from the start of the clip.

G. Mark-In/Mark-Out: These two brackets represent tools to mark the start and end points of a clip. You can either drag the orange markers to position a mark point or use the timecode for more precision. When a marker is positioned, click either the left or the right bracket to set the start or end point, respectively, of the clip that will play in the Timeline. Using these markers will not affect the original clip.

H. Split Clip: The scissors tool provides a more permanent edit than the marking tools. It will cut a clip in two, making two new clips. If the clip is in the Timeline, the scissors will cut that clip at the white marker, creating two separate clips in the Timeline that will play sequentially (see Figures 3.23 and 3.24).

If you cut a clip that you're previewing from a library (instead of first placing it in the Timeline), VSX5 will create two new clips and place them in the Library, in addition to the original clip. (See Figure 3.25.) Notice there are now two new clips in the Library, after you split one of the clips.

Figure 3.23
Before applying a cut.

Figure 3.24
After applying a cut.

Figure 3.25
Results of splitting a library clip.

Clips from either the Library or the Timeline can be edited in the Preview panel. Trimmed clips will not affect the original clip.

I. Enlarge: This toggle will display the Preview panel in a full-screen view. Once in full screen, click the icon again to return to the normal view, or press the Esc key.

J. Project vs. Clip Mode: This is a handy setting to use when previewing Timeline content. Select any clip in the Timeline to preview it. If Clip is selected, only that clip in that track will preview. If Project is selected, all the content at that point in time will preview. In other words, the content in all the tracks at that timecode point will play, not just the selected clip.

Isn't it amazing how VSX5 allows for so many tools and actions in the same window? It really does a good job at minimizing the use of multiple open windows and dialog boxes. The Timeline is no different. I'll cover that next.

Multitrack Timeline

THE THIRD AND FINAL SECTION of the main VSX5 interface is the multitrack Timeline. The Timeline is where you assemble the media clips to use in your video project. It is based on the progression of time. This line of time starts at zero on the left and progresses forward in time as you move to the right. 0:00:00:00 is the starting point. Time increases as the project plays and as the playback head moves to the right.

The biggest advantage of a multitrack Timeline over a single-track one is that you can instantly view where all your media items are located in relation to each other and for how long they're present in your movie. By utilizing the Project option next to the Play button in the Preview panel, you can also see how things are layered.

There are two Timeline views: the Multitrack view and the Storyboard view. What you'll see when you launch VSX5 depends in which view was showing when you previously quit the application. We'll cover the Storyboard view later in this chapter.

The Timeline in VSX5 allows you to layer assets in your movie project. This is called *overlay* and is the term in video production that refers to placing objects on top of other objects in a layered fashion. You may have heard of Picture-in-Picture (PiP). PiP works by laying one video clip over the top of another one. The order of tracks in the VSX5 Timeline starts from the top down, where the top-most track (the video track) serves as the background layer. Successive layers are built on top of each other by adding objects into the tracks below the video track.

Overlaid objects can cover a portion of the background video track or the entire track. Either choice allows you to set areas of transparency so that you can see portions of the background, or other layers, through the overlaid object.

Obviously, this layering property only affects visual elements, such as video clips, images, and text titles. Audio clips are not affected because you can't see them, but two clips playing concurrently will automatically blend, and the volume of the audio in each one can be set individually. The voice and music tracks are interchangeable. Voiceovers and music can go in either of the two audio tracks. You can also have audio embedded in any video clip you use and adjust the volume levels of any of those.

Figure 3.26 identifies the different tracks of the VSX5 Timeline. The main video track is the background layer. It will always display at full-screen size. Overlay tracks are layers on top of the video track background layer (PiP). Overlay tracks can be resized, reshaped, and animated, as well as have levels of transparency applied to them. All video and overlay tracks can contain a video, photo, graphic image, or just a solid color chip.

Figure 3.26
Multiple Timeline tracks.

Figure 3.27 points out tools in the Timeline that you'll be learning how to use in this and successive chapters. Following is a brief explanation of each. You'll have plenty of tasks using these tools, but feel free to try them out and see the results. Many of the tools will require content in the Timeline. Give them a try!

Figure 3.27
Timeline tools.

A. **Storyboard view:** Displays a Timeline view of assets in thumbnails, but still in the usual chronological order as the regular Timeline view.

B. **Timeline view:** This Timeline view utilizes multiple tracks, allowing for frame-accurate clip editing and layering of multiple file types to create an elaborate video project.

C. **Undo/Redo:** Allows you to undo and redo previous operations.

D. **Record/Capture:** Shows the Record/Capture Option panel, where choices include Capture Video, Import Files, Record Voice-overs, Take Snapshots, Screen Capture and more. New to VSX5 is the ability to create video screen captures. Many of these tools represent shortcuts to the Capture step features.

E. **Sound Mixer:** Launches the Sound Mixer and the multitrack Audio Timeline, which lets you customize your audio settings.

F. **Auto-Music:** This icon launches the unique feature in VSX5 that allows you to create multitrack, customized music.

G. **Zoom Adjuster:** Quickly zoom your Timeline in or out using a real-time, interactive slider.

H. **Fit Project in Timeline:** Adjusts your entire project to fit into the visible span of your Timeline.

I. **Project Duration:** Shows the duration of your project in timecode format.

J. **Show All Visible Tracks:** Squeezes all the Timeline tracks you're utilizing into a visible view on the Timeline.

K. **Track Manager:** Opens the Track Manager window where you can add additional Timeline tracks you may need in your project.

L. **Add/Remove Chapter Points:** Adds/deletes chapter points at the current playback head's location. Chapter points are break indicators that are carried forward to DVD creation to create separate chapters on your disc.

M. **Enable/Disable Ripple Editing:** Locks and unlocks tracks of any movement of any shift in time when you insert clips into other tracks. This allows you to control the shift of tracks as you insert new content. Locked

49

tracks will move to the right as content is inserted into other tracks, so as to maintain synchronicity. Unlocked tracks will NOT move.

N. Ripple Editing options: Displays menu of Ripple Editing options.

O. Individual Track Ripple Editing toggle: Enable or disable Ripple Editing on individual tracks.

P. Auto-Scroll Timeline: Enable or disable automatic scrolling of the Timeline so it follows along when a project plays.

Q. Scroll Timeline Forward/Backward: Manual Timeline scrolling. A scroll bar will also appear when there is content in the Timeline.

R. Timecode Locations: Timecode locations along the Timeline.

The Track Manager

The default multitrack Timeline view shows only a limited number of available tracks: one background, one overlay, one title, one voice-over, and one music track. This can be a limitation for many projects. Fortunately, VSX5's multitrack Timeline allows for up to twenty-one video tracks (one background and twenty overlay tracks), two title tracks, and up to four audio tracks (voiceover and music).

> Remember that although there are only two title tracks, titles can be added to any of the 21 video tracks, too.

Fortunately, you don't need to display all the tracks if you won't be using them all. The Track Manager lets you toggle their visibility and usage on and off. You can add and make tracks visible only when you need them so that they don't take up valuable screen real estate. To manage your Timeline tracks, follow these steps.

1. Click the Track Manager icon on the upper-left corner of the Timeline, below the toolbar (labeled as "K" in Figure 3.27).

2. In the Track Manager selection window, click to open the Overlay Tracks drop-down list. Highlight 3 in the list, as shown in Figure 3.28. Click OK. Your Timeline will update to show the additional tracks.

Figure 3.28
Adding Timeline tracks.

Table 3.1 specifies what library content types can be inserted into which Timeline tracks. Tracks are listed on the left. Along the top are the Media library media that can be placed in the tracks.

Table 3.1 Library Content Types

Libraries

Tracks	Media	Transition	Title	Graphic	Filter
Background	X[1]	X	X	X	X
Overlay	X	X	X	X	X
Title		X	X		X
Audio	X[2]				X[3]

(1) Video and photo media only, not audio

(2) Audio media only

(3) Audio filters only (which are located in a different panel and will be covered in Chapter 6)

The Storyboard View

The term *storyboard* might be familiar to you if you've seen TV specials that discuss how a movie was made, especially animated movies, like those from Pixar or Disney. Movie studios often have a room with walls covered by scraps of paper with drawings on them. They're almost always displayed in rows. These are concept drawings of a sequence of events for an upcoming movie. Together, they're called a *storyboard*. The board describes the story, hence the name.

The Storyboard view is also available in VSX5. Utilizing thumbnails displayed in sequence, it's the fastest and simplest way to add and organize the main video track because that's all it works with: the content that you have in the main (background) video track (video clips, graphics, titles and the transitions between them). It is not capable of displaying overlays or additional audio (outside of what's embedded in a video clip). It is meant to lay out the main ideas for your video project.

A big advantage of starting with a storyboard, besides quickly creating a sequence of clips in a desired order, is that this can be done in very little space. Whereas placing video clips in the Timeline view will display them in reference to their duration, the Storyboard view only places a simple thumbnail representation (similar to content in your libraries), despite how long the clip is. Therefore, you can concentrate more on the sequence of events and easily change them by simply rearranging the thumbnails through drag and drop.

After laying out your project concepts in the storyboard, you can return to the Timeline view. The Timeline will take your storyboard content and then convert it to the multitrack Timeline format where you can add more content and polish your timing with its frame-accurate abilities.

You can also view any project you've built in the Timeline back in the Storyboard view. This might make it easier for you to see and rearrange the big picture and then return to the Timeline to continue your work.

I won't spend much time discussing the Storyboard view, so in this short section, I'll show you how to operate the storyboard and take content to the Timeline. I'll also show you how to use basic content from the library. Since you'll just be using sample clips from the Media library, the story won't make much sense, but the concept will.

1. Click the Storyboard icon in the upper-left corner of the Timeline (labeled "A" in Figure 3.27). The Media navigation panel will auto-switch to the Media library.

2. Make sure the Video gallery of the Media library is visible by toggling that icon to the visible position (as a reminder, see Figure 3.29). You can also have the other media (graphics and audio) libraries visible, too; it won't matter. All the video sample clips' names start with the letter "V" for, uhh, video.

3. Use your mouse to drag and drop video clip V01 to the Storyboard, where it says Drag Video Clips Here.

4. Follow that with clips V08 and V17 to create a storyboard sequence of three video clips. Each clip could be an hour long or a minute long, but here, they only take up the space of a small thumbnail.

5. In the Storyboard, drag the night scene video to the end to rearrange the order of the clips.

6. In the Library Navigation panel, select the Transition library (the A|B icon). Small gray transition placeholder icons will then appear in the Storyboard between each video clip. These are the transition placement areas.

7. The Crossfade transition option should be visible in the default view of My Favorites. If it isn't, choose All from the Transition drop-down list. Drag and drop the Crossfade thumbnail to each of the gray squares between the video clips. Your view should look like that in Figure 3.30.

In here...   **Click here to view video clips**

Figure 3.29
Accessing the video Media library.

Figure 3.30
Storyboard view.

8. In the Storyboard view, double-click on the first transition. This will bring up the transitions Options panel below the Media library. This is how easy it is to access most of the options in VSX5.

9. Where you see the timecode display (currently showing 1 second), click on the 01 portion. It will start blinking to show that it is selected. Use the up arrow to change it to 2 seconds (see Figure 3.31). Repeat this for the second transition. Make sure that the second transition remains selected in the Storyboard.

Figure 3.31
Adjusting transition durations.

10. In the Preview panel, click the Play button. This will preview the selected transition only. See how nicely one scene fades into another?

11. Now select Project in the Preview window (to the left of the Play button). It will turn white when selected. This will ensure that the entire project plays, instead of just a selected clip. Select the Rewind (Home) button, and then click Play again. This time the entire project plays from the start.

12. Now you'll take your project over to the more detailed Timeline view. Click the Timeline button just to the right of the Storyboard button ("B" in Figure 3.27). Notice how much more room your media takes up here than it did in the Storyboard view?

    Also notice that content is only displayed in the video track (see Figure 3.32). If you were to add content in other tracks and return to Storyboard view, you would still only see content in the video track.

13. Now is the point when you should save your movie, which I'll discuss in the next section.

Congratulations, you've just learned the basics of using VSX5 to make your first video! Most of what you'll be doing from here on out will be based on these initial steps. There's still so much more to do and learn, though!

Figure 3.32
Timeline view comparison.

Saving Your Movie

WHEN SAVING A FILE, as opposed to sharing or exporting a movie, VSX5 creates a project file with the VSP extension. This file is actually an Edit Decision List (EDL).

Figure 3.33
Relink dialog box.

An Edit Decision List (EDL) is a small file that does *not* contain any content, but rather contains instructions on how to assemble the content, what clips or portions of a clip to use, where to place the clip in the Timeline, what filters to apply, and so on. These are the instructions for creating the sequence of events for your movie.

When you save a VSX5 project (File > Save), it creates an EDL with the .vsp extension.

As a result, when you reopen your project, the necessary content items must be present and in their original locations on your computer, with the same file names for the project to rebuild itself. If the content is not where it's supposed to be, VSX5 will ask you, via the Relink dialog box (see Figure 3.33), to relocate one of the files and then attempt to automatically relink the rest of them. If you moved files to several different locations, you will continue to be asked to locate missing files until they're all found. If VSX5 asks you to locate and relink a movie or asset you purposely deleted, then you can tell it to ignore the relinking process in the same dialog box.

When it comes time to output your project, VSX5 will use your project file, or EDL, to create your DVD, movie, or audio CD. VSX5 also does a pretty good job at recovering your files if your computer should lock up or crash. Fortunately, this rarely happens on a PC (yeah, right). When you restart VSX5, it will ask if you would like to open the recovered file. However, it may not include the most recent changes you made.

After you first save and name your project file, VSX5 will auto-save it every 10 minutes. This default setting can be changed. Go to Settings > Preferences. In the General tab, you can adjust this setting under the Project area (see Figure 3.34). You can both toggle the auto-save function on and off and set the time interval of how often it saves. Adjust this setting to suit your preferences.

To save your project, simply go to File > Save (see Figure 3.35) or Ctrl+S. In the dialog box, similar to most other applications, choose a file name and location. Oftentimes in this book, I will designate a file name and location for you. To save the same project under a different name, choose File > Save As instead.

Set auto-save time feature

Figure 3.34
Setting the auto-save feature.

Figure 3.35
Saving your project.

After we get serious about building video projects in VSX5, you will continue to build projects from previous chapters. Therefore, it's essential that you follow the instructions that mention saving your work. You will be naming them as Chapter 4, Chapter 5, and so forth. In subsequent chapters, you will be asked to reopen previous project to continue working on them.

Quick Quiz

1. What is an EDL and why is it used? (See "VideoStudio Moviemaking Terminology.")

2. What are the three main working panels in VSX5? (See "Touring the VSX5 Workspace.")

3. What are the three main processes to creating a movie? (See "Steps 1, 2, and 3: Capture, Edit, and Share.")

4. Name the six content libraries. (See "Content Libraries.")

5. What buttons in the Preview panel designate whether you see one track play or all tracks play? (See "The Preview Panel.")

Building a
Video 101

IN THE LAST CHAPTER, you learned where the main features are, how to use them, and how to assemble a movie. Congratulations! You're well on your way to learning VideoStudio Pro. It's not too scary, is it? Let's keep going. Now it's time to get a little more detailed on those basics and expand on the simple tasks covered in the introductory chapters. Now that you know how the application is set up and what each main area is used for, you can begin applying this knowledge to more precision editing.

This chapter will broaden your knowledge of acquiring content in the Capture step and organizing content in the various Media libraries. I'll focus on video and still image editing, as well as single and multi-trim video clip editing (so you can create multiple clips and splits from a single video). I'll also discuss saving and reusing edited clips for future use, adjusting the lengths of both videos and graphics, and best practices for using photos in video production.

You'll learn all this and more, so let's get going!

Setting Up Project Properties

T HE FIRST THING YOU NEED to do is designate the screen size of your project. Will you be making a widescreen (16:9) production or a standard (4:3) production? The videos you'll be using in this chapter are standard size ratio, so let's make sure the project is set up for this.

1. Launch VSX5.

2. Go to Settings > Project Properties.

3. In the Project Properties dialog box, under Edit File Format, choose MPEG Files from the drop-down list (see Figure 4.1).

Figure 4.1
Setting project properties.

You can choose either AVI or MPEG without much effect. MPEG will convert the files into DVD-ready content. AVI will keep the content in an untouched compatible format and provide you with specific window size options.

4. In the lower-right corner of the Project Properties dialog, click Edit. The Project Options dialog box will open.

5. In the General tab, under the Display Aspect Ratio drop-down list, choose 4:3.

6. Click OK twice to close both dialog boxes.

Adding New Content

S O FAR, YOU'VE JUST WORKED with sample clips that came included in the VSX5 libraries, and you'll be using many more of them throughout the book. Now it's time to learn how to import and use clips from the included lesson files. Before you do that, though, you should understand the various file types that can be used in VSX5. Not only are video files supported, but so are many animation files. Remember when I mentioned that VSX5 is not an animation application, but that it can work with outputs from animation software? You can import animation files from some Autodesk and Adobe applications, along with basic animated GIF files.

I'm highly confident that VSX5 will work with your video files, but you'd also be surprised at the file types it's compatible with that you probably have never heard of. The following lists describe the kinds of video, animations, and still images you can import into VSX5. Corel has always been a champion of file-format compatibility, and VSX5 is no exception.

Supported Video Formats:

▶ Microsoft AVI

▶ 3GPP (3GP), 3GPP2 (3G2): Multimedia files for cell phones

▶ Microsoft DVR-MS (.DVR-MS): Microsoft format for storing TV content recorded by Windows XP Media Center Edition, Vista, and Windows 7

▶ Autodesk Animation (FLC, FLI, or FLX)

▶ Animated GIF (GIF)

▶ QuickTime Movies (MOV or QT)

▶ MPEG (MPG, MPEG, MPV, MP2, MP4, or M4V)

▶ Ulead Image Sequence (UIS, UISX)

▶ Video Paint (UVP)

▶ Windows Media Video (WMV)

▶ Video Editor Project (DVP)

▶ VideoStudio project files (VSP)

▶ Hi-def: AVCHD, BDMV, H.264, HDV

▶ Others include M2T, M4V, MOD, M2TS, TOD, DivX*, RealVideo, and RM*. (It should also be noted that special software drivers are required for the DivX and RM formats.)

Supported Image Formats:

▶ Windows bitmap (BMP)

▶ Graphics Interchange Format (GIF)

▶ Joint Photographer's Experts Group (JPG, JPEG, JPE, JP2, JPC, or J2K)

▶ Portable Network Graphic (PNG)

▶ QuickTime movies (MOV or QT)

▶ Tagged Image File (TIF or TIFF)

- ► Ulead Photo Project, Object, and Sequence files (UFP, UFO, or UIS)

- ► PaintShop Pro images (PSP), PSPImage

- ► RAW camera formats (RAW, CRW, CR2, BAY, RAF, DCR, MRW, NEF, ORF, PEF, X3F, SRF, ERF, DNG, KDC, D25, HDR, SR2, ARW, NRW, OUT, TIF, MOS, and FFF)

- ► Other supported formats include CLP, CUR, EPS, FAX, FPX, ICO, IFF, IMG, MAC, MPO, PCD, PCT, PCS, PIC, PSD, PXR, RAS, SCT, SHG, TGA, WMF, , 001, DCS, DCX, ICO, MSP, PBM, PCX, PGM, PPM, SCI, WBM, and WBMP

For the next few sections, you'll be importing content into VSX5 from both the Capture and the Edit tabs and then organizing it into the appropriate libraries. But first, you'll learn how to organize and manage your media libraries using the Library Navigation panel.

Names of library clips may change once they're inserted into the Timeline. The preinstalled clips have shorter alias names applied to them. You can add alias names to library items just by double-clicking on the clip's title in the library and renaming it. In other words, the name of a library item may be different from the actual file name of it on your computer.

I mentioned this in Chapter 3, but it bears repeating for clarity. There is a difference between the terms *capture* and *import*. There is also a difference between importing and merely opening files. Importing media is the simple act of bringing digitally compatible files into VSX5. These imported files are already compatible with the software and do not need to be converted in order to be used.

Video that needs to be converted, on the other hand, needs to be captured. Even if the files are already in some digital format (e.g., digital TV or DV tape), they still need to be "wrapped" in a format that VideoStudio can understand and work with, usually AVI.

Using the Library Navigation Panel

You can use the Library Navigation Panel to create your own custom content libraries, which helps to keep different kinds of project media separate from each other. Content can be captured and/or imported directly into any custom library you create.

1. In the Edit step, select the Media library icon in the Library panel. The Library Navigation panel may or may not be open. If your view looks like Figure 4.2, click the Show Library Navigation Panel button to create a view like the one shown in Figure 4.3.

Figure 4.2
Click to open the Library
Navigation panel.

Figure 4.3
The Open Library Navigation panel.

2. Click the + Add button at the top of the panel. While the new folder is highlighted in blue, type **Chapter 4**. If it's not highlighted, double-click it. After doing so, you will see the media library (to the right) is empty (see Figure 4.4). Let's get some content in there. Make sure Chapter 4 is highlighted in the Library Navigation panel.

Figure 4.4
A new media library.

3. Click the Browse button at the bottom of the Library Navigation panel. In your VSX5 lesson folders, navigate to Photos > Buildings. Move the Explorer window over so you can see at least part of the empty media library. Drag and drop the photo LincolnNight.jpg right into the Chapter 4 media library. If the photo does not appear, make sure that the Photos icon is highlighted at the top of the library (you can still import the photo even if it's set to hide photos). Your view should look like the one shown in Figure 4.5.

Figure 4.5
New imported content.

Importing via the Capture Tab

You've just created a custom library folder, and you've already learned how to import content into it. Now it's time to use the Capture step to insert content directly into your new library. As I mentioned earlier, the Capture step is actually a little deceiving, as it includes both capturing and importing from specific sources and devices.

To import content directly into your new library, follow these steps:

1. Click the Capture tab at the top of your VSX5 screen. In the middle of the window, select Import from Digital Media. The Select Import Source Folders window will appear (see Figure 4.6). This window looks and behaves similar to your Windows Explorer navigation window.

Figure 4.6
Importing from digital media.

2. In the Select Import Source Folders window, navigate to Videos in your VSX5_LessonPlans folder > Videos folder and place a check mark next to the WashingtonDC folder (see Figure 4.7). Click OK.

3. In the Import from Digital Media window that appears next, you'll see the path to the WashingtonDC folder listed and highlighted. Click Start (see Figure 4.8) to preview all the video clips in this folder.

Figure 4.7
Select the WashingtonDC folder.

Figure 4.8
Click Start to display content.

4. Place a checkmark in the upper-left corner of the video called Fireworks2 (see Figure 4.9). Click Start import at the bottom, and the importing will begin.

Figure 4.9
Import selection window.

5. Once the importing status bars show that the process is complete, the Import Settings dialog box will appear (see Figure 4.10). Make sure Capture to Library is checked and Insert to Timeline is NOT checked. In the Capture to Library drop-down list, choose Chapter 4 and click OK.

6. Return to the Edit tab of VSX5. If it doesn't appear already, in the Library Navigation panel, choose Chapter 4 (under Samples) to view where the clip you just captured now resides. Unfortunately, the file name from the clip was not captured.

7. Click on the Fireworks clip file name. Change its name to **Fireworks2**. The name, though, will still revert back to the captured name when applied to the Timeline. Changing the name in a library does not actually change the file name, just its reference name while working in VSX5.

Figure 4.10
Importing to a custom library.

It's easy to understand why
you need to name the thumbnail in
the library of a captured clip. After all, VSX5
doesn't know what to name any of the clips
it captures, so it numbers them instead.
So why does it revert back to the captured
name when it's placed on the Timeline?
The original names of library items refer to
the original file name, wherever that file is
on your PC. If you rename a captured file
in the folder it is captured to, *then* it will
retain that name anywhere you use it.

8. Save your project (File > Save) as **Chapter 4. vsp**. Save it in either the default My Projects folder or perhaps in your lessons folder, so all your book files are centrally located. This saved file will now appear at the bottom of the File menu, so you can easily launch it again later.

Importing from a mobile device follows a similar procedure, but the window looks somewhat different. This capture procedure is instead located in the Edit step, using the Record/Capture icon between the Timeline and the Preview window. When your device is connected, it will be listed in the left column, with its downloadable content displayed on the right. Ctrl-select the clips you want to import and click OK. Again, you'll be asked into which libraries you want the clips placed.

Capturing Video

This section and the next, called "DV Quick Scan," have important information to learn, but following the steps is optional, as they are not common procedures (unless you want to have fun with your webcam!). I realize only a small percentage of readers have a DV tape camcorder or the ability or desire to capture from a digital TV source (extra hardware is required).

The procedure I'm about to show you is not integral to the rest of this chapter. If you have a DV tape camcorder or would like to capture a video of yourself from your webcam, this is the place to learn how to do it. Remember that capturing, as opposed to simply importing, involves converting raw video files to a usable format, and then importing them into VSX5.

1. Return to the Capture step and select Capture Video, the topmost choice in the center panel.

2. If you have a DV tape source, connect it to your PC and turn on to Play. If you are unfamiliar with how to connect a DV tape source, refer to the section "Connecting Your Video Source" in Chapter 18. If your source is connected correctly, the Capture Video button will be blinking in the panel.

3. If you would like to try this feature and have a webcam, choose HP Webcam from the Source drop-down list shown in Figure 4.11. This list also displays the other capture options. Select the one you're able to use. I chose Panasonic DV Device.

Figure 4.11
Selecting a webcam capture source.

Whichever Source option you choose, information about both your source and capturing settings will be displayed in the Information panel on the bottom portion of your screen. First on the list is the file name that the capture will be saved as. Second is the video size and quality settings. Third is the available space on your hard drive, fourth is the device name that it's capturing from, and last, the format the audio will be captured in.

4. In the Format drop-down list, choose DV if you would like the captured file to remain a basic RAW file that VSX5 can work with. It will add a "wrapper" to the file, making it an AVI file. Choose DVD to convert the file to a suitable one if creating a DVD is your goal, or an MPEG-2 file (MPG).

You will only see the DV option if you have a camcorder connected. If you do not, the only choice will be DVD.

5. The next drop-down list, Capture Folder, will be the location where the captured videos are stored. It is important to either choose your own location or remember this location. Video files are *huge,* and VSX5 doesn't always delete video files after you are done with them. Knowing where you can manually delete them will help you recover valuable hard drive space.

6. Next are your choices for representing your captured clips in VSX5. If you want them to appear in VSX5, make sure Capture to Library is checked; otherwise, they'll just be stored in the Capture folder. Then choose which media library folder to save them into. Click the plus sign (+) to add additional folders, just as you did back in the Library panel of the Edit tab.

7. Optionally, check the Split by Scene box to create a separate file every time there is a video break. This option is not available when capturing from a webcam.

8. Click the Options icon and select Capture Options. If you check Insert to Timeline, your captured video will be both inserted into the Timeline (at the end of any other clips), and, if you also have Capture to library unchecked, the video will be imported there, too. Don't worry about the Video properties under Options at this time. Click OK to close the small Capture Options window.

9. Click Take a Snapshot to save a JPEG of the current frame and drop it into the Capture library at the top of the page.

10. If you know you want to capture all of your DV tape, starting from where the playback head is, or your webcam, click the blinking Capture Video button. When you're done, click the same button again that now says Stop Capture. Your newly captured video clips will show up in the library at the top.

11. Close the Capture Video section by clicking the X on the far right of the panel. You will return to the main capture choices, and your captured clips will be placed where you directed them.

12. Save your project.

DV Quick Scan

Regarding capturing from a DV tape, the Capture Video feature is great if you know you're going to capture straight through. But what if you would like to review and choose which scenes to capture before actually capturing them? This is where the DV Quick Scan feature comes in. Quick Scan will scan your tape and provide thumbnail views without actually saving any of the video at first. You can then select which scenes you want to save, then capture, and import them into VSX5.

1. Select DV Quick Scan to open the DV Quick Scan dialog box (see Figure 4.12).

Figure 4.12
DV Quick Scan dialog box.

2. In the upper-left corner of the dialog box, you'll see a small Preview window showing the current frame of your DV tape being displayed on your camcorder, along with the familiar controls you saw in the Edit tab's Preview panel.

   In the Device drop-down list, you should see your DV camcorder listed. If it's not and if the Start Scan button at the bottom left is not blinking, your camcorder is not connected correctly. Make sure you're using a FireWire connection (not USB) and that your camcorder is on and set to play.

3. Choose your format again from the Capture Format drop-down list, either DV AVI or DVD (MPEG-2). Then choose your folder from the Capture Folder drop-down list.

4. In the Scan Scene area, choose whether you want to scan the tape from the beginning or from its current position. In the Speed drop-down list, you can select how fast to scan it at. Choose 1X if you want to view along with the scan. Otherwise, choose the Maximum Speed option.

5. Click the Start Scan button on the bottom left.

6. You can either wait until the tape is scanned in its entirety or click Stop Scan when you're done. All the thumbnails that now appear represent separate scenes you recorded. A scene is separated by when you turned the camera to Pause or to Off and back on again.

7. All the scenes are checked by default, and they will be converted when you press Next. If you don't want some of the scenes, Ctrl-click on the ones you do not want. When finished, select Unmark Scene at the bottom (see Figure 4.13).

8. Click Next. Your scenes will now be converted for use in VSX5.

9. When the clips are finished being captured, the Import Settings dialog box will appear (refer back to Figure 4.10). You will have the same options that you did before of where to import the clips.

10. Save your project.

So there you have it. VSX5 provides excellent capabilities for capturing and creating video files suitable for your projects from a variety of sources. Next I'll show you how to acquire clips via the Edit tab.

Importing via the Edit Tab

Unless you're capturing and importing RAW video content, you should be importing via the Edit step. For the rest of the lessons, all the files in your Lessons folder are already in the format that you need them to be in.

We've already practiced this procedure once, so this short section will be a reminder for the rest of the lessons. Here, you'll use common importing procedures, such as locating the folder where your media resides and placing the content into custom libraries. You'll also bypass importing to a library, and instead import and place content directly into your Timeline; but then you'll also set the clip up again for reuse.

Figure 4.13
Selecting scenes to capture.

To import a clip directly into your Timeline, follow these steps:

1. Return to the Edit step.

2. Go to File > Insert Media File to Timeline > Insert Video. Locate and open Fireworks1 in the WashingtonDC folder. Notice that's it's placed in your Timeline, but it's not in any of your video libraries. As I explained earlier, this is a nice shortcut, but since the clip is not in a library, it's not handy if you plan on using it again. But have no fear; you can still place it any of your libraries. I'll show you this next.

3. To place Fireworks1 into a library, open the Chapter 4 media library from the Library panel. Drag and drop the Fireworks1 clip from the Timeline into your Chapter 4 library next to Fireworks2. You can also drag and drop to place Fireworks1 before Fireworks2 in your library, if you'd prefer to keep clips in order. Now Fireworks1 is available if you want to use it again. Better? Better!

Tip

Any clip from the Timeline, with any number of effects or edits applied to it, can be saved for reuse just by dragging it into a gallery or library.

4. At the bottom of the Library panel (make sure the Media icon is selected), click Browse and return to the WashingtonDC videos folder. Pressing the Shift or Ctrl key, select both DC1 and DC2 (see Figure 4.14), and then drag the two clips into the Chapter 4 library area. This is one method, again, for importing clips into any displayed gallery.

Figure 4.14
Drag and drop clips into a library.

5. At the top left of the Chapter 4 library area, click the Folder icon (see Figure 4.15).

6. In the Videos > WashingtonDC folder, select Fireworks3 and click Open. This is another method to acquire clips for your project. You should now have five video clips and one photo, all stored in the newly created Chapter 4 Media library. These clips are LincolnNight.jpg, and videos Fireworks1, 2, and 3, and DC1 and DC2.

7. Save your project.

Figure 4.15
Opening clips into a library.

Alright, with the exception of a TV and screen capture (we'll try screen capture in Chapter 11), you've now learned and practiced every known method of acquiring and importing content into VSX5. The next section will cover the different trimming choices that can be done to individual video clips.

One last, but boring, method to import assets is similar to the Insert to Timeline method. You can also use File > Insert Media File to Library > Insert Video/Digital Media/Photo/Audio choices. Snore.

Editing Video Clips

YOU'RE NOW FAMILIAR WITH getting content into VSX5: capturing RAW content, importing converted, ready-to-use content into the libraries, and importing content directly onto the Timeline, bypassing the libraries. This section will show you how to edit your content, both in the libraries and those already placed on the Timeline.

Specifically, you'll learn how to use the Single Clip Trim and Multi-Trim Video windows, adjusting durations by changing the start and/or end points of a clip, changing the playback speed, splitting a clip by its individual scenes (if it has more than one scene), copying and reusing clips, and finally color-correcting a clip. Most of these features are located in the Options panel, which launches automatically when an asset is double-clicked on, so you'll get very familiar with using this area. Let's get started.

Although you can leave a blank space in every other Timeline track, VSX5 will not let you leave a blank space between clips or at the very beginning of the main Video track.

You can, though, leave the entire main Video track empty and just work in the other overlay tracks. Working only in overlay tracks allows you to make video clips any size (as opposed to only full-screen) and position you like and place them over a blank background.

A background that is blank will instead display a solid color designated in the Preferences > General tab under Preview Window. This color defaults to black.

Adjusting Clip Durations in the Timeline

There's more than one way to adjust the length of a video clip. The first method you'll use is the easiest and fastest, but it can be also the least accurate—adjusting a clip manually after it's placed on the Timeline. You might think that all you can do is shorten a clip, but there are a couple of circumstances where you can actually lengthen a video clip.

1. You should still only have the clip Fireworks1 in your Timeline (six clips in the Chapter 4 library, but only one video clip in the actual Timeline). Click the Fit Project in Timeline Window icon, just to the right of the Timeline zoom slider (see Figure 4.16). This will make the entire clip visible in the Timeline, instead of it extending off the right edge. You should now see the right end point of the clip.

Makes clip fit to view

Figure 4.16
Bringing the entire project in view.

2. You can trim the duration (snip off an end) of a clip in the Timeline by simply dragging either end to shorten it, again, without affecting the original clip. Drag the left side to shorten the start of a clip and drag the end to shorten the end of a clip. Click once on Fireworks1 in the Timeline. Move your cursor over the vertical orange bar at the very end of the clip and, watching the timecode feedback attached to your cursor, drag it to the left until the clip is at the 44.00 second mark and let go (see Figure 4.17). The results are shown in Figure 4.18.

3. Save your project as **Chapter 4** into your Lessons folder.

...To here   Move this...

Figure 4.17
Shortening a Timeline clip (before).

After

Figure 4.18
Shortening a Timeline clip (after).

CAUTION

Remember I just said you can lengthen a video clip under certain circumstances?

After trimming a clip in any of the Trim windows, you can return it to its original length in the Timeline by dragging the end of it back out. This will become clearer in future lessons, but basically, you can undo the shortening of a clip by dragging it back out in the Timeline.

This method, though, only works on the end of a clip in the Timeline, because there is essentially no room to push clips on the left to the left to make room. This can be fixed by first placing the clip in an overlay track, giving you room on both sides of the clip for length adjustment.

There is also a method to lengthen a clip beyond its original length, but it will slow down the playback speed. I'll show this later in this chapter.

Single-Trim Video

Single clip trimming a video segment just means taking an existing clip and changing the start and/or end point. You just did that in the last section, manually, in the Timeline. Another method is to apply this trim before adding the clip to the Timeline using the Single Clip Trim dialog box. The tools in this dialog are similar to those in the Preview panel that you learned about in Chapter 3. What's new is a Jog Wheel you can use to move a clip along.

1. In the Chapter 4 Media library, double-click the DC1 clip. This opens the clip in the Single Clip Trim window.

2. Using Figure 4.19 as a guide, use either the Jog Wheel or the white Scrubber arrow (or both) to go to timecode 02.10. At the 02.10 mark, click the Mark-In bracket to set the start point of this clip.

Position to here   Mark-In   Mark-Out

Use this...   or this...
to position clip

Figure 4.19
Single trimming a video clip.

3. Go to timecode 08.00 and click the Mark-Out point. Click OK. The Single Clip Trim dialog box will close, the clip will be updated in the library, and the results will display in the Preview window.

The original clip has not been altered at all. It still contains its original length. The only difference, as evidenced in the Preview window, is that only a small portion of it will play in your Timeline and project.

4. With the clip selected in the library, click Play in the Preview window. You'll notice the trim marks are also present in the Preview window. Drag and drop this clip from the library to the right of the Fireworks1 clip in the Timeline.

5. Save your project.

Tip

Here is an example of where you can lengthen a video clip. Because this clip, now in the Timeline, still has its original full length available to it, you can grab the right or left end and extend it, reinstating some or all of its original length. If you try this out, be sure to press Ctrl+Z to undo it and return it to the shorter length you created above. There are also undo and redo arrow icons in the upper-left area of the Timeline.

Split Clip by Scene

Normally, when you capture clips, they are already and automatically separated by scenes into separate clips. Scene splits are designated by when the camera was turned on, turned off, or paused.

Occasionally, though, you'll have a video clip that seems to have separate scenes but is still all in one clip. Maybe you would like these separated, perhaps for the purpose of adding chapter breaks or transitions in between. The Split by Scene feature in VSX5 will do that for you. Here's how it works.

1. Using any one of the import methods you recently learned, import the video clip JewelScenes into the Chapter 4 Media library, found in your Videos > WashingtonDC folder.

2. With this new clip selected in the library, click the Open Options Panel icon in the lower-right corner of the Library panel (see Figure 4.20) to open the Video Options panel.

Figure 4.20
Accessing the Options panel.

3. Click Split by Scene to open the Scenes dialog box. Here two scenes in this clip should already be listed in the Detected scenes area. (If there aren't two scenes, click the Scan button in the lower-left corner.) See Figure 4.21. Click OK.

If needed　　...To open this　　Click here...

Figure 4.21
Scenes dialog box.

4. In your Chapter 4 library, in addition to the original JewelScenes clip, there are now two new ones, each of which are parts of the original, separated at their scene breaks. Unfortunately, they have the same names. Fortunately, there is an easy way to tell them apart. Click each of the titles in the library to edit their names if you like.

5. You should have three clips named JewelScenes. Select each one and look at the Preview window. The first one should show a full-length clip (indicated by the scrubber line). Each of the other two should show a section of the original, the first part, and then the second part.

6. Save your project.

Changing the Playback Speed

Speeding up or creating a slow-motion video clip is usually relegated to more expensive video editing software tools. Yet this feature is included in VSX5 and is very simple to use.

1. With the Fireworks1 clip selected in the Timeline, open the Options panel and click Speed/Time-lapse. The Speed/Time-lapse dialog box will appear (as shown in Figure 4.22). Select the Video tab if it does not open by default.

Tip

You can also access the Options panel by double-clicking a clip in the Timeline.

Figure 4.22
Accessing playback speed options.

2. In the middle of the dialog box, change the Speed value to 200%. This will increase the clip's playback speed and shorten the clip's Timeline length by 50%. This happens because the frame rate will double and cause the clip to finish in half the time. Click Preview to play it. The clip now plays in half the time, and the fireworks show is one giant finale! (You will play more with the Speed/Time-lapse feature in Chapter 12.)

3. Click OK. The clip in the Timeline should now be half of its original length. The library clip, though, remains unaffected.

4. Select Edit > Undo or click the undo arrow in the Timeline (or press Ctrl+Z) to undo the previous step and return the clip in the Timeline to its previous length.

You can also create this effect directly in the Timeline, but this time let's slow the clip down.

1. On the zoom slider in the upper-right corner of the Timeline, click twice on the minus (–) magnifying glass to zoom out and create more room in the Timeline.

2. While holding down the Shift key, grab the right end of the Fireworks1 clip and drag it to the right until it's about double its length.

3. With the clip still selected, rewind and play it in the Preview window. It now plays slower and with a very eerie sound. The only downside is that this method doesn't allow for the same accuracy that the dialog box does.

4. Undo this step to return the clip back to its original playback length.

5. Save your project.

Multi-Trim Video

VSX5's Multi-trim Video feature takes the Single Clip Trim feature a step further. Multi-trim Video lets you create multiple mini-clips out of one long clip in a single process. All at once, you can make multiple trim edits to a single clip and add these to a library.

1. Place DC2 into the end of the Timeline in the same track after the other clip.

2. With DC2 still selected, open the Options panel and choose Multi-trim Video (as shown in Figure 4.23). The Multi-trim Video window will appear.

Figure 4.23
Multi-Trim Video dialog box.

3. Click the Mark-In bracket to place a marker at the start of the clip. Go to timecode 06.06 and set a Mark-Out point. This new, smaller clip will be added to the Trimmed Video tray in the bottom of the Multi-trim Video window.

Tip

As a reminder, use the white Scrub marker to go to the general frame location quickly. Then use the Jog Wheel and/or the previous frame and next frame buttons to home in on the exact frame you want.

4. Go to timecode 16.05 and set a Mark-In point. Set a Mark-Out at 24.28.

5. Set a Mark-In at 29.06 and Mark-Out at 35.03. You should now have three clips in the Trimmed Video tray, and your dialog box should look like the one in Figure 4.24.

6. Click the Play Trimmed Video button to preview your three clips.

Click to Preview

Figure 4.24
New Multi-Trim Video clips.

Tip

Invert Selection at the top of the Multi-trim Video dialog box selects the clips you *did not* trim. Select this to use the parts of the clips you trimmed off after multi-video trimming instead. Sometimes it's easier to first trim off the parts you don't want to use, and then choose the ones you want from what remains.

The Ad-Zapper tool in the Multi-trim Video dialog box is a pretty cool feature. If you captured video from your TV/VCR/DVR, Ad-Zapper looks for a 2- or 3-second gap of black frames when commercials begin and end. It uses this gap to corral the ads and delete them. Because of the very short gap, Ad-Zapper default sensitivity setting is on High.

7. Click OK. The clip is now split into three pieces on the Timeline with the unwanted portions removed. Beware, though, that you now have three clips in the Timeline with the same name. Again, though, the original clip in the library is unaffected.

8. Save your project.

Copying Clips

There are two ways to use the same video clip twice in your Timeline. The obvious method is to just bring another one down from the library. The other option is to make a copy of it right there in the Timeline, and then drop the copy into its new location. Let me show you how to do the Timeline method.

1. Select the last of the three newly trimmed DC2 clips in the Timeline. Right-click on it and choose Copy. The clip will now "stick" to your cursor. Move the copied clip to the end of the video track, and then left-click to drop it. Double-click on it to bring up the Options panel (if it isn't already open). Check Reverse Video back in the Options panel. This will make the second clip play backward.

2. Repeat the previous step with the second DC2 clip in the series, and then again with the first DC2 clip to reverse all the DC clips. The video should pan up the Washington Monument and then back down again. Preview the results.

3. Save your project.

Reusing Edited Clips

Just because you trimmed a video clip doesn't mean you can't trim it again and use the same and/or different parts of it somewhere else. The original information is still retained in the original library clip, and you can change the part you want to use at any time without affecting what you trimmed off and used previously. In other words, you can use a trimmed clip, and then trim it again to make a new one without affecting the previous one. Let me show you what I mean.

1. Click the Fit Project in Timeline Window button in the upper-right corner of the Timeline (refer to Figure 4.16).

2. Select DC1 in the library (not the Timeline). You'll notice the previous trim is still evident in the Preview window. Move the Mark-Out point all the way to the right. Insert a Mark-In point at 13:00. Drag DC1 from the library to the end of the Timeline. Although you reused the same clip from earlier in the Timeline, you're now using a different portion of it, again without affecting the first trim you did on it or the original clip's length!

> Notice that any new edit replaces an old edit, but not the original clip in the Library, and it doesn't affect what you've already placed into the Timeline. Pretty cool, huh?

3. Return to and select the first DC1 clip in the Timeline (the second clip in the Timeline sequence), and drag it into the Chapter 4 library (you may want to close the Options panel first if it is not already closed). Now you have both versions of the clip you created available to reuse at any time.

4. Add the Fireworks2 clip from your library to the Timeline right after all the DC1 clips (the end of the Timeline).

5. Save your project.

Color-Correcting a Clip

VSX5's advanced editing features allow you to do more than just trim a clip. One of the features in the Options panel is the ability to fix a video clip, similar to what you might do to a photograph in an image editing application. The Color Correction feature lets you adjust items like white balance, hue, saturation, brightness, contrast, and gamma.

1. Double-click the last clip in the Timeline, and select Color Correction from the Options panel.

Color Correction has many options to choose from. White balance is the process of removing unrealistic color casts so that objects, which are white in reality, are correctly rendered white in your photo. There are several ways to tell the software how to create the best balance. They include designating a perfect white color in a photo (using a color picker); telling it what type of lighting was used in your photo by choosing a light type (such as shade, overcast, cloudy, daylight, fluorescent, or tungsten); using a manual temperature setting (warm to bring out reds and cool for blues); adjusting individual Hue, Saturation, Brightness, Contrast, and Gamma controls; and, *my* preference, choosing the Auto-Adjust options. What's great about VSX5 is that any color adjustment will be applied to an entire video clip and rendered in real time.

---

2. Test any of the possible settings for your personal preference. Feedback is immediate. Use the undo arrow at the lower right to return all sliders to their defaults.

3. Select the Auto Tone Adjustment check box. Then from its drop-down list to the right, choose Brightest (see Figure 4.25). Click Play to preview. The results are rendered and played back in real time.

4. Save your project.

Figure 4.25
Color-correcting a video clip.

Using Still Images

ADDING IMAGES TO YOUR movies is just as easy as adding any other media element. All you need to do is drag and drop a photo or illustration directly into any of the video tracks. Videos and stills are interchangeable. You can import them the same way too, using the Browse button, drag and drop, or File > Insert Media File to Library method.

Because photos used in videos are often viewed on TV screens, and HD TVs at that, it's always recommended that you use photos with the highest resolution possible. Larger image sizes help as well.

Isn't an image's size the same as resolution? Nope, afraid not. Image size refers to the physical print size of the photo, such as 8×10 inches. Resolution refers to the quality of that photo, such as 72 dpi (dots per inch) or 300 dpi. Increasing the image size will not increase the resolution; in fact, it will do just the opposite.

If you increase an image's size in inches, the same resolution will just be spread over a larger area, and the quality will drop. Think of it as placing a drop of ink on a piece of paper and then spreading that dot over a larger area. It gets thinner and loses saturation, and it becomes lighter in color. Decreasing an image's size in inches will make the image smaller but in turn squeeze the pixels together, increasing the quality (increasing that drop of ink's concentration). Therefore, an image that's designed for a webpage will not look good when projected on your TV because a webpage image is a much smaller file and is designed for a much smaller viewing area. Keep this in mind when adding photos into your video projects.

Another consideration is the aspect ratio of a photo, or the width vs. height. Any ratio is fine, as long as it matches the ratio of your video project. You don't want a rectangular video interspersed with square photos, right? VideoStudio can fix this by making everything fit your project ratio. Just be aware that photos might be stretched or squeezed to fit. But at least you can preview the results before committing to using them.

Adding Photos to a Video

Handling photos or illustrations (line art) in VSX5 is exactly like managing video clips. They're imported into the same Media libraries as videos and audio clips. Back in the section "Adding New Content," you saw the list of graphics formats that VSX5 can work with. Most of your images will likely be in the JPEG format, but it's nice to know that so many others will work, too.

1. In the Media library, click both the Hide Videos and Hide Audio Files icons at the top. This will narrow down the library view to show only still graphics.

2. Import the photo US_Capitol.jpg from the Photos > Buildings lesson folder into your new Chapter 4 photo gallery.

3. Place the photo into the Timeline just after the first video clip.

4. Zoom into this portion of the Timeline by clicking twice on the plus (+) magnifying glass to the right of the zoom slider. Drag the right end of the clip so that the duration reads about 5 seconds (see Figure 4.26).

5. Save your project.

Figure 4.26
Extending the photo duration.

I'll show you the effects of using standard clips in a widescreen project in a future chapter.

Adding a Solid Background

Occasionally, you may want to display something in your video project that either doesn't take up the entire screen or doesn't interfere with any background activity. You may want the viewer to concentrate only on a title or a collection of small photos scattered on the screen. The issue with this is that video editing software requires that something, anything, fill up the entire screen, because this designates the overall screen size. This is where a solid color, such as a color chip, can come in handy. These solid colored backgrounds included in VSX5 can take the place of no background, and they can be much less distracting.

Solid backgrounds have many uses including

▶ A background for a title

▶ A blank space between any two clips in the main video track

▶ Creating a frame around a smaller video clip

▶ A background for a montage of small, overlaid photos or video clips

▶ A pause between two scenes

The following steps will show you how to add solid backgrounds and how they're useful.

1. In the Library panel, select the Graphic library. Choose the Color gallery from the drop-down list (as shown in Figure 4.27).

Figure 4.27
Accessing the Color gallery.

2. Grab a purple color chip (any color will do, actually) and drop it at the beginning of the main video track. All the other clips will make room for it by moving to the right.

3. Set the duration to about 10 seconds by either dragging the end out like you did previously or by double-clicking the chip to open the Options panel and setting the duration there.

4. Go to the Title library. Grab any bright animated title and drop it into the title track underneath the purple color chip (no need to edit the text). Also, drag the title's duration to 10 seconds (it will snap to the end of the color clip's length) so that it matches up with the color chip.

5. Double-click on the title clip you just laid down in the Timeline to make it appear in the Preview panel. Then double-click on the text in the Preview panel to make it editable. In place of Lorem ipsum, type **Our Trip to D.C.**

Click somewhere else in the Preview panel to exit the text editing mode, but leaving the text block selected. Manually reposition the text block on the screen, if you like (see Figure 4.28). Make sure Project is selected in the Preview window, not Clip. Rewind your movie and play to preview your animated title.

Figure 4.28
Using a solid color background.

6. Return to the Color gallery and drop a different color chip than the last time and place it after the first video clip in your Timeline. Again, the other clips will shift to the right to make room. Play this section. Not too exciting, right? It does, though, create a blank space if you need it. As you remember, you cannot have an actual blank space in the background video track, so this is a way around that.

7. Double-click on the chip you just laid down to bring up the Options panel. Set the duration to exactly 0:01:00:29 (see Figure 4.29) to set the duration of the new color chip.

Figure 4.29
Using the Options panel to set Color Duration.

8. Select the Fireworks1 video clip in the Timeline. Drag the clip *straight* down into the Overlay track beneath it and let go. The rest of the clips in the Video track will shift left to fill up the blank space left by Fireworks1. The Fireworks1 clip now becomes an overlay on top of the color chip background and should line up with it exactly. The video is also now reduced to a smaller size. Make sure they also line up exactly.

9. As mentioned, the background video clip is now an overlay clip and no longer occupies the entire screen. Make sure the Options panel is open to the Attribute tab. If not already available, double-click on the video in the Preview panel to bring up the corner resize handles. Drag any yellow corner to resize the clip larger, if you like. (Important! Make sure your cursor shows a double-ended arrow when resizing!) Grab the middle of the selection to reposition it so that the background is nicely sized and centered in the border frame.

Grabbing the yellow corner (instead of the green corner inside the yellow corner) will maintain the aspect ratio. You can undo any mistakes with Ctrl+Z and redo with Ctrl+Y. Your screen should look similar to that shown in Figure 4.30.

10. Save your project.

Tip

In the Attributes tab of the Options panel, you can use the Alignment options to position the overlap clip more precisely.

Figure 4.30
Using color as a border.

Quick Quiz

1. What feature allows you to store specific project content aside from other content? (See "Using the Library Navigation Panel.")

2. Why would you use the Capture step as opposed to just importing into the Edit step? (See "Importing via the Capture Tab.")

3. How can you save an edited clip to use later? (See "Reusing Edited Clips.")

4. Name at least two purposes that a solid color background can be used for. (See "Adding a Solid Background.")

Video by Numbers with

Instant Projects

O KAY, SO IT'S NOT TRULY INSTANT.
It's not like Cup-a-Soup, where you just add
water and it transforms into a fully nutritional
dorm room culinary delight, but it comes pretty darn
close in terms of making a movie. The simplified and
upgraded Instant Project feature in VSX5 has all the
ingredients to create a slideshow, video introduction, short
movie, or conclusion. All you need to add is the hot water, uh,
I mean content.

Each Instant Project uses placeholders that include backgrounds,
frames for your slides, video clips, text titles, and music. Each
media object has a set default length of time that you can adjust
if you desire, but you don't have to. You just need to swap out
the placeholder content for your own. An Instant Project is the
reverse of adding a template theme to a DVD or movie project.
In an Instant Project, the template comes first, and then the
content. With a DVD, you create the content and then add a
theme around it before burning it to disc.

Instant Projects can be used for video projects, but because of the way they're laid out, it makes more sense to use them for slideshows. Outside the intros and conclusions, all the placeholders have rather short lengths. They can certainly be lengthened, but you'll have to make sure your other tracks are set for Ripple Editing. That way, anything inserted or lengthened in the middle will move ALL the other tracks forward accordingly so that everything stays synchronized.

Many of the placeholders also contain pan and zoom effects that add somewhat of an animated effect to stills. Videos can be created with Instant Projects, too; they just require a little more editing on your part. You'll create an "instant" slideshow first, and then a short video using the Instant Project feature.

Setting Up an Instant Project

THE FIRST STEP IN CREATING an Instant Project is to choose a template. Doing so is easy, but there a lot of options to choose from in various categories—over 140 templates total. Categories are not separated by design, but rather by function, or where you'll want to use them in your project: in the beginning (introduction), middle, end (conclusion), or throughout the entire project. There is also a custom list where you can place those you've made or templates you've edited and would like to reuse. The middle category provides the most complex templates, so let's just jump in and try one of those.

1. Launch VSX5 or choose File > New Project.

2. Open the Track Manager. Make sure all the drop-downs only have one track listed (see Figure 5.1). I want you to see how adding an Instant Project template will automatically add the necessary additional tracks for you. Click OK.

Figure 5.1
Track Manager icon.

3. Click the Instant Project icon in the Library Navigation Panel (see Figure 5.2). The Instant Project list will appear. Take some time to tour the template choices in the various categories. You can preview templates in the usual Preview window. Especially notice the category differences. The Custom category is reserved for projects you create and want to use in the future, which you'll learn more about at the end of the chapter.

Figure 5.2
Instant Project Navigation panel.

4. Let's go for it and use a rather complex template. Choose the Middle category, and then choose the template that looks like a forest background with a black border around it (see Figure 5.3). It should be numbered T17. Drag the template to the start of your Timeline.

Preview it here   Choose this one

Figure 5.3
Choosing a template.

5. Save your project as **Chapter 5-slideshow**.

There are a few things to notice in the Timeline. *All* necessary additional Timeline tracks have been added automatically. A bunch of placeholder clips for your photos have been placed at just the right increments. Notice that the background video track is just a black color chip. You learned previously about using these, not only as blank spaces, but as frames for when content in overlay tracks doesn't take up the entire background. Something has to take up the complete background, and the black chip does just that.

> Don't freak out about the layout—this is going to be much easier to customize than it looks, I promise you! It'll be like painting by numbers. You'll only need to work in the overlay tracks and the title track. Changing out the background chip and music track is purely optional but can be done if you like.

6. View the structure of the template as it plays. Click the Play button in the Preview panel and notice the different layers and timing involved. Notice what happens in the Preview panel as the playback head moves down the Timeline.

Tip

If you lose track of where you saved your project file, you can still open it easily by relaunching VSX5 and choosing the file name from near the bottom of the File menu.

7. All the clips in your Timeline might be highlighted (surrounded by orange borders) because they're all selected. Click in a blank area of the Timeline to deselect everything. Fit your project to Timeline view.

8. Double-click any of the placeholder clips in Overlay track 1 (the first track below the background video track). This opens the Video Attribute Options panel. You'll notice that the Picture-In-Picture filter has been added (see Figure 5.4). This filter (video effect), as a result of the Instant Project template chosen, was used to automatically create custom frames around the pictures and the reflections below them, evident in the Preview panel. (It's also a filter you can customize, but I'll cover this more in Chapter 8.)

Added with Instant Project

Figure 5.4
Picture-In-Picture filter.

Now you understand how an Instant Project is chosen, how it's loaded into the Timeline, and how track assets interact with each other via overlays and video filters. The next section will cover filling in the placeholders with content.

Creating a Custom Slideshow with an Instant Project

THE FIRST THING YOU NEED to do is gather the content you want to add into your Instant Project. Since the Instant Project has everything you'll need except your slideshow photos, that's all you'll need to gather and insert. For this part of the lesson, you'll use the Landscape photos.

Follow along with these steps to learn how to create a quick, but professional, slideshow using the VSX5 Instant Project feature.

1. Go to the Library panel, and create a new folder called Chapter 5. Just like you did in creating the Chapter 4 folder, click the + Add area at the top of the panel and name the new folder **Chapter 5**.

2. Making sure Chapter 5 is still selected in the panel, click Browse at the bottom. Navigate to the Lesson Plans > Photos > Landscapes folder.

3. Select all the photos and drag them into the Chapter 5 library, which should look like the one shown in Figure 5.5.

Figure 5.5
Instant Project photos.

4. Follow this next step closely, even reading it a couple times first. Put the Timeline's playback head in the middle of the first clip (named #2) in Overlay track 1 (see Figure 5.6). From the Chapter 5 library, grab the corresponding #2 photo. Hovering it over the #2 placeholder clip, press the Ctrl key on your keyboard. The info on the clip will change to +Replace clip. Let go of your mouse to replace the clip, and *then* release the Ctrl key. In a couple seconds, you'll see the results in the Timeline (see Figure 5.7).

Figure 5.7
Clip replacement results.

Playback head here

Figure 5.6
Placing an instant slideshow image.

There is a second method for adding content to the template. Right-click on the first clip in Overlay Track 1 (not the background Video track) and choose Replace Clip > Photo (see Figure 5.8). This inserts files straight from your PC file explorer into the Timeline. However, as mentioned before, this method doesn't make these files available for later use via any of the media libraries.

Figure 5.8
Replacing a clip.

You may have just noticed that the clips resort back to their original file names when they're inserted into the Timeline. Once again, this happens because the library only *references* the original files.

If you were to move a clip from its original location on your PC, the library would show it as a broken link. The library needs to know where the original clip is in order to work with it.

It all has to do with that EDL I discussed previously (the Edit Decision List that contains the project instructions, but not the content). If you want to change the file names in both the library and the Timeline (that is, the clips themselves), right-click the clip in the library and choose Locate on Computer. You will be taken, via the Explorer, to the clip's location, where you can rename it.

Let's now change the text titles from "VideoStudio" to something more appropriate.

1. Double-click the first clip (the first "VideoStudio") in the title track to bring that title to the forefront. Double-click the text in the Preview panel to highlight it for editing. Drag across its length to select all (or press Ctrl+A). Type in **From Boston...** to replace the text.

2. The text Edit Options panel has popped up to the right. In the Alignment selection of the Edit tab (which will be covered further in Chapter 9), click the bottom, center choice to place the text at the bottom of the Preview window (but still above the white square). Apply this alignment procedure for all the text you edit in this project.

5. Repeat step 4, adding all the other photos to their corresponding placeholders (photo #1 into placeholder #1 and so on) throughout the entire movie. Fitting the Timeline to view will help you see that you placed them all correctly. Rewind the project and play to preview. Pretty cool, huh?

6. Save your project.

3. Manually slide down the third text clip in the Timeline to start at about the 46-second mark. It doesn't need to be exact, just close. Repeating step 1, rename the text **To Lake Tahoe**.

4. Move the second text clip to start at close to the 39-second mark. Change that to read **To Texas...**

5. By grabbing the right end, extend the first and third title clips to roughly double their length, or to around 8 seconds long. The cursor will provide feedback for you.

6. Change the last text clip (at the very end) to **The End**. Align it as previously mentioned, but leave it at its current length.

7. Save your project. Your Timeline should look like the one shown in Figure 5.9.

8. Go to the Share tab. Click Create Video File.

9. Choose WMV > WMV HD 720 30p. Name it **My Instant Slideshow** and place it in your Chapter 5 lessons folder. On my middle-of-the-road PC, rendering this file will take about 10 minutes. When finished, it will be added to your Chapter 5 Media library and start playing automatically. Stop it if you like. Go find the file outside VSX5 and double-click on it to view in WinDVD or another movie viewer.

Tip

Since most slideshows aren't exactly nine slides long, you can modify your show by deleting any unused placeholders or adding new sections.

Delete sections by selecting any in the Timeline and pressing the Delete key. You can also extend your slideshow by adding another Instant Project before or after the current one, and again, taking out the stuff you don't need.

Another great shortcut is to right-click on an existing clip in the Timeline, choose Copy, and then move your mouse to a new location and click to drop it. Then, as before, replace the content for it, as you did in the "Copying Clips" section in the previous chapter.

Figure 5.9
Completed instant slideshow.

Creating a Custom Movie with an Instant Project

CREATING A MOVIE with an Instant Project, as you might suspect, is very similar to creating a slideshow. After all, you're inserting media, just different media, but it might need a couple of extra adjustments to make it work. Replacing a video clip into a fixed length template clip will shorten that video clip to fit the length of the template clip. You may not (probably not, actually) want that. But that can be fixed.

There is one very important adjustment we'll need to set before proceeding. By default, each of the Timeline tracks operates independently of all the others. By this, I mean any content added to one track will not affect content in any of the others as far as timing is concerned. That can create a synchronization problem. If you have a title that is perfectly aligned with a particular video or graphic and you drop another clip before that video or graphic, those will move to the right to make room, but the title in the title track will not, *unless* Ripple Editing is turned on.

Ripple Editing allows you to insert clips into the start or middle of the Timeline while automatically moving other clips (including empty spaces) to the right accordingly, to maintain the synchronicity of all your other Timeline assets. Let's set that up for this project.

1. Back in VSX5, go to File > New Project. Save your slideshow, if prompted.

2. On the very far left of the Timeline, click the Enable/Disable Ripple Editing icon to turn on this feature. See Fig 5.10. It will highlight a brighter white when you do.

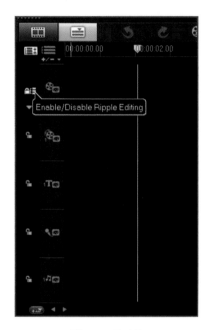

Figure 5.10
Enabling Ripple Editing.

3. Click the small down-facing arrow just below the Ripple Edit icon and choose Select All. This will lock and turn on ripple editing for all the tracks in the Timeline. See Figure 5.11. You'll notice you can also choose to lock individual tracks if you need to.

Figure 5.11
Ripple Editing all tracks.

Figure 5.12
Instant movie template choice.

Now we're ready to continue. So, let's create an instant movie, but with video clips this time, and see how it differs from an instant slideshow project.

To avoid creating an unnecessarily long movie for this short section, and since I'm sure you'll get the point with just a few clips, you'll use a shorter template this time.

1. Select the Instant Project library panel again. Under the Complete category, choose the template shown in Figure 5.12. It might be numbered T24. Drag it to the start of the Timeline, like you did last time.

2. Save your project as **Chapter 5_Instant Video**.

3. Fit the project to Timeline view.

4. Open your Chapter 5 library. Make sure the Video content will be visible via the Show Videos button at the top.

5. From the Videos > Balloon_Trip folder, browse to import clips Balloon-2 through Balloon-7 into your Video library. Click the Hide Photos icon at the top so that only your videos are displayed. You might also see the video clip (slideshow) that you generated in the last section. You can keep it, or you can select it and press Delete. It will only delete the VSX5 reference to it, not the file itself.

6. As you did with the slideshow Instant Project, replace the placeholder clips with the Balloon videos in sequence. Start with Balloon-2 over Placeholder 2 in the background video track. Drag the clip over the placeholder. Hold down the Ctrl key, then, first release the mouse, then the Ctrl key. **Before** trying the next clip, first read through step 8.

7. Some of these imported clips are too short. Some are shorter than the template clips, and that's a problem. Try Balloon-3. When holding down the Ctrl key to replace, instead of seeing +Replace Clip, you'll see Replace Clip (Source Duration Too Short). Each time you encounter this, cancel the replace process by simply letting go of your mouse button.

The next few steps are very precise, so be sure to read through them carefully first.

In canceling the replace process mentioned in step 8, be sure to let go of the mouse first to return the clip to the library. If you let go of the Ctrl key first, the clip will still be added to the Timeline in between placeholders 3 and 4. If this happens, Undo it by pressing Ctrl+Z or use the Undo arrow on top of the Timeline.

8. In the library, right-click on Balloon-3 back and choose Properties. Notice the duration is 6.206 seconds. Click OK. Double-click on placeholder 3 in the Timeline. In the Photo tab (the placeholder is a photo, not a video) that pops up in the Options panel, notice that the duration of the template placeholder clip is 7 seconds. This identifies the issue I mentioned earlier: The video clip is shorter than the template clip. The template will not accept any clip that is shorter than itself.

    With placeholder 3 selected in the Timeline, use the Options panel to shorten the duration of the placeholder clip to 6 seconds. Attempt to replace it with the video clip again. You should now be successful.

Make sure you're swapping out the photo clips in the Timeline, not the transitions in between them. Also, be aware that the Properties setting will display a clip's length in seconds and tenths of seconds, whereas the durations displayed in the Options panel and the Timeline are in seconds and frames. One half second is about 14 frames.

9. Replace placeholder 4 with Balloon-4.

10. Balloon-5 and Balloon-6 will have the same "clip too short" issue. Repeat step 8 to correct the issue. Look at the video clip's length first and then adjust the placeholder's length to the nearest second *below* that. For example, Balloon-5 is 5:14 seconds in length. Adjust placeholder 5 to 5 seconds and try replacing it again. Repeat the procedure for Balloon-6. Balloon-7 will not need adjusting. Stop after adding the last balloon video (#7).

11. Placeholder 8 is not needed. Select it and press the Delete key. The transitions on either side will also be deleted.

12. Save your project.

13. Select the Balloon-2 clip in the Timeline. Extend (not move) the right end as far to the right as it will go to increase the length. This will extend that clip to its full length (albeit not that much longer). Repeat this with all the other clips you replaced. This ensures that the videos will still play their full length and makes the placeholder lengths equal the video clip's lengths.

As you do the length adjustments, notice that clips in the tracks below will shift to the right to maintain the timing of the project. This is the effect of Ripple Editing!

Tip

If you remember from previous discussions, the full clip's length is available at any time, and adjustable, on the Timeline and in the Library. The original clip is never destroyed. The length shown in the Timeline is what will actually play, independent of the original clip's length.

14. In Overlay Track 1, replace placeholder 1 with the last video clip, Balloon-7. Do not adjust the duration. Notice how the video automatically conforms to the picture frame size. Play this section to preview it. See Figure 5.13.

15. As you did with the slideshow, change the text of both titles in the title track to something more appropriate. I used "Balloon Festival" and "Safe Landings." Like last time, don't bother changing any of the text formatting, and you can even leave the text positioned where it is already. Your Timeline should look similar to that shown in Figure 5.14. Be sure to save your project.

16. As before, export your movie as WMV > WMV HD 720 30p (the Share step). Preview it in WinDVD or a similar playback application.

...Displays it here   Placing this clip here...

Figure 5.13
Video in a picture frame.

Figure 5.14
Instant video Timeline.

Reusing Your Custom Instant Project

A GREAT BENEFIT OF combining VSX5's Instant Project with its clip replacement (as opposed to hip replacement) capabilities is the ability to save and reuse your Instant Projects along with the adjustments you made with them. It's especially helpful if you've added customization, such as your own music track, transitions, text formats, and perhaps additional video effects.

You can export and save any project you create into the Instant Project template library, specifically into the Custom category, where it can be reused as easily as using a new one. This can be helpful, for example, for business use when you need to create consistently designed videos for marketing or training.

The following steps will show how to convert any existing project into an Instant Project that you access from the Instant Project template library and reuse again and again.

1. Make sure the Chapter 5_Instant Video project you just created is open.

2. Go to File > Export as Template.

When you click on Export as Template, a message appears asking if you would like to save the current project. You must click Yes to proceed.

3. In the Export project as template dialog box, use the slider to select a frame in your movie that will be used as a thumbnail preview for the template custom gallery. I suggest selecting a frame that shows the design of the template, rather than the content itself.

4. Under Template path, click the small button on the far right and browse to the destination where you want to save your templates. Choose a place where you're not likely to move it. See Figure 5.15.

Figure 5.15
Exporting a project template.

5. Name your template and click OK. You will see the Project Successfully Exported as a Template dialog box. Click OK again.

6. Go to File > New Project to create an empty Timeline for your new template project.

7. To add your new project to the Instant Project template list, open the Custom gallery of your Instant Project library. Drag your new custom template into the Timeline. See Figure 5.16.

8. To delete a custom Instant Project template, right-click on the thumbnail in the custom gallery and choose Delete. You can only delete custom templates this way.

So, creating a custom Instant Project is really like just saving a normal VSX5 project. It looks exactly the same as the video project you just created with all its content, custom adjustments, and so on. Instead, though, you save it inside the Custom gallery of the Instant Project library for organizational purposes.

Figure 5.16
Using a Custom Project template.

Quick Quiz

1. Name a few of the various kinds of template layouts available in the Instant Project template list. (See "Setting Up an Instant Project.")

2. How can you change the name of a clip in the library without affecting the clip's original file name? (See "Creating a Custom Slideshow with an Instant Project.")

3. What's the downside of importing a clip directly into the Timeline? (See "Creating a Custom Slideshow with an Instant Project.")

4. What shortcut key do you hold down to drop and replace an existing clip in the Timeline? (See "Creating a Custom Slideshow with an Instant Project.")

Making Some Noise
with Audio

PRIOR TO THE 1920S, silent films were almost always produced with subtitles, the universal "language" of silent films. Today, in foreign films, subtitles are present along with the regular audio. But back then, subtitles were the only choice. All that changed in 1927 with the release of the first part-talkie movie *The Jazz Singer*, followed in 1928 with the first all-talking feature *Lights of New York*. Now the "silent" part could be replaced with spoken dialogue and the ability to convey emotions and excitement. This was huge!

Audio is an important part of any video project. It adds personality and customization through music, narrative, and sound effects. VSX5 allows you to have multiple audio tracks, which then let you utilize audio from files included in VSX5, from your own collections, CDs, voiceovers recorded directly in VSX5, screen captures, and music and sound effects from the included and customizable Quicktracks by SmartSounds.

VSX5 contains four fairly interchangeable music and narration tracks. Audio clips can be shortened, stretched, level-adjusted, and surround-sounded. Other adjustments include playback speed, peak levels, tempo, noise reduction, and much more. With the customizable Quicktracks, you can even turn specific instruments on and off to set varying moods. A most excellent, recent feature is the ability to take advantage of Dolby audio techniques, including multitrack surround sound.

In this chapter, you'll learn about almost all of these audio adjustments. For ones that I don't specifically cover, you'll at least know where they are so you can try them on your own. You'll learn how to manage the various audio tracks, add and edit audio from a variety of sources, separate audio from its video counterpart, create stereo from a mono audio clip, and even share an audio-only piece from your video project.

These lessons are all about sound, so you'll need an audio CD for this chapter. Grab a CD of your favorite music.

Managing Audio Tracks

I N VSX5, YOU MANAGE audio tracks the same way as video and title tracks: by using the Track Manager to select which ones to display and activate. The following steps will show you how to set up your Timeline in preparation for adding and editing audio.

1. If you're not there already, launch VSX5.

2. As you've done before, open the Track Manager from the icon in the upper left of the Timeline area.

3. Choose 3 in the Music Tracks drop-down list. You should now have all four possible audio tracks selected. Click OK.

4. Click Show All Visible Tracks. This will give equal viewing area to all your Timeline tracks, instead of emphasizing just the video tracks. If you don't see all the Timeline tracks, click the icon again, as it's a toggle switch. Your Timeline should look like what's shown in Figure 6.1. It will also help to expand the Timeline vertically by stretching the panel upward a little again by grabbing the separator at the top of the Timeline.

Show visible tracks · Track Manager · Audio tracks added

Figure 6.1
Timeline view showing all audio tracks.

Adding Audio

ALTHOUGH ADDING, importing, and creating audio in VSX5 has many similar characteristics to adding and using other media file types, the various sources and techniques do have differences that you need to be aware of. This section will cover choosing audio files from the included VSX5 audio samples, acquiring files from your computer, and an audio CD, recording audio directly into a video clip, and splitting and using an audio clip separately from a video clip. It's a lot of different techniques, but all are easy to pull off.

Accessing the Audio Gallery

Just like the rest of the media libraries, the Audio gallery in VSX5 already includes a nice selection of preinstalled, royalty-free music and sound effects samples. Sample music clips start with the letter "M," and sample sound effects start with the letter "S." Did you catch the high-tech reasoning there? You add them to the Timeline just as you would any other media clip, except they will be added to one of the four audio tracks.

In previous versions of VideoStudio, the Audio library had a dedicated place in the Library Navigation panel (between the Preview and Library panels). Now it is included in and accessed as part of the main Media library, along with videos and photos.

These steps will show you how to access the Audio gallery in VSX5.

1. In the Library Navigation panel, select the Media library at the top and then the Samples gallery.

2. Click Show Audio Files to make your Audio gallery visible. When it is yellow it is in the On position. If the audio files disappeared, the switch was off. Click it again. See Figure 6.2.

Figure 6.2
Accessing the Audio library.

3. Select a few of the clips and preview them without adding any to the Timeline just yet. Unfortunately, the clip names are not descriptive of their content. You'll get the opportunity to use some of these later in the chapter.

Adding Audio Content from Your PC

Let's review this process of acquiring audio from your PC, even though it's almost identical to adding other media files you've imported. As usual, though, there's more than one way to do this.

1. Go to File > Insert Media File to Timeline > Insert Audio > To Music Track #1. (See Figure 6.3.) The clip you select will be added with its start point where the playback head is, so make sure your project is at 00:00:00:00.

Figure 6.3
Adding audio directly into the Timeline.

2. In the Import dialog box, click on the Files of Type drop-down list and view the multitudes of audio formats that VSX5 will work with.
    Navigate to the Music folder of your lessons, select the clip called Hawaiian Music, and click Open. The music file will be inserted into Music Track 1. As you can see, the file goes into the Timeline, not into your Audio gallery. You can, though, drag it into your Audio gallery if you want.

3. Using the Library Navigation panel, create a custom library called **Chapter 6**.

4. Drag and drop the music clip, from the Timeline, directly into your new Chapter 6 library. It is now reusable for other projects. You could also have placed the music into the Audio gallery portion of the Media library.

You can also right-click inside *any* Timeline track and choose Insert Audio > To Music Track 1.

Adding Audio from an Audio CD

What's nice about using music from your CD collection is that, unlike digital media purchased online, CDs are rarely copy-protected, and the music can be easily "ripped" for use in your VideoStudio projects. However, be advised that by "ripping" your audio CDs, you are violating copyright laws by making unauthorized copies of your music.

In VSX5, importing a clip from an audio CD is exactly the same as importing any other media file.

1. Make sure your newly created Chapter 6 library is displayed and audio files are visible by clicking the Show/Hide Audio Files icon at the top. Insert any audio CD you like into your CD/DVD tray.

CAUTION

You may have to close any dialog boxes or CD players that auto-launched on your computer before moving to step 2.

2. In the Audio library, click the Import Media Files icon at the top, the folder icon next to the Show/Hide icons. The Browse Media Files dialog box will appear. Locate and open the CD that's in your CD/DVD drive. See Figure 6.4.

Select   Preview

Figure 6.5
Previewing tracks in the Browse media files dialog box.

Figure 6.4
Opening your audio CD.

3. Although the tracks may not be named by their song title, this import method allows you to select any track and preview it in this dialog box before you import it (see Figure 6.5). This play to preview feature is not available using the Browse method back at the bottom of the Library panel. Find at least one song (or several using Shift- or Ctrl-select) you want to rip from your CD, and click Open to place them into your Chapter 6 library.

In the earlier versions of VideoStudio, audio clips were placed in both the Library and the Timeline. Thankfully, the new method only imports clips into the Library.

Adding Voiceover Narration

All is not lost if you forgot to add some appropriate (or inappropriate) commentary into your video while you were shooting it. In VSX5, you can add narration anywhere in your project afterward, too. The best part is that recording it separately means it will go into a separate track from your video, where you can edit it or even delete it and try again.

There are several things to consider before recording directly into VSX5.

▶ Turn off the TV and eliminate any outside/background noise, if possible. Tell the kids to go outside and play.

▶ Use the recording level meter in the Adjust Volume level window to test and adjust the volume of your voice.

▶ Will you just be using the built-in microphone on your laptop? If so, get as close to it as possible, but don't yell into it. Talk normally.

▶ Do you have an external microphone or a headset with a recording arm that you can connect to your PC? If so, use it, but again, test the recording levels first.

▶ Recording levels can first be adjusted to get within the correct range via your PC's Control Panel. Operating systems may vary, but go to the Control Panel > Sound > Recording, and select the recording device you are using. Recording levels should be adjustable there.

Tip

You can also separate existing audio from a video. I'll show you how this is done later in the chapter.

Following are the steps to record your voice as a narration directly into a video project.

1. Delete any music you have in the Timeline.

2. Click the icon in the library to Show Videos. Go to your Chapter 4 library (you'd better still have it!), and insert Fireworks2 into the main video track starting at the beginning.

3. Move the playback head in the Timeline to around the 5-second mark (the Preview window will tell you when you're there). Click the Record/Capture Option button in the Timeline toolbar (see Figure 6.6). In the Record/Capture Option pop-up window, click the Voice-over icon.

Figure 6.6
Record a voiceover.

4. The Adjust Volume window that appears works very simply. Use it first to test the recording level by speaking normally into your recording device while watching the bars spread out from the middle. If the bars get farther than halfway and start turning red, the level is too high.

5. Click Start and record a short 3- or 4-second introduction to the fireworks show, such as, "Welcome to the fireworks show from the steps of the Lincoln Memorial!" Press Esc or the spacebar when you're done.

6. You're welcome to try a couple times until you get it right. I did. Use Ctrl+Z to undo each one you don't like.

7. Your recording is automatically placed in the voice track of the Timeline. Rewind, select Clip, and play the selection to preview.

8. If you don't like it, click the undo icon in the Timeline and try the steps again. If you do like it, preview it again, but with Project selected in the Preview panel to test the combination of your voice and the fireworks. (There is a really good chance that the fire-works clip has drowned out your narration. Don't worry, you will fix this later in the chapter.)

9. Drag the new audio clip into your Chapter 6 library to use later. Select the label under the thumbnail, and rename it **Fireworks voiceover**.

10. Save your project as Chapter 6.

Adding Audio Using Auto Music

Corel has partnered with the audio technology and content company SmartSound to include a collection of royalty-free music clips using its product called Quicktracks. There are several great features in Quicktracks. First, any clip can automat-ically trim, or even extend, to your project's length in a natural, realistic manner. Second, these clips can be edited for style, tempo, genre, and more. Some even allow you to choose which instruments in the clip you want to play, setting the mood, so to speak. These features are collectively referred to in VSX5 as Auto Music.

In this section, you'll select and add some Auto Music clips, but you'll actually edit them a little later in the chapter.

Click the Auto Music icon in the Timeline (see Figure 6.7). The Auto Music panel pops up over the library similar to an Options panel. There seems to be a lot going on here as far as choices go, so let me explain them. The five drop-down lists allow you to choose different audio clips and then variations thereof. They are separated in a hierarchical fashion: Scope > Filter > Subfilter > Music > Variation.

Figure 6.7
Accessing Auto Music.

Let's start with a look at the Scope drop-down list. (For the purposes of this discussion, make sure to keep Owned Titles selected, because choosing another option will affect the appearance of the other lists.)

Feel free to click Play Selected Music at any time to preview an Auto Music clip.

► **Owned Titles** include all the Quicktrack audio clips that were included with your copy of VSX5.

► **SmartSound Store** allows you to preview clips from the company SmartSounds, and then purchase and install them right into this panel.

► **Music Multi-layer** displays clips that will allow you to toggle different instruments on and off to set various musical moods. Clips with this ability in the Music drop-down list are designated by asterisks.

► **Music Single-layer** are clips without the individual instrument editing ability.

► **Sound Effects** are functionally self-explanatory. These need to be purchased separately, though, from the sample SmartSounds that come included with VSX5.

Tip

To purchase and download additional Quicktracks from SmartSound, click the SmartSound Quicktracks icon in the Auto Music panel, and then proceed to the Internet tab.

Options in the Filter list let you isolate clips by Album, Composer, Instrument, Intensity, Keyword, Release Date, Style, or Tempo. Setting the Filter choice will alter what's available in the Subfilter, Music, and Variation lists. Leave the choice at Style for now.

The Subfilter list lets you narrow down the Filter choices and will affect what options are available in Music and Variation. Options in the Music list result from your choices in the previous filtering lists, and those choices affect what's available in the Variation list. The options in the Variation list depend on your choice in the Music list.

The following steps will show you how to choose and apply a SmartSound.

1. Click the Auto Trim check box to make the audio clip fade out naturally at the end, no matter what length you make it. This is one of the key benefits of using Quicktracks.

Tip

As a reminder, the Auto Music choices are narrowed down in the following hierarchical order: Scope > Filter > Subfilter > Music > Variation.

2. Select the clip, Scope > Owned Titles, Filter > Intensity, Subfilter > All −5 Intensity(s), Music > The Great Escape, and Variation > Persevere (as shown in Figure 6.8).

3. Rewind your project. Fit your project to Timeline view.

4. Click Add to Timeline from the Auto Music options panel. It will add this clip to Music track 1. You'll notice that the audio clip is the same length as the project's length. The Auto Trim check box is the reason for this. Play it to preview. You may notice the music is difficult to hear over the fireworks. You'll fix this in the "Adjusting Clip Volumes" section later in the chapter.

Figure 6.8
Choose this variation of a Quicktracks clip.

5. Save your project.

Splitting Audio from a Video Clip

Splitting (or separating) the audio portion from a video clip allows you to either delete it (thus muting your video and shrinking the file size somewhat) or edit the audio by adjusting volume levels or adding filters and effects separately from the video clip it came from. You can also shift the location of the audio clip along any of the audio tracks, in essence, making the audio start before the video starts or have it end after the video ends. (This is explained further in the Tip on J and L cuts on the next page.)

Any audio split from a video can *only* go into the voice track, not a music track. Technically, this is because audio from video, more often than not, contains people talking and other environmental noises, as opposed to music. You can move it afterward to another track. Because of this, the Voice track needs to be clear to perform this video/audio split operation. Therefore, you might need to move whatever is in the Voice track down to another audio track before splitting a video's audio portion to make room.

The following steps will guide you through the process of splitting the audio portion from a video clip.

1. In the Timeline, move the voiceover clip (not the music clip) straight down to a lower, empty music track. Make sure you move the voice clip straight down to keep it in the same time location.

2. Double-click the Fireworks2 video clip in the Timeline (the only video in the Timeline) to bring up the video Options panel.

Tip

A shortcut to step 2 is to right-click on the clip in the Timeline and select Split Audio.

3. Choose Split Audio. The audio track of the Fireworks2 video clip will now be in the voice track of your Timeline. See Figure 6.9.

4. Save your project.

Splitting audio from here...   ...will place the audio here

Figure 6.9
Timeline view of a split audio clip.

Tip

Special effects can be performed by applying what the industry calls *J and L cuts.* These are adjustments that separate the audio portion of a clip so that it can be shifted either to the left or to the right on the Timeline, independently of the video clip. (You'll often experience this when watching a movie or TV show, hearing a waterfall or a car revving, for example, before it actually appears onscreen.)

The shapes of the letters J and L represent the shape of the video vs. the audio portion in the Timeline. The J represents the audio that starts before the video, and the L represents the audio that extends beyond the end of the video clip. It depends on which way you move the audio in relation to the video along the Timeline.

You can also accomplish the same task by just cutting off the first few and/or last few seconds of a video clip after the audio is separated. You may, though, have to add a blank filler video clip (such as a color chip) as a placeholder for blank areas in the start of your main Timeline track because you can't have a blank space in that track. You will be using filler spaces in the main track in future chapters.

Editing Audio in the Main Timeline View

S OME AUDIO EDITING is accomplished in the Music & Voice panel. These include volume adjustments, setting a fade-in/fade-out, and applying audio filters. I'll explore the first two here. Audio filters will be covered later in the chapter.

Adjusting Clip Volumes

Adjusting audio clip volume levels lets you set the volume of individual audio clips, improving the mix of your multiple audio and video clips, and overall project volume levels. This can be useful if, say, the fireworks are too loud and don't allow you to hear an added voiceover or music track, hint, hint.

These steps will show you how to manually adjust the overall volume level of an audio clip.

1. Double-click the audio clip in the voice track that was split from Fireworks2 to bring up the Music & Video panel.

2. Open the Volume control meter by clicking the down arrow to the left of the Fade-In icon (see Figure 6.10). Decrease the level to about 50%. You will see numerical feedback in the field to the left of the meter. You can either type in the amount in the field next to the meter or lower the vertical slider in the meter itself. Typing in the amount will be more accurate. Click outside the field to set the value.

Figure 6.10
Accessing the Volume meter.

3. Repeat step 2, but instead increase the volume of the Quicktrack music clip to 200%. This will put the fireworks and music on a much better mix where you can hear almost equal values of each. Do not change the volume of your voiceover yet.

Double-clicking a Quicktrack in an audio track will display the Auto Music options instead of the Music & Voice panel, but they both will have a volume control meter.

4. Play at least part of your project to preview the new audio settings. Save your project.

Tip

You can bypass the Volume meter and type a specific numeric value into the field next to the meter. The benefit of using the meter, though, is the peak level feedback you get if you go too high. The field will go from green to yellow to red as levels increase. The higher values of yellow and especially red will indicate possible distortion on playback and even skips (clipping).

Trimming Audio

Trimming audio is done in the same way as trimming video. The following steps, although you won't apply them to the project, will show the various methods for trimming audio clips in the Timeline.

1. Fit your project to the Timeline view.

2. Grab the *end* of any audio clip and shorten it by dragging to the left. Undo.

3. Grab the *start* of any audio clip and shorten it by dragging to the right. Undo.

4. Double-click The Great Escape music clip to bring up the Auto Music options. In the timecode (above the Scope drop down), highlight the number 33 so it blinks. Type in 15 to shorten the clip's time to 15 seconds. Tap your Enter key to lock it in. As you can see, there are many similarities between trimming audio and trimming video. There are still other ways to adjust the length of an audio clip. Keep the track at 15 sec for the next section.

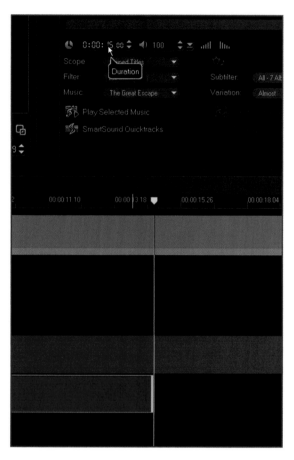

Figure 6.11
Shortening an audio clip.

Stretching Audio Clips

Wait, what? You can stretch an audio clip? Actually, in VSX5, you can! Adjusting audio playback length might be necessary or desirable if you want to match it to the length of a video clip. Logic says you shouldn't be able to, but there are two ways to do this.

▶ Use a Quicktrack. These "smart" sound clips are designed to end fluidly, no matter what the length.

▶ Adjusting an audio playback speed between 50% and 150% will change the length without noticeable changes in pitch. It will instead play a clip at a slower tempo, which will still sound (mostly) natural.

CAUTION

You cannot adjust the playback speed of a Quicktrack clip.

These steps will show you how to stretch certain audio clips.

1. Double-click the Fireworks audio clip in the Timeline. In the Music & Voice panel, reduce the volume of the clip to 0 (mute) so it won't interfere with the next steps.

2. Fit the project to Timeline view. Play the last few seconds of the music section you just shortened. Notice how the Music track still fades out naturally even though you shortened its length by half.

3. In the Timeline, drag-stretch The Great Escape audio clip back out to the end of the project. Play the last part of the track again. Notice how, again, it fades out naturally. This is one of the beauties of Quicktracks.

4. Mute the music track, as you did to the Fireworks audio in step 1.

5. Double-click the voiceover clip in the Timeline you created.

6. Select Speed/Time-lapse. Time-lapse does not come into play with audio tracks, but playback speed does. These two features just happen to be bundled together. Change the Speed setting to 150%. (See Figure 6.12.) Click the Preview button right in the Speed/Time-lapse window.

   Notice that although its tempo is faster because of the increased playback speed, the pitch remains the same—in other words, no chipmunks! You can alter playback speed from 50% to 200% without noticing any pitch change.

   Change the speed setting to 50%, and preview it again. That should lull you to sleep!

Figure 6.12
Adjusting a clip's speed.

7. Click Cancel or return the Speed setting to 100% and leave the Speed/Time-lapse window. Play the voiceover again in the Timeline to make sure it plays normally.

8. Return the Fireworks audio level back to 50% and the Music track audio level back to 200%.

9. Save your project.

Adjusting Audio Fade-In/Fade-Out

Background music that starts and ends gradually is commonly used to create smooth transitions between clips, the same way that video clips oftentimes fade out and the next one fades in to eliminate abruptness. Since the Quicktrack we added has this effect built-in, we'll apply a fade on the Fireworks audio instead.

Simple audio fades are easy using the Music & Voice panel. More complex fades can be done in the Sound Mixer. You'll play with the Sound Mixer a little later in the chapter.

1. Double-click the Fireworks audio clip to bring up the Music & Voice panel.

2. In the Music & Voice panel, click both the Fade-in and Fade-out icons (see Figure 6.13). Preview the start and end portions of your project. It might be a little tough to notice any differences, since it's rather quick, but preview it anyway. I'll show you where the actual settings take place and how to adjust them shortly.

Figure 6.13
Fade-in and Fade-out controls.

Setting the Mood in Quicktracks

Quicktracks not only contain the ability to auto-fit audio clips to any length, but some of the tracks are multilayered, giving the ability to turn on and off different instruments (or layers) to control which ones play. You can control layers through specific instrument choices or preset mood settings.

If you've ever worked in a photo editing application that allows you to work with objects on different layers, this feature is similar to that. When you hide a layer in the photo application, certain objects or effects will temporarily disappear in your photo or illustration. In the multilayered Quicktracks, hiding a layer mutes an instrument or group of instruments.

1. Return to the Auto Music options by double-clicking on The Great Escape music clip in the Timeline.

2. Choose Scope > Music Multi-layer. In the Music list, your choices are now narrowed down to those with asterisks in front of them. These are the customizable, multilayered choices available to you.

3. In the Filter list, choose Composer. Open the Subfilter list. Do you know any of these people? Me neither. Go back and choose Filter > Style instead.

4. Choose Subfilter > Orchestral, Music > Feature Presentation, Variation > Majesty. Click the Play Selected Music button in the panel to preview. Ah, so soothing!

5. Select the Set Mood icon.

6. Move the Strings slider to the left to turn them all the way down. Click the Play button in the Mood Properties window to preview the change (see Figure 6.14). You can play around with the other instrument settings and then click the Play button to see how different levels change the sound and the mood.

Figure 6.14
Setting the mood.

Now let's experiment with different settings.

1. Return the Strings to the previous setting in line with the other instrument levels. Turn Trumpet, Horns all the way down. Preview again. Nice, huh? And easy, too! Click OK.

2. Delete the music in Music Track 1 (not the Fireworks audio!) to make room for a different Auto Music track. Rewind your project to the beginning.

3. The Auto Music panel should still be open. If it is not, click the Auto Music icon in the Timeline toolbar to reopen it. Choose the following settings in the Auto Music panel: Scope > Music Multi-layer, Filter > Instrument, Subfilter > All-12 Instruments, Music > Clear Vision, Variation > Soar. In the Mood Properties dialog, choose Drums & Bass from the Mood drop-down list at the top. Preview it, and then click OK.

4. Rewind your project. In the Auto Music panel, click Add to Timeline. Increase the Volume level to 200% so it can be heard above the noise of the fireworks.

5. Save your project.

Editing Audio in the Sound Mixer

THE MUSIC & VOICE PANEL contains a selection of basic audio clip editing features, which are oftentimes sufficient, as long as the edit pertains to the entire clip. What if you want to make more precise adjustments? How about multipoint adjustments? This is where the Sound Mixer comes in handy. The Sound Mixer allows for more precise control, including editing volumes at multiple points along the Timeline, as well as stereo and surround sound effects.

The Volume level on regular audio clips (as opposed to Quicktracks) in VSX5 is handled by adjusting the height of a horizontal line that runs the length of the clip in the Timeline. You can place a "pin" (keyframe) anywhere along that line to lock the volume in place, while still allowing for adjustments all around it. Move the line up to increase the volume or down to decrease it. Moving the line gradually down to zero at the end creates the fade-out effect you're now familiar with. Increasing it at the beginning creates a fade-in.

This is also where you can create stereo audio by designating which channel plays individual audio tracks. An advanced Dolby 5.1 Surround Sound feature even allows an audio track to "swim" between two or more channels at your discretion.

These steps will show you how to add precision volume adjustments to audio clips.

1. Click the Sound Mixer icon in the Timeline toolbar to go to the Audio Timeline view. (See Figure 6.15.) Audio in all the tracks is represented by a straight horizontal line running down the middle of each track. This indicates that volume levels are at 100%, except for the fade-ins and fade-outs we created earlier. In the audio tracks, you'll see both the horizontal volume indicator line and actual audio waveforms below that. Audio waveforms designate very precise audio levels at any point in time. The wider the vertical reach, the louder the audio. (See Figure 6.16.)

Figure 6.15
Accessing the Sound Mixer area.

Volume Levels

Fade-In　　　　　　　　**Waveform**

Figure 6.16
Timeline Audio view.

The point where the volume changes direction is called a *keyframe*. Keyframes can be added very easily, and you'll be applying them here and in other locations in your projects going forward.

Keyframes can also be used to indicate other changes, such as for animations. In this audio rubberband situation, they work like pins to hold the line in place while level changes can occur on either side of it.

2. Click Show All Visible Tracks to expand the Track view (icon underneath the storyboard icon). Select the Clear Vision audio clip in the Timeline to display the audio options.

3. Select the Attribute tab in the Options panel. You can see that clip volume control and Fade-In/Fade-Out controls are located here, as well.

4. See the horizontal lines running down the middle of all the clips? A selected clip's audio line will be pink. Clips that are not highlighted will be a light green. These lines indicate volume levels. A line down the middle indicates a volume level of 100%. A higher line indicates a volume level above 100%. A lower line, a level below 100%. These lines are often referred to as *rubber bands* because of the rather elastic properties they contain.

   In the selected music audio clip, look at the pink rubber band part on the far left. Its upward path from the bottom indicates the volume's gradual fade-in. In the Attribute panel, click the Fade-In control to turn it off and notice the visual change. Undo the change.

5. On the far right, where the fade-out begins, drag the second to last keyframe "pin" and move it straight left to make the fade-out more gradual and longer time-wise (see Figure 6.17). The exact location need not match the screenshot. Make sure the rest of the rubber band remains level by gently adjusting the pin up or down.

Volume level change point　　　**Slide keyframe to left**

Figure 6.17
Adjusting a fade effect.

Using a combination of the zoom buttons and the bottom scroll bar, zoom into the portion of the Timeline that shows the voiceover clip. Let's lower the Music track's volume where it coincides with the voiceover so that you can hear the voiceover a bit better. As opposed to previous methods that laid down volume level keyframes (pins) automatically, in the following step, you'll add these keyframes (pins) manually. (You should read the steps before proceeding.)

1. Using Figure 6.18 as a guide, in the music track (not the Fireworks audio), click once to place a keyframe at both the start and end of where the voiceover below it starts and ends. Your cursor will turn into an up-facing arrow when it's over the right spot.

2. Place another keyframe just before the first keyframe and just after the second one you just placed.

> **CAUTION**
>
> If you inadvertently move the rubberband up or down when setting a keyframe, you can readjust the line by moving the keyframe up or down. Just make sure you grab the keyframe you set. If you miss the keyframe and click the line, you'll add another keyframe.

3. Move the two center keyframes down as far as they will go. (Do not drag down too far, or you will drag the keyframe off the track and delete it. If this happens, click again on the rubberband to replace it.) You have just caused the music to gradually and temporarily mute while you speak and then raise back up to 100% afterward.

4. Preview your changes and save your project.

Figure 6.18
Adjusting volume levels with keyframes.

Splitting a Stereo Track

Audio files sometimes separate the vocals or music from the background and put them in different channels (stereo). The Duplicate Audio Channel feature in VSX5 allows you to separate the two stereo channels and then mute or play just one or the other channel. Unfortunately, it's not as easy as just telling which channel you want an audio clip to play from (right or left). Although not that difficult, you need to use the special Duplicate Audio Channel feature.

First, you'll duplicate a stereo audio clip (in the background, not on the Timeline itself) so it splits the instruments currently playing in one track, into two. Next, you'll tell which channel (left or right) you want to play by muting the other channel so only one of the channels (and thus one set of instruments) plays (left or right).

Confused? Let's try it and see if we can eliminate that confusion. So you can hear the differences better, you'll create a new project and only use it for this section.

1. Save your Chapter 6 project and open a new one (File > New).

2. Import the other audio clip, called Audio Duplication, from your music folder, straight into the Timeline (File > Insert Media to Timeline > Insert Audio > To Music Track #1). Play it to preview it. Listen closely. If your PC has stereo playback, you should be able to distinguish those guitars playing in the left channel from those playing in the right channel.

3. Open the Sound Mixer again using the icon at the top of the Timeline.

4. Highlight the music tack in the Timeline and open the Attribute tab in the Options panel. Click the Duplicate Audio Channel radio button and select the Left radio button (see Figure 6.19).

Figure 6.19
Duplicating an audio channel.

5. Preview the clip again. Notice that only one set of guitars, coming from the left channel, now plays.

6. Now select the Right channel radio button and play the clip again. Notice how only the other set of guitars is now playing.

7. Reopen your Chapter 6 project without saving the current one.

Now wasn't that easy? I think it was quicker to do it than it was to explain it! But, you get the idea now? Good, let's move on.

Creating Traveling Stereo from Two Mono Tracks

Not only can you separate and isolate an entire track into one channel, but with the Surround Sound Mixer tab, you can alter the adjustments over time, interactively and in real time, to create an effect of audio repeatedly traveling from one speaker to another. Let's try this feature and others in the Surround Sound Mixer tab.

1. Open the Settings menu at the top of your screen. Make sure Enable 5.1 Sound is disabled (*not* checked). This will (when enabled later) add additional audio playback options beyond stereo.

2. Still in the Options panel, select the Surround Sound Mixer (SSM) tab next to the Attribute tab.

3. Rewind your project and select the music audio clip. The music track will now be highlighted in the SSM tab (see Figure 6.20). Play your project (as opposed to a clip) and watch the reaction of the three meters. There's one for each channel and a volume (VU; VU = Volume Units) meter to indicate the volume changes in Music track 1 when playback gets to the voiceover clip. This resulted from the volume level changes you made earlier.

Figure 6.20
Surround Sound Mixer tab.

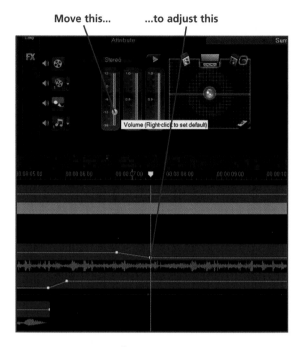

Figure 6.21
Adding audio keyframe using volume adjustment.

4. Select the Fireworks audio track. With the playback head somewhere other than over the voiceover, add an audio keyframe. Move the playback head again a little further down, away from the new keyframe.

5. Move the Volume slider (left-most VU meter) in the SSM panel up or down (see Figure 6.21). When you do so, notice that another keyframe is created and placed according to your Volume setting.

6. Undo until the two new keyframes disappear. I just wanted you to be aware of the other level adjustment method.

7. Rewind your project, and select the Fireworks audio clip in the voice track.

You're now going to make the audio in this track move back and forth between the right and left channels, in real time, while it actually plays. To do this, you'll be moving the big red dot in the middle of the speaker "room" on the Surround

Sound Mixer tab (see Figure 6.22). Be sure to read the following steps in their entirety first. Also, make sure that Project is selected (this won't work with Clip). Don't worry that your Fireworks audio clip is no longer selected in the Timeline. It is still selected in the SSM panel.

Tip

A red dot in the Surround Sound room indicates the voice track is selected. If it's blue, a music track is selected.

You can also use the Play button in the SSM tab to preview your clips.

Interactive stereo control

Figure 6.22
Real-time stereo adjustment.

1. Place your cursor over the red dot in the SSM tab. Press the spacebar to play your project. While your project plays, slowly move the red dot back and forth. Do this for the entire clip. Do it slowly. You might actually be able to hear the audio move between your speakers as you perform this operation.

2. Click the spacebar at any time to stop the process, or you can let it go until the end.

3. When finished, the track's rubberband will be littered with keyframes (as shown in Figure 6.23), indicating changes in channel playback location. Rewind and play your project to preview it. You should hear the audio move from left to right to left, and so on. You will also see the stereo indicator move back and forth when you preview it.

4. Undo once with Ctrl+Z and save your project. The next section will expand on this SSM feature in a more advanced way.

Tip

Luckily, choosing Undo will undo this entire process, instead of just removing one keyframe at a time.

Figure 6.23
Surround sound audio adjustment.

Using 5.1 Surround Sound

VSX5 and the Dolby 5.1 Surround Sound feature take audio channel mixing to a whole new, higher level. It works similarly to the real-time stereo mixing you did in the last section, but instead, Surround Sound allows for interactive audio mixing of up to six separate channels (5 channels and a sub-woofer, which only handles bass/low frequencies). Of course, you will need to have an actual surround sound system set up in order to take full advantage of this feature afterward. If not, you can still at least go through the motions of how it's done and save it for surround sound playback.

1. Go to the Settings menu and select Enable 5.1 Surround. Click OK in the message box warning you that playback will be altered and previous edits and previews will not be carried forward.

2. Select Music track 1 in the Timeline, which is the Quicktracks clip. In the SSM tab, the bottom-left Music icon will be selected no matter which of the three available Music tracks are chosen. It represents all of them. You can select a different music track by clicking the down arrow to the right of the Music icon (see Figure 6.24). Keep it at Music track 1.

3. Instead of just adjusting stereo channels by moving the indicator back and forth, you'll now adjust center speakers and sub-woofers of your surround sound system by moving the indicator *all around* the "room." Mouse over the two VU meters to the left of the Surround Sound room to see an indication of what each one adjusts (see Figure 6.25). These two extra VU meters (sliders) adjust the extra speakers in a surround sound system.

Figure 6.24
Selecting a different music track.

Figure 6.25
Surround Sound adjustments.

4. As you did in the "Stereo Adjustments" section, make sure that Project (not Clip) is selected. Place your cursor over the blue dot in the center of the Surround Sound Mixer room and press the spacebar to play your project. This time, though, move the blue dot in a circular motion around the room, but as before, slowly.

5. Continue until the project is finished playing. Rewind and play to preview, noticing how the blue dot now moves around the room, simulating true surround sound!

6. Leave the Surround Sound Mixer panel by clicking on the Sound Mixer icon in the Timeline toolbar and return to the Timeline view.

7. Save your project.

Applying Audio Filters

AUDIO FILTERS IN VSX5, although perhaps not nearly as fun to apply and view as video filters, still provide important tools for audio repairs and some special effects. Audio repairs can come in very handy for both casual fun videos and business presentations. Less than optimal quality video may not be a project killer, but poor audio can be. Pops, clicks, hisses, and hums can be annoying and irritating to your listeners.

Many of the audio filters in VSX5 have options for customization. Many of them are provided by NewBlue, a third-party software provider who develops add-on tools for medium and high-end video production. Having them included in VSX5 for audio and video effects at no additional charge is a major bonus for you.

Following are some steps to try a few of the Corel and NewBlue audio filters.

1. Open the Options panel for the Fireworks audio clip by double-clicking it in the Timeline. In the Music & Voice panel, click the Audio Filter icon. (See Figure 6.26.) The Audio Filter dialog box will open.

Tip

You can also right-click on the Timeline clip and choose Audio Filter to jump straight to the task.

Figure 6.26
Select the Audio Filter option.

2. Select Echo in the Available Filters area, and click Options. Under the Defined echo effects drop-down list, choose Long Repeat. (See Figure 6.27.) Click the Play button in the Echo window to preview. Scary, huh? Repeat and preview with the Stadium choice. Click Cancel twice to close the Filters windows.

3. Select and play just your voiceover clip in the Timeline. It might need some polishing, but let's have some fun with it first. With it still selected, open the Audio Filter dialog box again. Choose Pitch Shift and then Options. Crank it to one end and preview. Repeat with the other end of the spectrum. Remember how adjusting the speed of this clip previously did not change the pitch one way or the other? With this audio filter, you *can* change the pitch. Click Cancel.

Figure 6.27
Setting the Echo audio filter.

Unlike the NewBlue filters, Help within the default VSX5 Audio Filters is accessed through the regular VSX5 Help file instead of within each filter.

4. Select NewBlue Audio Polish and click Options. Click the question mark (?) to bring up helpful instructions on how to use it and what it affects. You can repeat this with each of the NewBlue audio filters to quickly learn more about what to recognize in an audio file that the NewBlue (and the VSX5 filters for that matter) can reduce or completely fix for you. Close this help window.

5. Back in the NewBlue Audio Polish window, click the P next to the question mark to view and try the selected presets for this filter, previewing each in the same window.

6. Find a setting to your liking and click OK. Click Add to add this filter to the list on the right. Click OK to close the window and apply the effect.

7. Save your project.

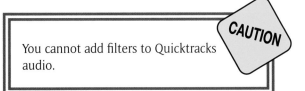

You cannot add filters to Quicktracks audio. CAUTION

Exporting Audio-Only Files

PERHAPS YOU HAVE A video recording of an important lecture, or you mixed some great audio pieces together in your video project and would like to save just the audio portions for a podcast or CD. Using the Create Sound File feature will allow you to isolate all the audio tracks as one and export them as a dedicated audio file, independent of what else is contained in your project Timeline.

1. Before we share our audio portion, let's return to the Quicktrack selection we used earlier. Double-click music track #1 to return to the Auto Music area. Return to the following settings: Scope > Owned Titles, Filter > Intensity, Subfilter > All –5 Intensity(s), Music > The Great Escape, and Variation > Persevere. It will update the current clip automatically without having to manually reapply it.

2. Go to the Share Step tab at the top of the screen.

3. Select Create Sound File. Open the Save As Type drop-down list. Here you will see four options where you can save your output:

   ▶ **MPEG-4 Audio Files (.*mp4):** MPEG-4 is designed to deliver DVD-quality video at lower data rates and smaller file sizes. In this case, choosing this type will only apply the features to the audio portion that it encodes in the AAC audio codec.

   ▶ **Ogg Vorbis Audio Format (*.ogg):** According to Wikipedia, Ogg is a free, open container format maintained by the Xiph.Org Foundation that is unrestricted by software patents and is designed to provide for efficient streaming and manipulation of high-quality digital multimedia.

   ▶ **Microsoft WAV files (*.wav):** Though a WAV file can hold compressed audio, the most common WAV format contains uncompressed audio in the linear pulse code modulation (LPCM) format.

   ▶ **Windows Media Audio (*.wma):** A proprietary technology that forms part of the Windows Media framework. Microsoft claims that audio encoded with WMA sounds better than MP3 at the same bit (sample) rate. Again, that's what Microsoft claims...

4. Save your file as MPEG-4. Double-click the file in the place where you saved it to preview the results.

Quick Quiz

1. What do multilayered music clips in the Quicktracks collection allow you to do? (See "Setting the Mood in Quicktracks.")

2. How do you make a mono audio track into a single-channel stereo track? (See "Creating Stereo from Two Mono Tracks.")

3. In the Sound Mixer view, what is the item called that, when placed on the Timeline, allows you to change the direction of an audio clip's volume? (See "Editing Audio in the Sound Mixer.")

4. What feature allows you to create active stereo and multispeaker arrangements? (See "Using 5.1 Surround Sound.")

Keeping It Unique with

Video Effects

NOW THAT YOU'VE LEARNED how to assemble video and audio clips and edit these assets, it's time to have a little fun with them. This chapter will cover how you can apply special effects that will give your project a uniqueness all their own. You'll expand your knowledge on using special effects by adding transitions between clips, fading clips on entrance and exit, as well as adding the Pan & Zoom effect to photos.

Pan & Zoom allows you to better integrate photos into a video project by giving them an animated look. You'll learn about video overlays, or what is sometimes called Picture-In-Picture, and even chroma key effects like what the weatherman uses on TV when he points to the weather map. (You do know that he's not actually standing in front of the map, but standing in front of a large blue or green screen, right?)

Adding Transitions

I'VE ALREADY TOUCHED on transitions somewhat. Transitions are used to, umm, transition from one clip to another, eliminating sharp scene breaks. Of course, you rarely see these effects in movies. Hollywood is more apt to use audio J cuts instead, where the audio for the next scene starts before the video does. But transitions are certainly acceptable and almost expected in home and business video projects. Transitions are an easy way to add effects to your movie. Their application can be made even easier by automating the process. Most of them are customizable, too!

Although you've added transitions in previous chapters, these steps will show you a few more methods and tweaks you can use when applying transitions.

1. Open the project you created in Chapter 4. Click Show All Visible Tracks so that the top two video tracks expand somewhat. If it does the opposite, click it again.

2. Move your Timeline to where all the short clips occur (see Figure 7.1). Feel free to zoom in or out a little to make them all fit your Timeline's view.

3. Go to the Transition library (see Figure 7.2). Select All from the gallery drop-down list.

Figure 7.2
Accessing transitions.

Figure 7.1
Current Timeline view.

4. If it isn't already there, add the Crossfade transition to My Favorites. Here's how. In the All gallery, select the Crossfade transition thumbnail. Transitions are generally in alphabetical order. You'll see a preview of it in the Preview panel. Click the Add to My Favorites button (see Figure 7.3). The Crossfade transition will now appear in the My Favorites list in the gallery drop-down list. Add the MaskE transition in the same way. Add two or three more transitions of your choice to My Favorites.

Did you notice that your project became a little shorter? This occurs because the ends of each of your clips need to overlap a bit so that one clip can blend in with the next one. In other words, it's necessary to see one clip fade out at the exact same time the next one is fading in, hence the necessity to overlap and the additional shortening of the overall length.

Tip

You can also right-click on any transition and select Add to My Favorites.

Figure 7.3
Adding a transition to My Favorites.

5. From the gallery drop-down list, go to your My Favorites list. Select the Crossfade transition. Just to the right of the Add to My Favorites icon, click the Apply Current Effect to Video Track icon. A tooltip will appear when you pause your mouse over it to indicate you have that right icon selected. The video track (and only the video track) of the Timeline now has the Crossfade transition applied between each of the video clips. Feel free to preview a section of your Timeline.

6. Select the very first transition in the main video track, after the first color chip. (You may need to zoom in a bit to see it better.) Delete it.

7. Save your project as **Chapter 7A**.

Play the last part of the section of the Fireworks1 clip in the Video Overlay Track 1. Notice that it ends abruptly and overlaps with the next clip. Let's see if we can fix that, too.

1. Fit the project to Timeline view. Double-click the Fireworks1 clip in the Timeline to bring up the Options panel. Open the Edit panel and shorten the clip to 57 seconds.

2. Open the Graphic library from the Library Navigation panel by clicking the icon under the Title icon. Go to the Color gallery.

3. See the same color chip you used as a background in the video track? Drag and drop that same color chip into Overlay Track 1 at the end of the Fireworks1 clip. See Figure 7.4.

Figure 7.4
Adding a color chip.

4. Drop the Crossfade transition between the end of the Fireworks1 clip and the new color chip. The new color chip should now end at the same time as the one in the main video track. See Figure 7.5. Play this portion to preview it. It should play a lot smoother now.

Figure 7.5
The added transition.

Tip

Steps 2 and 3 were made easier because the default length is 3 seconds for color chips and 1 second for transitions. The length for each can be edited, of course.

Tip

Transitions can also be added automatically any time two clips are overlapped in the Timeline.

1. We need some more content for this section, so create a custom library called **Chapter 7**. Then import the videos Jewels1 through Jewels3 into the Chapter 7 library from the Videos > WashingtonDC folder.

2. Go to Settings > Preferences > Edit. Under Transition Effect near the bottom, in the drop-down list, choose a default transition you like. I chose MaskE because it's also in My Favorites. Click OK. This will designate which transition is used in the next step.

You can also check Automatically Add Transition Effect, which will add a transition every time you place two clips just *next* to each other in the Timeline. However, this is not necessary for the current overlapping procedure. I keep this unchecked unless I have a specific project I need it for.

3. Making sure you only have Jewel1 selected in the Chapter 7 library (instead of all three), add it to the very end of your project into the background video track. Zoom into the new clip. Add Jewel2, but do so while slightly overlapping on Jewel 1. Your overlap will determine the length of the transition effect. Refer to Figure 7.6 and the next tip. Try to create an overlap of 1 second. The MaskE transition will automatically be added between the two clips.

Figure 7.6
Autotransitions when overlapping clips.

Tip

When you overlap the clips, an additional number will appear in parentheses next to your cursor. Each number represents a frame: for example, 01.08-00 means an overlap of 1 second and 8 frames.

4. Repeat the previous step with Jewel3 by overlapping it with Jewel2.

5. Return to the Transition library. Highlight the MaskE transition in the My Favorites gallery to preview it. Notice how it performs.

6. In the Timeline, double-click on either of the MaskE transitions (zoom in if it'll help select it) you just auto-applied. The Options panel will open.

7. Click the Customize icon and change the selection in the Path drop-down list from Fly Right to Slither. (See Figure 7.7.) Click OK, and then preview this change. Unfortunately, you cannot set this customization as the transition's default, or add this customization to all the transitions at once.

8. Save your project.

Figure 7.7
Customizing a transition.

Adding Overlays (Picture-In-Picture)

VIDEO OVERLAYS, COMMONLY called *picture-in-picture* or PiP in the TV world, are videos placed and played on top of other videos. These produce layers in a movie, much like an image editing application might create layers of images and objects for a unique effect. Where PiP implies a video taking over just one corner of the screen, video overlays don't have this restriction. Overlays can take over the entire screen and can even contain invisible parts that allow the background layer, or other overlay layers, to show through. (This latter effect is called *chroma key* and will be discussed in the section "Applying a Chroma Key Effect" later in this chapter.)

Overlays can be of any size, which may completely cover the background video track. You can also do many of the same things to an overlay clip that you can to a background clip, including adding borders, effects, and filters. Unique features that you can apply to an overlay clip include such items as transparencies, masks (making only certain portions transparent), and animating the overlay across the screen. Let's try these.

In this section, you'll add overlay objects and learn how to integrate them into a scene.

1. Go to File > New Project. This time you'll be using some nice HD clips. Make sure your Chapter 7 library is selected and all three Show Media icons at the top are active (yellow).

2. Click the Import Media Files icon at the top, instead of the Browse import feature. Locate the Videos > Balloon_Trip folder.

3. In the Browse Media Files window (yes, I know it's confusing that it says "Browse" when you're not actually in the Browse feature, but you're still "browsing" nonetheless), choose All Video Formats from the Files of Type drop-down list. Import all seven of the video clips (Shift-select all of them) and click Open. (See Figure 7.8.)

Figure 7.8
Selecting file import formats.

4. Return to the same Browse Media Files dialog box as in step 3. Choose All Image Formats from the same Files of Type list, and import all six images into the Chapter 7 library.

5. Selecting All Audio Formats, repeat again to import the one audio WAV file.

Tip

A shortcut for importing all the formats is to choose All Formats in the Browse Media Files dialog and select all (Ctrl+A), and then click Open, but it was much more fun torturing you instead.

6. Add HD-Travel_Start.wmv to the start of the Timeline's Video track. Zoom to fit. Save your project as **Chapter 7B**.

7. Add the intro family.jpg into video Overlay Track 1, so its end aligns with the end of HD-Travel_Start.wmv.

8. Put the MAP.jpg in the same Overlay track right before the intro family.jpg. Drag the start of the MAP clip backward until its length is 4 seconds long (see Figure 7.9). Preview the results. It doesn't look so impressive floating right in the middle of the screen, does it? Well, we can actually alter the shapes of the photos so they fit onto the TV screen in the background.

9. Place the playback head in the middle of the MAP.jpg overlay clip and select (click once) the MAP photo in the Timeline. The MAP photo in the Preview panel should have eight yellow sizing handles surrounding its frame. (Note that the *corners* have small green handles *inside* the larger yellow squares.)

10. In the Preview panel, click the middle of the clip and drag to reposition it so that its upper-left corner fits into the upper-left corner of the TV screen (not the TV frame, but the screen inside it). See Figure 7.10.

Figure 7.9
Extend MAP.jpg back to 4 seconds in length.

•

Figure 7.10
Positioning the Map jpg on the TV.

Figure 7.11
Use the green handles to skew image frame.

11. To reshape the rest of the map to fit inside the TV screen, reposition the other three small *green* squares to fit into the nearest TV screen corners. Be sure to grab the green squares *inside* the yellow squares. The green ones are the skew handles. The yellow handles are for resizing only. See Figure 7.11.

> Your cursor will turn into a single arrow when using the green handles for skewing and turn into a double-headed arrow when using the yellow handles for resizing.

12. Figure 7.12 shows the finished placement. Notice how the green squares become larger as they leave the comfort of their yellow square partners. To see the results more clearly, select Project in the Preview panel. That will hide all the handles so you can more easily see the results. You'll need to do this frequently for accurate adjustments. Select MAP in the Timeline, or Clip in the Preview panel, to return and continue editing. It might take a few tries to get the positioning the way you want it, so don't despair.

Now you need to do the same manual resizing to the intro family photo. Or do you?

Figure 7.12
Skewed image to fit.

Copying Attributes

We all love the copy and paste feature, right? VSX5 goes a step beyond copying and pasting objects, clips, and so on, by also being able to copy attributes/ options from one clip to another, thereby saving multiple steps of reapplying the same size, shape, position, and other options. In VSX5, you can also now selectively choose which attribute(s) to paste from one clip to another. This is a feature that will come in very handy for you.

1. Right-click on the MAP clip in the Timeline and choose Copy Attributes.

2. Right-click on the intro family clip to the right of MAP and choose Paste Optional Attributes. The list tells you what options may (or may not) be in the clip you copied from, that you can paste into this other clip. Keep all the attributes selected (even though not all are being utilized). Click OK. Bam! The intro family photo should now be placed inside the TV screen in the same location and shape as the MAP illustration.

Tip

If you know you'll be copying all the attributes from one clip to another, you can bypass the Paste Optional Attributes window by simply right-clicking and choosing the Paste All Attributes option instead.

Animating an Overlay Clip

One of the many advantages of putting assets into an Overlay track is having the ability to move or animate this smaller video window around the screen. This section will show you how to place your overlay clip onto a path that it will follow over time. You cannot create your own path from scratch, but there are quite a few preset paths to choose from.

1. Zoom the Timeline out a couple times. Add another copy of the MAP image from the library to the Timeline, at the end of the HD-Travel_Start clip in the background layer. Follow that with the videos Balloon-2 and Balloon-7, but do not overlap them.

2. In Overlay Track 1, drop Balloon-5 so that it starts at the same time as Balloon-2. Follow that with Balloon-4 and Balloon-3. Using the feedback adjacent to your cursor, like you did when overlapping to add a default transition, overlap Balloon-4 onto Balloon-5 by 1 second to add your default transition. Do the same thing with Balloon-3 onto Balloon-4. (See Figure 7.13.) The background video track and Overlay Track 1 should now end at the same time.

Figure 7.13
Current Timeline view.

3. One at a time, right-click each of the three clips you just put down in Overlay Track 1. Notice that the first clip has Fade-Out checked, the next one has both Fade-In and Fade-Out checked, and the third one has Fade-In checked. This is due to the transitions you added. Do not uncheck them.

4. Select Balloon-5 in the Timeline. Using the yellow resize handles in the Preview panel (*not* the green skew handles), resize the clip to about the size you see in Figure 7.14. Position it to the lower-left corner area of the screen. Remember to stay inside the *safe zone* (the thin rectangle inside of the Preview panel).

Ever see a commercial where some of the words or other graphics are cut off on the edges? Keeping graphics and text within the safe zone will guarantee full viewing on all TV screens. The safe zone area, indicated by a thin border line, occupies the center 90% of the screen, giving a 5% border all around. Action safe zones are narrower, and title safe zones are even narrower, by 5% each. Luckily, with the advent of better quality and flat panel displays, this issue has been much reduced. A 10% safe zone for everything will usually be sufficient.

Figure 7.14
Resizing the overlay.

5. Right-click on the resized Balloon-5 (as opposed to Maroon-5) clip in the Timeline and choose Copy Attributes. Paste All Attributes to Balloon-4 and Balloon-3.

6. Reselect Balloon-4 in the Timeline and position it to the top center of the Preview panel and position Balloon-3 to the lower right. When you select any one of them, the others will disappear, since none of them plays at the same time relative to the others.

7. Double-click Balloon-5 in the Timeline. In the Attribute panel, under Direction/Style, choose the Enter and Exit directions, as shown in Figure 7.15. Also, click both the Fade-In and Fade-Out icons. Apply the same choices to Balloon-3 (the last one). Save your project.

Figure 7.16
Rotate animation settings.

Figure 7.15
Direction and fade animation settings.

Figure 7.17
Set the pause duration.

8. For Balloon-4 (the center one), select Enter from the bottom left, Exit to the bottom right, and then select Fade-In and Fade-Out *and* both Rotate options (see Figure 7.16).

9. In the Preview panel for Balloon-4, notice the horizontal blue bar? This represents the pause duration where the clip is not moving, the duration between its entrance and exit. Adjust the orange end points to extend them about halfway to each left and right end. This will make the clips enter and exit more quickly and remain in place longer (see Figure 7.17). Make the same changes to Ballon-5 and Balloon-3.

10. Rewind and play your movie to see your progress thus far.

11. Save your project.

In the Attribute panel, except for filters, the options you see can only be applied to an overlaid clip.

Adding Borders to Overlays

Adding borders to items in an overlay track is akin to adding a picture frame (which you'll do later on). Although perhaps not quite as decorative, it does help to differentiate the clip from its background.

1. Double-click Balloon-5 in the Timeline. Select Mask & Chroma Key in the Attribute panel. The Mask & Chroma Key options contain additional features beyond the "weatherman" feature. The first adjustment sets clip transparency, the second adjustment creates a border, and the third lets you choose a border color (see Figure 7.18).

Transparency   Border   Border color

Figure 7.18
Mask & Chroma Key panel.

2. There are three ways to enter either a transparency or a border thickness value.

   ▶ Change the value by typing it directly into the field.

   ▶ Use the arrows to the right of each field to move the values up or down incrementally.

   ▶ Use the slider to the right of the incremental field.

   For Balloon-5, enter a value of 3 for the border thickness. The resulting change in the Preview window will be immediate, showing your new border.

3. Click the color chip just to the right of the Border fields (it should currently be white) to add a border color that accents the clip. Choose a color from the Corel Color Picker (see Figure 7.19). It's quite extensive in its choices. Click OK to any dialog boxes.

Figure 7.19
Choosing a border color.

4. Repeat the previous steps to add borders for clips Balloon-6 and Balloon-4. Be sure to add a border thickness along with your border color.

5. Save your project.

CAUTION

Do not copy and paste attributes to the other two clips, as the clip's current location will transfer as well as the color.

Pan & Zoom Effects

AN & ZOOM EFFECTS are a great way to add motion to still images. Take the History Channel, for example. Many of its episodes include footage from before the era of video, when much of modern history was recorded on film or can only be depicted in photos and illustrations. So how do you appeal to an audience used to seeing motion on TV, the computer, and handheld devices? Simple—make the pictures move! While zooming just allows you to emphasize a particular part of an image, panning *and* zooming entails moving across the face of an image to gradually reveal the story behind the picture.

The rest of this section will guide you (gently, I hope) through the process of setting up pan and zoom effects in VSX5. It can be complicated, but follow the steps precisely and perhaps read through each step before executing it.

1. Open the Track Manager. Set your Overlay Tracks to 3. Click OK. Make sure the photo gallery is visible in your Chapter 7 Media library.

2. Center your Timeline where the last three overlays you just placed are. In the Chapter 7 library, click the Show Photos icon, if not already selected, and add the photo overlay1.jpg to Overlay Track 2 starting at the 16 second mark. (See Figure 7.20.) Extend it to a length of 4 seconds (by dragging the end out or using the Options panel). Add overlay2.jpg after overlay1 and extend it to 4 seconds. Repeat with overlay3.jpg.

Figure 7.20
Adding another overlay.

3. As you've done recently, overlap photo overlay2 onto overlay1 for 1 second to again add the default transition. Repeat by overlapping overlay3 onto overlay2.

4. In the Preview panel, select and resize overlay1 in the same way you did the three overlaid video clips. Place the overlay in the bottom *center* of the preview screen. Add a white border with a value of 3 by double-clicking it in the Timeline and selecting Mask & Chrome Key.

5. In the Timeline, copy the attributes of overlay1 onto overlays 2 and 3.

6. Double-click on overlay1 in the Timeline. Go to the Edit panel and check Apply Pan & Zoom. In the drop-down list just below the check box, select the last choice in the second row. Click outside of the selection area to accept this choice. (See Figure 7.21.)

Figure 7.21
Choosing a Pan & Zoom preset.

7. For overlay2, choose the first Pan & Zoom option in the second row. Click Customize. The Pan & Zoom dialog box will open (see Figure 7.22). The Pan & Zoom window is similar to what you'll see when customizing video filters in the next chapter, so learning this here will give you a great head start. This is probably the most complex area of VSX5, so if you can conquer this, you'll be able to handle anything else in the book.

The Original panel on the left is where you'll set up visual cues and settings. The Preview panel on the right lets you see the results of your settings from the left side. The Timeline below the panels is similar to your video Timeline, allowing you to view results at different points in time.

Figure 7.22
Pan & Zoom window.

The icons above the Timeline allow you to drop keyframes so that your effect can change direction and/or attributes at that point in time. The Pan & Zoom dialog box will have different features, depending on the effect you choose.

8. Let's use the tools to exaggerate the current animation (see Figure 7.23). Make sure the playback is at the beginning. In the Original panel, resize the yellow-cornered bounding box so it covers only the mom's face. You'll see feedback occurring in the right panel. Back in the left panel, the red cross represents the center of the right-side view in the currently selected keyframe. Move it so Mom's face is centered.

9. The other crosshair (that's white, NOT red) represents the position in the last keyframe, or the end of the Pan & Zoom effect. Click it. It will now turn red and your playback head will move to the end. You can now adjust the ending position. Each time you click a white cross, it will convert to a red cross, because the clip moves to that frame and because it now represents the current frame.

If you move the playback head between the start and end points of the effect, another crosshair will display. This represents a position between the start and end. You can, if you so desire, add another keyframe here and change any of the available attributes, like direction, zoom, and transparency.

Using Figures 7.24 and 7.25 as your guide, set the first and last frames similar to what you see there.

Figure 7.23
Using the Pan & Zoom window.

Start center point   Start frame size   Start view

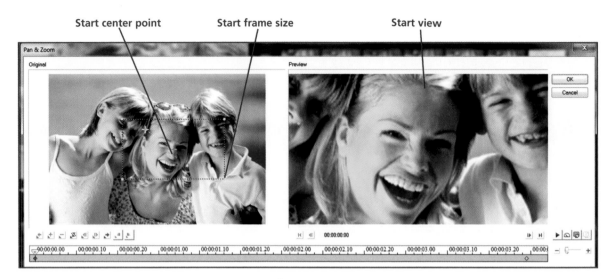

Figure 7.24
Starting Pan & Zoom view.

End center point   End frame size   End view

Figure 7.25
End pan and Zoom view.

10. Rewind and play to preview right in the Pan & Zoom window. Click the Play button to both start and stop the pan effect. Click OK when finished previewing to close the Pan & Zoom edit window.

11. Double-click overlay 3, check Apply Pan & Zoom, and then go to Customize again. It will default to the first preset in the drop-down preset list. Click the Go to Last Frame button (lower right of the Preview window on the far right just to the left of the Play button).

12. Narrow and reposition the bounding box to close in more on the family's faces (see Figure 7.26). Reposition the red cross so you see all four family members. This will create an animation opposite of the one in Overlay 2. Preview it, and then click OK.

13. Rewind your project and preview your work to this point. Save your project.

Figure 7.26
Adjusting a Pan & Zoom end point.

Adding Embellishments

EMBELLISHMENTS IN VSX5 allow you to add design interest to clips, scenes, and stills. They can take on several forms and functions. You have decorations (about 40 of them) that are similar to Christmas ornaments and fun, scrapbooking-like clip art—objects you could scatter around your screen to add some personal touches.

Embellishments also include picture frames (more than 40). Picture frames have the great feature of being a mask. Think of it as a Halloween mask, where the cut-out eye holes allow you to see what's on the other side. Place any of the picture frames in an Overlay track, and any part of it that's white (the eye holes) will be transparent, letting the underlying content show through.

Flash animations (about 70) include both animated decorations and animated frames. Flash animations are what's known as *resolution-independent graphics*. You can make them any size or shape you like, and they will still look great—no pixilation, no jagged lines, and no jagged edges.

Also included in this category are the color backgrounds (chips) you applied in Chapter 4. Frames and objects are pretty self-explanatory, so let's add a couple of Flash animations instead.

1. First, you'll need to extend the MAP image in the middle of the Timeline's video track while ensuring all the clips in the other tracks move forward accordingly; otherwise, they'll be out of sync when you add a clip to the middle of any of the other tracks. Exactly like you did in Chapter 5, enable Ripple Editing and turn it on for all tracks.

2. Double-click the MAP image in the main video track (not the overlay track). In the Photo tab of the Options panel, set the length to 6 seconds and press Enter. All the other tracks should've moved to the right accordingly. If not, undo and revisit step 1.

3. Close the Options panel. Select the Graphic library, and then select the Flash Animation gallery from the drop-down list (as shown in Figure 7.27).

4. Place MotionD05 (the compass) into Overlay Track 2 (leaving Overlay Track 1 empty) directly under the MAP image. Adjust it to be the same length as the MAP image in the video track. In the Preview panel, size MotionD05 smaller and place it into the upper-left corner. Make sure to keep it within the safe zone. (See Figure 7.28.)

Figure 7.27
Select the Flash Animation gallery in the Graphic library.

Figure 7.28
Adding a Flash animation.

5. Repeat step 5 with MotionF02. Place this decoration in Overlay Track 3 directly under, in line with, and with the same duration as MotionD05. This time, do not adjust its size.

6. Rewind this section and preview. Nice, huh?

7. Save your project.

Tip

You can create and add your own decorations. Using the same Import icon you use for other media, you can import objects and frames of various file formats, including JPG, GIF, BMP, PNG, and PSP files. You can also import a Flash SWF into the Flash Animations gallery. There are some video tutorials that show this on Corel.com and YouTube.com.

Applying a Chroma Key Effect

A CHROMA KEY EFFECT is a fancy term for setting a transparency (a mask) based on color. You might be familiar with the terms blue screen and green screen. This technology is commonly used in the movies and on news programs to project an image or video onto a different background, giving the illusion that someone or something in the foreground is part of the background, intending to show that everything is together in one scene, when it's really not.

Most Hollywood or TV productions will put up a solid blue or green wall in the background and then tell the computer to place a different image anywhere that blue or green color appears—in other words, make that color transparent and display something instead. In the weatherman's case, it's the weather map. In a movie, it might be an alien planet's landscape or outer space. Any objects in the foreground will remain visible unless they also contain that same background color. If they do, they will also be transparent. (Wear a blue shirt against a blue screen and your torso will become invisible.)

Using a computer, the two layers (foreground and background) are combined and broadcast together on a single layer. VSX5 can create this effect. The challenging part for you, if you want to use this effect, is to shoot a video that has a solid color background that can be selected to be transparent. The background can be any color, not just blue or green. A nice feature of VSX5 is that you can select a range of a color, so the transparent color doesn't have to be the same color value throughout the entire background. This helps when you lack the budget of a Hollywood movie stage.

Let's see what effect you can produce with the clips you have so far. The trick is to find a clip with a smooth, solid-colored background. The clip you apply a chroma key effect to must reside in an overlay track.

1. Double-click the last clip in Overlay Track 1, Balloon-3, to bring up the Options panel. In the Preview panel, move the clip to the upper-left corner, but stay within the safe zone. It'll be better to view the clip on this part of the background.

2. In the Attribute panel, click Mask & Chroma Key. Check the Apply Overlay Options box. Make sure that Type > Chroma Key is selected.

3. VSX5 will automatically choose what it thinks the color is that you want to be transparent, and it will apply the chroma key effect immediately. To make sure it selects the correct color, click the eyedropper (next to the

Similarity color chip) and click on the sky in the overlay clip. Click the eyedropper tool again to turn it off. (You might see that too much of the background has become transparent. You'll fix this next.)

4. The best results will come from choosing a range of the eyedropper's selection. It's really selective on a per-image basis. To the right of the eyedropper, use the slider/input field to enter a value of around 30. You might need to use the eyedropper after this to click on the sky again. Once again, this is different for every clip and depends on where you click the eyedropper. Feel free to adjust the settings until you get the desired effect. The background will change in real time as you adjust the slider. See Figure 7.29 for the desired results.

5. Save your project.

Figure 7.29
Setting a chroma key transparency.

Tip

To get the best chroma key effects in a low budget situation, try hanging a solid color sheet as a backdrop, remembering that the color of anything in front of it cannot be the same color as the backdrop, or in that color's range setting. If that happens, parts of the foreground, including your subject, will also become transparent.

Applying a Mask Effect

A MASK EFFECT IS SIMILAR to a chroma key effect, but it's a predesignated transparency style instead, similar to a picture frame. Place the frame on an overlay track and only what's inside the frame (the white parts) will automatically show through. It's not unlike the Flash animation frame you applied earlier in this chapter. You can also create your own mask frames in applications like PaintShop Photo Pro or Photoshop. (See the "VideoStudio" section in Appendix B for a short video tutorial on creating a mask frame.)

To apply a mask effect to your video, follow these steps.

1. Double-click on Balloon-5 in the Timeline (Overlay Track 1).

2. In the Attribute panel, select Mask & Chroma Key. Check Apply Overlay Options. In the Type drop-down list, select Mask Frame (see Figure 7.30).

3. From the list that shows up, scroll to preview the many choices; then choose one you like. Select one to apply to the clip. See Figure 7.31. (Any attached border will be deleted.)

Figure 7.30
Selecting Mask Frame.

Tip

Clicking the plus sign (+) in the lower right lets you add a mask of your own. So, once you create one in PaintShop Photo Pro or Photoshop, this is how you would import it. The minus sign (−), or delete mask frame, is only available for ones you've imported, not any of the ones included in VSX5.

4. Skipping the clip that has the Chroma Key effect, apply mask frames to Balloon-4 and all three photos under that in Overlay Track 2.

...to view this

Choose this...

Figure 7.31
Select an option from the Mask Frame list.

5. Save your project. You'll be adding more to this project in future chapters. You should now have two saved files from this chapter: Chapter 7A and Chapter 7B.

6. Go to the Share tab, and choose Create Video File. Select WMV > WMV HD 720 30p. After it's finished rendering, open and play the file so you can see how the results of your hard work play at the proper speed and fluidity.

Exporting Selective Tracks

NOW IS A GREAT TIME to introduce a quick new feature in VSX5. You can now, very easily, designate which tracks will render out to a final movie. By clicking the small icons (the ones with the "eye") on the far left of the Timeline, between the padlocks and the tracks themselves, you can "hide" individual tracks from playback and/or rendering out. There might be several reasons you'll want to do this.

▶ Save out only one audio track, maybe just the music, by hiding the rest when sharing a sound file.

▶ Sometimes it's easier to disable a track than it is to mute a sound or temporarily cut video, graphics, or titles for testing purposes.

▶ Testing the effect of overlays by hiding a track of one of them and showing another one.

▶ Creating subtitle tracks of different languages, and then hiding all but one language for each project.

1. Move MotionD05.swf that's in overlay track 2 straight up and place it into overlay track 1. See Figure 7.32.

Figure 7.32
Move Flash Frame Upward.

2. Click the Disable overlay track (eye) button in overlay track #2. See Figure 7.33.

Figure 7.33
Disable Overlay track.

3. The results are shown in Figure 7.34. Export a movie as you did in step 6 of the previous section to see the difference, if you like.

4. Make all tracks visible again and save your project.

Figure 7.34
Overlay track disabled.

Quick Quiz

1. What's the easiest way to reuse attributes from one clip and apply them to another? (See "Copying Attributes.")

2. What's a great way to add motion to a still image? (See "Pan & Zoom Effects.")

3. Name the four types of decorations available in VSX5. (See "Adding Embellishments.")

4. What are the pitfalls to avoid when creating chroma key effects? (See "Applying a Chroma Key Effect.")

Chemistry Experiments with

Video Filters

THIS IS THE CHAPTER on video filters that are located in the Filter library, identified by FX in the Library Navigation panel, as opposed to the previous chapter on video effects.

Why did I name this chapter the way I did? Video filters, unlike video effects, can be layered and mixed together for different results that can be greater than the sum of the individual elements, akin to a chemistry experiment. Even the order in which they're layered will affect the final results.

Filters are effects you apply to clips to change their style or appearance. Filters can be creatively applied to enhance your clips or be used to correct flaws, such as making a clip look like a painting or improving its color balance. You can apply multiple filters to a clip. Rearranging the filter layers, or the order in which they're applied, will affect the final result. A filter on the top layer of the filters list will alter the clip differently than if it were on the bottom layer. (This has nothing to do with Timeline tracks behaving as layers.) You can also toggle applied filters on and off to preview their effect or combined effects. Only checked filters will be applied in the final rendering process, so you can experiment using all kinds of possibilities.

All the effects you'll work with in this chapter are in the Filter library. Because there are so many, I won't explain or cover them all, but you'll get to use some of the pretty cool ones, such as AutoSketch, Lensflare, Picture-In-Picture by NewBlue, Old Film, and some cool weather effects. Feel free to try the rest of them on your own. Luckily, the animated previews give you an excellent idea of what to expect from them, and applying and previewing them requires just a couple of steps.

Video filters are very easy to apply. All you do is drag the thumbnail choice from the Filter library and drop it directly onto any video or still clip in the Timeline. Double-click that clip to bring up the Options panel, and the filters you applied will be listed, rearrangeable, editable, and customizable.

Using Keyframes

I'VE TOUCHED ON THE IDEA of using keyframes a couple times already, but I'll cover it in more detail now because a better understanding of them becomes even more important in this chapter. A *keyframe* (also described previously as a *pin*), most commonly used by animators, is a particular frame on a Timeline that designates where an animation, or effect, will start or end, as well as how it might change attributes by then heading in another direction or setting. Keyframes can be any number of frames apart (such as 5, 10, 20, etc). There is always a keyframe at the beginning and at the end of an effect or any Timeline.

After keyframes are designated, an animation software application, or a special team of artists (in-betweeners or tweeners, for short), will then create the frames in between, so that the sequence will progress from one keyframe to the next while keeping the motion looking smooth and natural. This allows the head artists to concentrate on the key aspects and turning points of a story and pass on the minutia to someone else or, in VSX5's case, your computer.

In VSX5, you'll place keyframes wherever and whenever you want a filter to change direction. This directional change can be for any number of reasons, such as a change of direction, color, size, shape, or other factors that affect your video clip.

AutoSketch Filter

THE AUTOSKETCH FILTER was new to VideoStudio Pro X3 (version 13), and it is amazing! This filter, working with still images or videos, will animate a tracing of the image over time. Then it fills it in with color. The shorter the clip, the faster it draws. The longer you stretch the clip out, the slower it will trace. It's also customizable for color, shade, pen width, and accuracy.

1. Open project file Chapter 7B and resave it as **Chapter 8**. Make sure the Options panel is closed for now. This will allow you to view more of the Filter library content.

2. From the Chapter 7 custom library, add Balloon-7 again to the end of the video track. You'll now have two of them in a row. Deselect this new clip, so it's not highlighted.

3. Now you'll need to move some of the overlay clips so they don't get in the way of what you'll be doing next. Shift-select all six overlay clips under Balloon-2 and Balloon-7 (Balloon-5, -4, -3, overlays 1, 2, 3). Move them forward in time, down the Timeline, so that the beginning of Balloon-5 lines up with the start of the second Balloon-7 (see Figure 8.1).

4. Select the Filter library from the Library Navigation panel. Choose All from the gallery list (see Figure 8.2).

Move these tracks down the Timeline

Figure 8.1
Adjusting the Timeline.

Figure 8.2
Selecting the Filter library.

5. From the Filter library, drag and drop the AutoSketch filter (remember, they're in alphabetical order) onto the *first* Balloon-7 clip in the Timeline.

6. In the Preview panel, click Play to view the results. (Because you just edited a single clip with your filter, the clip should be selected by default.)

Although Balloon-7 is a video clip, the AutoSketch filter will use only the first frame of the clip as the basis for its tracing and treat the entire clip as a still image, based on that first frame. In other words, the video itself will not play, just a sketch of the video using only the first frame.

7. Go to the Attribute panel for Balloon-7 (double-click the Balloon-7 video clip). The AutoSketch filter you applied is in the list of applied filters on the left (see Figure 8.3). Click Customize Filter to be taken to the AutoSketch customization window.

Figure 8.3
Video filter list in the Attribute panel.

This window is similar to the one you used in the last chapter to edit the Pan & Zoom effect. The differences are the custom settings at the bottom left. But the viewing windows are the same (with the Original view on the left and the Preview window on the right) showing how your settings will be applied. The Preview panel should start out blank, because the filter hasn't begun sketching anything yet. Playback controls are under the Preview window, and keyframe controls are under the Original window.

8. You can test the different settings on the lower left, such as Accuracy, Width, and Darkness, but the one I find most useful and noticeable is the Color setting, which changes the tracing pen color.

Click on the black color chip, and the Corel Color Picker will open. In the top row, click the blue color chip, and then choose a light to medium shade of blue in the main panel. (See Figure 8.4.)

Figure 8.4
Choosing an AutoSketch color.

9. Click OK to close the Color Picker window. Click the Play button to preview the effect in the Preview panel. Click OK again and preview the clip in your Timeline. You can change the filter to use another color value if you like.

10. Save your project.

Tip

In the lower right of the Corel Color Picker, you'll see a Web Safe check box. This is the value given to Internet browser colors that were used back in the era of 256-color (8-bit) displays and are written in HTML code. When setting the background color of a web page (among other graphics), coders and web design software applications will use these values to set the colors.

Check the Web Safe box under the Hex value and watch the colors in the main panel change. Some of the color chips are replaced with ones that are web-browser compatible, or what's called *web safe colors*. There are 216 colors considered to be web safe. The rest (the difference between 256 & 216) were used for the computer's operating system.

Although most designers still use web-safe colors for items like backgrounds, text, and buttons, embedded photos and videos don't need to adhere to this palette. Therefore, you're welcome to ignore this feature.

In conclusion, Corel has a habit (neither good nor bad) of keeping old features just in case platform shoes make a comeback.

Lensflare Filter

LENSFLARE IS OFTENTIMES an unwanted characteristic of bright light reflected or scattered around inside your camera lens. Most commonly, this occurs when shooting into the sun—when the sun is in the frame or the lens is pointed in the direction of the sun. This artifact can be eliminated by using a lens hood, umbrella shade, or similar device.

Lensflare filters, on the other hand, are purposefully used to add sparkle to a photo or video clip. They can be used to add sparkle on a lake or add reflections from the sun, stars, street lamps, or Christmas lights.

To add sparkle to a video clip, follow these steps.

1. From the Filter gallery, drop the Lensflare filter onto the clip Balloon-2 (the pickup truck) in the Timeline's main Video track. (It might make it easier to find the filter if you first close the Options panel.)
2. Reopen the Options panel by double-clicking the clip in the Timeline. In the Attribute panel, open the Lensflare preset drop-down list (under the applied filter list), and double-click the first choice in the second row (as shown in Figure 8.5).
3. Click Customize Filter, which will open the Lensflare window. In the Original panel, with the playback head at the beginning of the Timeline, move the cross mark (currently in the upper-right corner) to right on top of the sun, inside the front windshield of the truck. The Preview panel on the right should update accordingly.

#1   #2

Figure 8.5
Preset choices for filters.

4. In the options area in the lower-left corner, choose 35mm Prime for Lens Type. Set Intensity at 50, Size at 50, and Extra Strength at 300. These are just artistic suggestions, so in the future you can choose your own. For now, though, use these settings.
5. Above and to the left of the Timeline, click the Reverse Keyframes icon (refer to Figure 8.6). This will reverse the entire sequence, make the sun appear dimmer at the end (instead of brighter), and set the filter at a speedier, exaggerated mode.
6. Click OK and preview this portion of your project, using the Clip play feature. Notice how the sun seems to set much more quickly than normal.
7. Save your project.

Click to reverse keyframes   Select this   Choose these settings   Move crosshair to here

Figure 8.6
Lensflare filter customization.

Picture-In-Picture Filter

YOU'VE ALREADY DONE Picture-In-Picture (PiP) effects by laying down clips in the overlay tracks. So why is this any different? Several filters from a third-party software developer, NewBlue, are now included in VSX5. One of them is an excellent PiP filter that adds almost infinitely adjustable 3D geometry, shadow, and reflection features. It takes the video overlay feature in VSX5 to a whole new level by expanding beyond just the overlay part.

These steps will show you how to apply and customize the NewBlue Picture-in-Picture filter.

1. First you will need to move a couple more clips to get them out of the way. In the Timeline, Shift-select overlays 1–3 in Overlay Track 2. Move them to Overlay Track 1 and center them under the first Balloon-7 clip in the main video track. Delete Balloon-5 in Overlay Track 1. Move Balloon-3 (currently at the end of Overlay Track 1) and center it under Balloon-2. Center Balloon-4 under the last Balloon-7 clip. Your Timeline should look like the one shown in Figure 8.7.

Figure 8.7
Timeline view after adjustments.

> Moving clips around a Timeline will not affect any filters or effects you've applied to them, except for how they might interact with clips in tracks below them.

2. In the Filter library drop-down list at the top of the Library window, select NewBlue Video Essentials II. The only choice is Picture-In-Picture. Drop this filter onto the last clip in Overlay Track 1 (Balloon-4).

3. In the Preview panel, make sure the desired clip is labeled Overlay Track 1. Right-click on the clip in the Preview panel and choose Fit to Screen (as shown in Figure 8.8). Fit to Screen will allow the effect to utilize all the screen space it needs (including reflections), even though, as you can see, the actual picture in the picture only needs a portion of the screen.

Figure 8.8
Picture-in-Picture clip placement.

4. In the Options > Attribute panel, click Customize Filter to launch the NewBlue Picture-In-Picture Edit window.

5. Did your eyes get huge? Yes, there are a lot of possible mind-boggling settings. But there are also a lot of presets to choose from to make it easy. Rewind the playback head to the beginning. In the bottom portion of the window, select the Gentle Reflection preset (see Figure 8.9).

Figure 8.9
NewBlue Picture-In-Picture window.

Just as in the VSX5-specific effects and filters customization windows, NewBlue filters also allow for animated adjustments using keyframe points where settings can change at any point in time (frame) for such items as direction, rotation, color, transparency, and the like.

6. This preset will automatically move the playback to the center of the clip (in the main Timeline, too) and add a keyframe.

7. In the NewBlue Picture-In-Picture preview window, select Play to preview. Watch both the Timeline and several of the small dials to the left change direction. Notice how these parameters change over time. At the keyframe in the middle of the Timeline, it will change again, but in the opposite direction. Click Play again to stop the playback.

A relatively new feature allows you to preview NewBlue filters in both the NewBlue customization window and the main screen's Preview panel at the same time.

8. Still in the NewBlue window, rewind the Timeline back to the beginning. Set the Rotate X field to −60.0. Try using the manual rotate dial. This is great when you want to preview possible choices. After trying that, type **−60** into the field directly under the dial, and press the Tab key. Set Rotate Y to 60.0. Click the Tab key to set. Preview it again.

9. Forward the Timeline to the very end and set the same fields to the same numbers from step 8. Rewind and preview the clip again. Notice how the values in this window interactively update. Also notice that because the settings are the same at the start and at the end, with a keyframe in the middle, the effect appears to loop and play without any abrupt changes, even when it restarts. Click OK to close the NewBlue customization window.

10. Preview this portion in the main Preview panel, and save your project.

Because of all that is going on, your project may not preview these combined effects very well, but when you save your video file at the end of this chapter, everything will come together and play very nicely.

Old Film Filter

I JUST WANT TO SLIP THIS SIMPLE one in because it's cool and used frequently in broadcast TV. Add a Pan & Zoom effect with this one, and you have another something from the History Channel. This filter adds items like different shades of sepia tones, film scratches, jittery affects, dust, and variations in lighting. As you'll see in this section, Old Film filters are great for making modern photos and videos look aged, giving them the appearance of days gone by, the times of black-and-white film, and even silent film.

These steps will show you how the Old Film filter can take a modern photo and easily age it by 100 years.

1. Since the image you're going to use has nothing to do with a balloon trip, save your current project and open a new project by selecting File > New Project.

2. In lieu of creating a library just for one image, import image #4 into the Chapter 7 library from the Photos > Landscapes folder. It's a photo of an old tractor sitting in a yard, currently in color.

3. Place the image into the Timeline and extend the duration to 15 seconds (see Figure 8.10).

4. From the Filter library, choose the Camera Lens gallery. Drop the Old Film filter onto the tractor (#4) clip.

5. In the Options > Attribute panel, from the drop-down preset list, double-click the second choice in the first row. Click Customize Filter.

Figure 8.10
Image for the Old Film filter.

6. With playback at the start, set the Scratch setting to 100%. Click the Go to next keyframe icon (see Figure 8.11). Since there are no keyframes anywhere in the middle, and as keyframes are automatically placed at the start and end points, clicking on this icon will take you to the very end of the Timeline. Set the Scratch setting to 100% again. This will maintain the same setting throughout the entire clip. Click OK to close the Old Film customization window.

Figure 8.11
Go to next keyframe icon.

7. Right-click on the clip in the Timeline and choose Auto Pan & Zoom so you can add an animated effect to the still image.

8. In the Options panel, go to the Photo tab. In the preset choices list under Pan & Zoom, double-click the last one in the second row, and then click Customize again.

9. In the Original window view, move both crosses *straight* down so they're both centered in the middle horizontal plane of the tractor, and keeping the line between the crosses as horizontal as possible. Use Figure 8.12 as a reference.

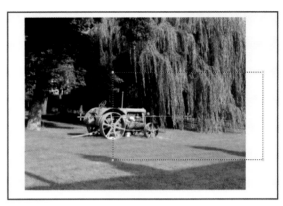

Figure 8.13
Pan & Zoom End view.

Figure 8.12
Pan & Zoom Start view.

10. Move to the end of the Timeline by clicking either the Go to Last Frame icon or Go to Next Keyframe icon. If you have trouble finding the right one, remember that pausing your cursor over an icon will display a tooltip that tells you what its function is. Center the tractor again as you did in step 9 (see Figure 8.13).

11. Preview your new settings by clicking the Play button in the Pan & Zoom window. Follow the crosshairs as they move across the Original panel to see exactly what's happening in the Preview panel. When you're satisfied with your settings, click OK to close the Pan & Zoom customization window.

> **CAUTION**
>
> When you have a clip (video or photo) selected that has a filter applied to it (and with the Options panel open), you will only see filters applied when the Attribute tab is selected. You will not see them in the Photo or Video tabs.
>
> Also, in the customization window, if you have multiple filters applied to a clip, you will only be able to see and edit the filter you're currently customizing.
>
> When you have Project selected in the Preview panel of the main window, all filters and effects will be visible.

12. In the main Preview window, rewind, select the preview choice, and play the clip. And, Bam, the History Channel!

13. Save the project, and name it **History Channel** if you like.

Applying Multiple Filters

VSX5 LETS YOU APPLY up to five filters to a single clip. VSX5 has some great weather effects, including clouds, lightning, wind, and rain that, when combined, can produce quite a storm. Let's see how much trouble you can get into trying some of these out. Your plan is to create a progressively worsening storm at the balloon festival. You might want to tie your balloon down...

1. Reopen your Chapter 8 project. Move Overlay clips 1, 2, and 3 straight down into Overlay track #2. Move Balloon-4 to the left and center it under the first Balloon-7 clip. (See Figure 8.14.) This will isolate the last Balloon-7 clip.

2. Open the Options panel for the second (last) Balloon-7 clip in the video track. In the Attribute panel, make sure that Replace Last Filter is *not* checked. Since you'll be combining and creating a video chemistry experiment using and mixing multiple filters, you don't want each new one you're adding to delete the previous one.

3. Open the FX > Darkroom gallery. Drop Brightness & Contrast onto the Balloon-7 clip. Go to the Special gallery. In the following order, drop the filters Cloud, Lightning, Rain, and then Wind onto the clip.

Figure 8.14
Isolating the 2nd Balloon-7 clip.

4. In the Options > Attribute panel, click the "eye" icons next to all the filters except for Brightness & Contrast to hide them temporarily (see Figure 8.15). If you see the "eye" next to the filter name, the filter is activated. Click the eye to turn filters off. It's a toggle switch. Click it again to turn them back on.

Figure 8.15
Turning off selected filters.

5. Click to highlight the Brightness & Contrast filter in the list and select Customize Filter. At the first keyframe, set the Brightness to 0 (0 is in the middle of the Brightness slider). At the end, set Brightness all the way to the left (−100). Preview the clip in this Preview window. It may seem too dark at the end, but we're going for the dark and stormy look, and the other filters will help reverse that somewhat. Click OK.

6. By toggling the eye icons again in the filter list, hide the Brightness & Contrast filter and show just the Cloud filter. From the Cloud presets drop-down list, double-click the first one in the last row and preview it.

7. Hide the Cloud filter and show the Lightning filter. In the presets list, choose the second one in the first row. Preview this one.

8. Hide the Lightning filter and show the Rain filter. Choose the last preset in the second row. Go to Customize Filter.

    Click the Advanced tab in the lower left. At the first keyframe, set Wind Direction to 100 (the rain will be heading into a direction of 100 degrees, or about 7 o'clock). Set Speed to 50.

    Go to the last frame and set Wind Direction to 180 and Speed to 100. This will give the impression of a harder driving, horizontal rain.

    While you're still at the last frame, return to the Basic tab. Move the Density slider to around 6000. Preview to see how the wind direction and density of the rain changes gradually over time. With the new rendering power of VSX5, the rain effect should play close to real time, even in preview mode. Click OK.

9. Hide Rain and show Wind. Choose the first preset in the second row.

10. Turn on all the filters by turning on all the "eye" toggle icons.

11. Preview Clip (not Project) in the Timeline. Notice that the effect of the Brightness & Contrast filter is not as evident, because it doesn't get very dark at the end like you had set it originally. This is because all the other filters are playing on top of it, layer-wise.

    Select the Brightness & Contrast filter in the filter list. Click the down arrow on the right side of the list until the Brightness & Contrast filter is all the way at the bottom of the list. Preview the clip again.

12. Preview it again in full screen view, click the Enlarge icon (see Figure 8.16). Looks to me like this balloon festival needs to be cancelled! Select the Enlarge icon again in the larger window (or press the Esc key on the keyboard) to return to the regular sized view.

Figure 8.16
Click Enlarge to preview at full screen.

Before you output this project, let's add a sound-track.

1. Rewind your project back to the start, and then click the Auto Music icon in the Timeline's toolbar. Choose the following: Scope > Owned Titles, Filter > Album, Subfilter > Core Foundations, Music > Clear Vision, and Variation > Rain.

2. Check the Auto Trim box, and then click the Add to Timeline icon.

3. Preview your project from the beginning. It might very well play jerky with everything going on. Playing it twice in a row oftentimes helps. Save your Balloon project.

4. Output your movie. Choose Create Video File and select WMV > WMV HD 720 30p. Preview it to see all your applied filters and effects occur in real time. You've done well!

With over 65 video filters in VSX5 to choose from and the presets and customization abilities that come with them, the resulting choices are practically endless. Although I couldn't cover all of them, you did learn how to choose them, order them, use easy presets, and edit specific parameters using keyframes, an important tool in any video editing application containing animation capabilities.

Feel free to read through this chapter again and use your own clips to experiment with any of the other filters available. Remember, you'll never destroy any of your original content. Have fun!

Quick Quiz

1. What are keyframes used for? (See "Using Keyframes.")

2. What do you do if you want to reverse the playback of a video filter? (See "Using Keyframes.")

3. What are some of the advantages of using the NewBlue video filters in VSX5? (See "Picture-In-Picture Filter.")

4. How many filters can you apply to a single video clip? (See "Applying Multiple Filters.")

5. When you're applying multiple video filters, what's the easiest way to test one out without involving any of the others? (See "Applying Multiple Filters.")

Making Statements

with Titles

I TOUCHED ON TEXT-BASED TITLES earlier in the book, but it needs to be reinforced here in the chapter that covers the topic. Titles, when using the term in video editing, can mean one of two things, and as a result, can be confusing. You will become familiar with both meanings and will know which one is being referred to in each instance (or at least in this book).

Text titles can be used interchangeably with movie titles. A movie title is a separate, single movie. For example, Netflix may advertise that it has over 10,000 titles. Of course, it is referring to the movies themselves, not text titles. You can import and combine several movie titles (or captured clips) into VideoStudio, but the output will still be another title. Yikes!

Text titles (within a movie) are text features usually applied in separate tracks (layers) in the Timeline. These can be a simple stationary phrase such as a title, a subtitle, or a moving phrase, such as a rolling title (e.g., credits). To relieve any confusion regarding the meaning of titles, any titles I discuss will be referring to text titles only. Movie titles, in this book, have been and will be referred to as videos, movies, and so on.

A couple versions before VSX5, text could only be placed into one of two title-specific tracks. These title tracks were always on the top layers of any movie—on top of any other video or graphic elements on the Timeline. You could have one title on top of, or pass over, another one, but this type of interaction could not occur with any other visual. New since VSX4, text can now be placed in any track but audio, including overlay tracks, and thus interact with any other visible element in your movie. Now you can have text pass behind a photo or video overlay, too!

In this chapter, you'll learn to create titles from scratch as well as use titles from the included samples. Then you'll edit both by adding and customizing title effects and filters. You'll learn the huge difference between the single and multiple titles options, as well as learn what's possible now that you can use titles intertwined in video and overlay tracks. I've even included a secret trick on how to create the famous *Star Wars* scrolling, vanishing title. Lastly, you'll learn how to create subtitles and discover what they can be used for.

Ready? Let's make some statements.

Title Rules

THERE ARE SEVERAL THINGS you'll need to know about placing titles in VSX5. These rules actually apply to all video editing, even in TV production. These rules involve where you place your titles on the screen and how they're formatted. This section explains these considerations.

Title Safe Area

There is a safe zone for graphics and action. When you double-click any item in an overlay track, you've noticed that the Preview panel displays a white border just inside the edges. This zone borders the inner 90% of the window, which excludes 5% on any one side. That's your action, graphics, and text safe zone. True, anything placed in the background video track will automatically extend beyond this zone to the edges, but important graphics and action should remain inside the zone whenever possible.

Font Considerations

Fonts are also an important item to consider when incorporating titles. The following information might make your eyes roll into the back of your head, but there are two ways TV signals are displayed: interlaced and progressive. You might be familiar with TVs that are available in 720p, 720i, 1080i, so on? The "i" stands for interlaced, and the "p" stands for progressive.

Interlaced monitors display only alternate horizontal fields at a time: odd then even, then odd, and so forth. They do it so fast, though, you can't see the difference unless objects are moving very fast or thin lines appear. When that happens, you might see a flicker effect.

The Hertz rate (Hz) determines how often these fields are refreshed per second (the higher the rate, the better). This is why when you pause some TVs or take a photo of a TV screen, you see unmatched horizontal lines. When you shoot a video of a TV screen, you see flickering horizontal lines. These lines often slide up or down the screen. This happens when the capture rate of the video is different from the field refresh rate of the TV. The rates are out of sync.

A progressive display, in contrast, receives both fields all at once. If you pause, capture, or photograph a progressive field display, the image will show both fields at once and produce a complete, seamless image. You can probably guess why a progressive signal is more desirable than an interlaced one and why products using it are more expensive. Why do I bother to mention this? Since most displays still use the interlaced choice, the type of fonts you use will become an important consideration.

VSX5 allows you to use any fonts that are on your system. Because of the interlaced field issue, you want to avoid fonts that have any thin (especially 1-pixel) horizontal lines. If you use these types of thin, wispy fonts, your title will flicker when displayed on an interlaced screen because one field will display it, but the next one will not. Next time you watch TV, especially commercials, closely watch for thinner fonts, as they may flicker ever so slightly. Once you see this effect for the first time, my guess is you'll be looking for it all the time.

You don't have to worry about this issue when your project will be displayed on a progressive field TV screen or your computer. All modern computer displays are of the "p" variety and are referred to as *progressive scan displays*. These include LCD/Plasma/LED TVs, and more.

Creating a Single Title

I N THE TRACK MANAGER, you have two title tracks available to you. With VSX5, you can also use titles in any of the overlay tracks. As with other media elements, such as videos, graphics, and audio, you can choose from either the samples that came included with VSX5 (or that you downloaded through the Corel Guide), or create your own. Let's start by learning how to create your own from scratch.

1. Launch VSX5 and open your Chapter 8 project. Save it as **Chapter 9**.

2. Open the Track Manager, and select 2 from the title tracks list. Click OK.

3. Make sure all your tracks are locked down for Ripple Editing. They should still be locked from the last time you worked on this project. If not, refer to Figures 9.1 and 9.2 as a review.

Click here...   to enable these...

Figure 9.1
Enable Ripple Editing.

Click here...   Select this...

Figure 9.2
Enable Ripple Editing on all tracks.

4. Go to the Graphic library > Color gallery and add a black color chip to the beginning of the main video track. All other clips should move forward accordingly. If they don't, revisit step 3. The chip will default to a duration of 3 seconds, which is fine.

5. Zoom into your Timeline to see the color chip sufficiently (see Figure 9.3). Make sure the Timeline's playback is at the very start.

Figure 9.3
Prepping to add a title.

6. Click the Title library icon to display all the built-in, preanimated, and customizable text title choices (see Figure 9.4).

Figure 9.4
Accessing the Title
Text feature.

7. Where it says "Double-click here to add a title," double-click where you would like to start entering your text—in this case, just above the "c" in "Double-click." As a result, the text insertion point will show up onscreen, and the Text Options panel will pop up with the Edit panel at the forefront.

   Most of the options are pretty self-explanatory with familiar text formatting tools, such as font, color, justification (left, center, right), spacing, rotation, and effects like borders, shadows, and transparency. You'll notice radio buttons for Single Title and Multiple Titles, with Multiple Titles selected by default. Select the *Single* Title radio button for now. Set your text insertion point again by double-clicking in the Preview window where you want to start typing your title.

8. Pressing Enter after each word, type **Our Summer Balloon Trip,** so you have four lines of text all in one text container. Click and drag your cursor back over the text to highlight it. This will allow you to set the formatting using the tools in the Options > Edit panel.

9. Using the T drop-down list (which shows all available fonts), choose a font that has at least a medium thickness. Fortunately, the list also displays examples of what the font looks like (see Figure 9.5). I chose an Impact font. If you don't have this one, I suggest Arial Black or something similar. Select the Align Center option above the T font list. Your title will center itself relative to the entire window.

10. Select a light blue or light green font color by clicking the small white color chip under the T font list. Next, choose a font size of 36 and set the line spacing to 100.

Figure 9.5
Choosing a font for your title.

11. Click outside the text once; then click and drag to select just the words Summer and Balloon and make them a darker green. This shows that you can format individual words (individual letters, too!) in a single text block. Your text might look something like what's shown in Figure 9.6. If it doesn't, it's okay; you may have chosen a different font. Adjust the formatting options until your title looks similar.

12. Use your mouse and alignment options in the Edit tab to position the text similar to Figure 9.6. You want a space at the bottom of the current text to add another single line of text in the next section.

Figure 9.6
Example of a single title.

Creating Multiple Titles

USING THE SINGLE TITLE option means you can have only one text box at any point in time in the same title track. You can have multiple titles in a single track, but only if they don't overlap. Adding the extra title track (for a total of two) meant you could overlap only two titles at most. In past versions of VideoStudio, one quirky feature that helped folks get around the two-title (and thus only two over-lapping titles) track limitation was that you could have multiple titles within a single title clip. But now in VSX5, there are two ways to have multiple titles that go beyond the two-title track limitation. One way is to use the new feature of inserting titles in the video track and overlay tracks. The other is the older way, which is still available, using the Multiple Titles feature. I'll show you how the latter feature works.

This section will teach you how to add titles in a way that's similar to adding single titles, but then also adding multiple ones, using the same time frame (the same clip) and in the same track. Let's continue the steps from the last section.

1. Click outside the current text to deselect the text block. Oh wait, you can't. It remains active with the insertion point still blinking where you left it. Click Project instead of Clip. This will deselect the active text block in the Preview panel and place the text clip in the Timeline the same default length as the color chip. Title blocks also default to three seconds in length.

2. Double-click the text clip in the Timeline. Try to reposition the text block in the Preview panel. Hmmm, you can't do that either. All it does is reselect the text for editing. Click Project again. (I really am about to make a point here!)

3. Rewind your project to the beginning. With the Title library selected, you'll see the familiar "Double-click here to add a title" instructions. You can create another title, but it will only go into the second title track (don't do this).

   What you've encountered are the limita-tions of the Single Title option.

4. In the Timeline, double-click on the title you created. In the Options panel, click the Multiple Titles radio button. Click Yes to the alert box. The previous title you made is now surrounded by a smaller border, indicating it's no longer taking up the entire screen and there is now room for additional titles. See Figure 9.7.

Figure 9.7
Setting up the Multiple Titles option.

5. In the Preview panel and with the playback at the start, double-click to place another insertion point directly under the other text (but above the safe zone border) and type **Vancouver, Canada**. Using the same tools as you did for the previous text, format the new line to something different, but keeping it something that fits size-wise and is aesthetically pleasing.

Tip

If you select a text block once in the Preview window, formatting will change the entire text string. If you double-click a title, formatting will only affect text you have first drag-selected.

6. Deselect the text, reselect it, and position it under the other text (click titles once to select and move, twice to edit the text itself). Even though you still have Align Center selected, the new text only aligned itself relative to the new text box, not the entire Preview window. After placing it, use the Alignment box choices in the Edit tab to precisely center it near the bottom. Another characteristic of multiple titles is that each is its own customizable text block, independent of any others and of the Preview window.

So, just when you might think that having only two title tracks is a limitation, you find out that you can actually have as many titles as you want in a single title track. The Timeline will even reflect the two titles you have. It should say, "Our Summer Balloon Trip | Vancouver, Canada". I recommend just keeping multiple titles selected all the time, as I can't think of any instance where you'll need the limitations of the single title setting.

Tip

Although it seems that you can create as many titles as you'll need using just one title track, you will want to take advantage of the two available tracks when you want to have them occur at two different time frames but still overlap. For example, you might want one title to display from 0 sec to 5 sec and another one from 3 sec to 8 sec. You'll need to use two tracks for that. The multiple title feature will not allow you to have titles with differing start and end times in the same clip.

Customizing Your Own Titles

A S YOU CAN SEE FROM the previous section, using the Multiple Titles option is the way to go. You don't even have to take advantage of it each time, but keeping it selected will ensure that it's readily available. Let's continue taking advantage of the Multiple Titles feature. This section will show you how to add some cool text formatting and maybe even a little animation.

1. Click once to select the top Our Summer Balloon Trip text group. In the Alignment area of the Edit tab, click the up arrow in the top row. This will place the top line of the text at the top center of the title safe area.

2. Click the Border/Shadow/Transparency icon (see Figure 9.8). Click the Shadow tab. Select the Drop Shadow option (second "A" from the left). Adjust X & Y to 7.0. Click the color chip and set the shadow color to white. It will appear gray, since its transparency is mixing with the black background. Keep all other settings the same. Click OK.

3. Go to the Options > Attribute panel. The Animation radio button should already be selected. Check Apply to activate it. A whole slew of animation choices will appear.

4. In the adjacent drop-down list, choose Pop-Up. In the preset list, choose the first option in the last row. (See Figure 9.9.) Preview your clip. When finished, double-click on the clip in the title track again.

Figure 9.9
Animation settings.

5. Next to the preset drop-down list, click the Customize Animation Attributes icon (the one showing a double-T). In the Unit list, choose Character. Leave Pause at No Pause. Under Direction, choose the down arrow (at the top). Click OK. This will designate the title's animation on entry and will only apply to the "Our Summer Balloon Trip" portion of the title.

Figure 9.8
Advanced title formatting.

6. Add the same animation preset to the Vancouver text by first selecting the text once and checking Apply in the Attribute tab. Choose the Pop-Up option and the first choice in the last row in the preset list again. In Customize Animation Attributes, choose the up arrow (at the bottom).

7. Preview your text block. Notice that, because these two text blocks are in the same clip in the Timeline and utilizing the Multiple Titles feature, they both behave differently but also complete their animations at the same time. Save your project.

Tip

You can use grid lines to help you position and line up text. Near the bottom of the Edit tab, check the Show Grid Lines box. The small icon to the right of the check box will open an options window where you can set choices, such as grid size (spacing), grid type (solid, dash, dots, and so on), grid line color, and whether or not you want your items to snap to the grid lines for increased precision.

This grid feature is also available for any objects placed in an overlay track, except that the grid is accessed via the Alignment icon in the Attribute tab of the Options panel.

Adding Title Effects

ALTHOUGH YOU CAN APPLY any video filter to a title, VSX5 has special effects just for titles. A cool feature of this is that you can apply an effect or filter along with the animation, so you can really go wild. But although you can apply separate formatting and animations to each title in the same multiple titles track, you cannot do so with a filter/effect. A title effect, just like a video filter, is applied by dropping it on the clip in the Timeline, so it affects everything in that clip, including the multiple titles that might be in there. Let's see what happens when you apply filters to titles.

1. In the Timeline, select Balloon-2 (the pickup truck—you might want to zoom out a bit). Go to the Title library, but do not choose one of the samples. You'll create a title from scratch instead.

2. Making sure the clip playback is at the beginning, create a title near the bottom of the Preview panel that says, "We're Finally Here!" Click outside the text box to deselect it. This will still keep it highlighted for positioning and formatting. Formatting and animation will default to your last settings.

Feel free to format the title as you like. I used the same font and color as the first word in the first text block at the project's start. Increase the font size to about 45 (size results will depend on your font) so it fits across the page. If your text extends too far, lower the font size a bit until it fits. Set alignment to the bottom center.

3. In the Attribute panel, click the Filter radio button. Title effects will now appear in the Filter library. Drop the Oil Paint filter onto the "We're Finally Here!" text in the Timeline. Make sure Replace Last Filter is not checked. Do the same thing with the Zoom Motion filter.

I realize that there may be confusion with regard to filters vs. effects. Selecting the Filter radio button in the Attribute tab to activate the Title Effects gallery of the Filter library can sound counterintuitive. Just understand that the terms *effects* and *filters* in many cases can be used interchangeably. What I've attempted to do is call the icons and libraries as they are titled in the VSX5 software.

5. In the Timeline, stretch the duration to match the length of Balloon-2. Your Preview panel should look similar to the one shown in Figure 9.10 at the end of the clip. Save your project.

Tip

If you use a color from the Corel Color Picker (accessed from the color chip icon in the Options panel) and then can't find it when you want to use it again, note either the R-G-B or the H-S-B values in the Corel Color picker window from the previous choice. You can then use these values to create the identical color by adding those values into the same Color Picker.

4. In the Attribute panel, move Zoom Motion to the top of the list. Preview your project in this portion. Because of the complexity you've added, it may preview slowly. You can just move the playback head manually to see how it looks at various points. It will, of course, play fine in your exported movie.

Figure 9.10
Applied title effects.

Using Sample Titles

AS WITH MANY FEATURES in VSX5, there is an alternative for those of you who lack either the time or the creative ability to make titles from scratch. The Title library has about 35 premade titles, all with stylized formatting and built-in animations that can still be customized to your liking. Perhaps the formatting isn't so tough to set yourself, but the animations can be. With the next steps I'll show you the benefits of using the title samples that came with, and that you downloaded to, VSX5.

1. Make sure Ripple Editing is still enabled and that all tracks are locked. Add a black color chip in the background video track between Balloon-2 and Balloon-7. Extend its duration to 6 seconds.

2. Drop a Crossfade transition at the start and end of the chip clip (yeah, that made me snicker, too). Under the Balloon-2 clip in the background video track, adjust Balloon-3 so that it starts at the same time as Balloon-2.

3. Go to the Title library and select the Lorem Ipsum title. Oh wait, they *all* say Lorem Ipsum. Okay, use what might/should be the 23rd title in the library, the one with the 60s look of colored text on a blue oval. Add it to the Timeline right after the title you just made. See Figure 9.11.

Figure 9.11
Applied sample title.

4. Extend its duration to 4 seconds to match the end of the color chip.

5. This sample is also a multiple title, meaning you can format different portions of it separately. Select the word "Lorem Ipsum" in the Preview panel. Change it to "And Away. . ."

and change "dolor sit amet" to "We Go!" Preview the project in this area. Although you can change the formatting and animation style, leave them all untouched here. No sense in messing with perfection.

Using Titles in Overlay Tracks

A S MENTIONED PREVIOUSLY, a newer feature is that you can now place titles in any track but audio tracks. This gives you the ability to extend beyond the previous limitation of only having two title tracks (even though the Multiple Tracks option helped). This includes the background video track, overlay tracks, and of course, the title tracks themselves. The following steps will show you how to work with titles in other tracks.

1. First of all, you need to adjust the position of some Timeline clips again to make room for the next title addition. In the Timeline, move the overlay clips 1–3 from Overlay Track 2 straight down to Overlay Track 3. Move Balloon-4 from Overlay Track 1 straight down to Overlay Track 2.

2. Move the playback head to the start of the first Balloon-7 clip (select the clip in the Timeline and click the Home button in the Preview panel). Select the Title library. Drag

the very first choice from the gallery and add it to Overlay Track 1 so that its start aligns with the start of the first Balloon-7. Place the title at the start of the transition before the Balloon-7 clip, not the clip itself.

3. Go to the Options > Attribute tab and uncheck Apply so there are no animations applied to this clip.

4. Replace the placeholder text with **Family**. Select the text for formatting. In the Edit tab, to the right of the font selection drop-down list and just above the Alignment area, is the Select a Title Style Preset drop-down list. Click it and choose the first option in the fifth row (see Figure 9.12). This will set the font, color, and border for this title. These presets only add text formatting styles, not animation styles, such as you might obtain from the Samples library.

Figure 9.12
Applying a preset title style.

5. Notice that the text block in the Preview panel has resize handles. Instead of guessing and reguessing a font size, click and drag one of the *yellow* corner handles so that it's about half the size of the preview screen (see Figure 9.13). Position the text in the center of the window by clicking the center alignment choice in the Edit panel.

6. Extend the title's length to match the length of the first Balloon-7.

7. First preview the title clip, and then preview the project for the section you just created. Save your project.

Figure 9.13
Current title view.

Creating a *Star Wars*–Type Title

NEW TO VERSION X3 of VideoStudio was a rolling credit type style. It does not have a *Star Wars* animated text style, though, where the text appears to fade into a vanishing point at the top. I know we *all* want that feature! There is currently no way to edit the rolling credit field or any other text gallery object to do this, but there is a way around it.

For additional effects, upgrade to the VSX5 Ultimate version to get an elaborate set of video and text effects that include similar *Star Wars*–like effects.

In this section, I'll show you how to create a movie that can then be created, reimported, and then tweaked to make a *Star Wars*–type rolling credit.

1. Create a new project.

2. Open the Title library. Drag the sample that resembles a rolling credit (shown in Figure 9.14) to the start of your project. (It's the one called Lorem ipsum. No wait, it's the one that shows multiple lines of text moving vertically from below the bottom of the screen to past the top of the screen.)

   Because of the new feature in VSX5 of adding titles to almost any track, you can drop the title right into the background video track. Do that. Because your Timeline is empty, this clip will, by default, go to the beginning of the background video track.

   Because of the effect it contains, this clip extends longer than the default 3 seconds. Extend it to 20 seconds long instead.

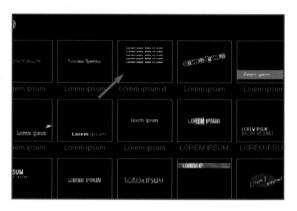

Figure 9.14
Rolling credit selection.

3. Double-click the clip in the Timeline to select the title in the Preview panel. Change the font to Arial Black and the font size to 26. Double-click it in the Preview panel to edit the text. Click and drag-select all the text (or use Ctrl+A to select all) so that what you type next will replace it.

   Type in something to the following effect. You may have to click outside the text box and move it up occasionally to continue adding additional text. Just make sure that afterward the text box is centered onscreen. The rolling effect will take care of the rest.

   Your most dramatic effect will result from text that reaches all the way across the screen, so use long names! Press the Enter key to add more lines. Here is an example:

The End

A (your name) Limited Production

Producer
(your name)

Director
Supercalifragilisticexpialidocious

Assistant Director
Whatshisface's Assistant

Starring
The Force
The Rebel Alliance
A small cast of real actors
A large cast of fake actors
and a
Bunch of other People

(Add more if you like…)

4. Choose the Align Center text choice at the top of the Edit tab and any of the three align center choices from the Alignment box in the Options panel (Align top center, Align center, Align bottom center), and then preview the clip. Cool, huh? But you're not done yet. It scrolls, but it doesn't *Star Wars* scroll. Go to the Share tab and choose Create Video File. Select WMV > WMV HD 720p. Name it **StarWarsText** and save it in your lesson plans folder.

5. Save your project as **Scrolling_Title**. Reopen your Chapter 9 project.

6. Add a black chip to the end of the main video track. Extend it to a length of 20 seconds.

7. As a result of sharing your video, your StarWarsText movie will be saved in your video library. Drag it to the first overlay track under the color chip. Adjust either clip so the lengths match up.

8. Select the Star Wars clip in the Timeline so that it highlights in the Preview panel. You will now adjust the top-left and top-right green skew handles inward to narrow them at the top. Your cursor will again be a single arrow instead of a double arrow. If you click and move the wrong one, click the undo arrow in the Timeline toolbar.

Pull each green skew handle at the top corners (only!) horizontally about 2/3 of the way toward the center yellow resize handle. Your screen should look similar to what's shown in Figure 9.15.

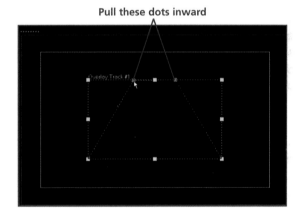

Figure 9.15
Skewing the text window.

9. Right-click inside the clip in the Preview panel and choose Fit to Screen. This will make sure the scrolling text fills the screen for maximum effect.

10. Rewind and preview this portion of your project. Pretty cool, huh?

11. Save your project.

You might be wondering why the background color chip was necessary and why you couldn't just put the Star Wars file into the background video track. The reason is because you can't reshape/resize anything in the Video layer. By default, anything in the background video track must fill the entire screen. Adding the color chip was the perfect fix for this situation.

Creating and Using Subtitles

YOU PROBABLY ALREADY know what subtitles are. They were first used in silent films before the time of talkies. They're used today in foreign language films so that the viewer can understand what's going on in a film where the language is, well... foreign. Subtitles are also used to describe other sounds that indicate action, such as clapping, crowd cheering, thunder, or in old Batman programs, Bam, Pow, Zowee (am I showing my age?). These are not to be confused with dubbed movies where the audio is someone speaking in a language you understand while the onscreen lips move to another language. (Think old Godzilla movies...)

Subtitles are akin to captions on photographs and can be used for captions on video, too. When using image editing software to add captions to photos, you just have to type in the caption. The software will then automatically place the captions in the identical location and use the same format for each of the images. Most don't give you a choice of text formatting options. Subtitles in VSX5 are handled the same way, except that you're using text on video clips and you *can* customize the formatting. Type in what you want to say and VSX5 will place the subtitle in the same screen location in each scene. This location is usually centered on the lower one-third of the screen. (The *lower third* is actually a TV production term for a graphic placed in the lower area of the screen, though it's not necessarily the entire lower third as the name suggests.)

The subtitling feature in VSX5 still requires you to create the titles with the desired duration and timeline locations. You then select the titles and save them as a special subtitle file. When reimporting them, VSX5 will use the timecode settings it saved with the subtitle file to place the titles in the same time locations where they were previously laid. In this case, though, they'll all be placed in the same positions onscreen and you can then set text formatting when you import them.

This feature works best with longer movies, where the process and time required for batch formatting and precise placement outweighs doing it manually. There are also specific applications for working with subtitles, including Subtitle Workshop by URUWorks that supports the VideoStudio subtitle format (VSF).

Since the lesson videos have little or no dialogue, the subtitles you'll create will actually be more like captions, or descriptive phrases, but this is still easier than manually placing text in the same spot each time.

First, though, you'll need to do some Media library housekeeping.

1. Open a new project.

2. Open the Media Library Navigation. Right-click on the Chapter 4 folder and select Rename. Change its name to **Washington DC**. Change the name of the Chapter 7 library to **Balloon Trip**.

3. Notice that in the Balloon Trip library, there are three video clips that would be better organized if they were in the Washington DC library, namely the videos Jewels1–Jewels3. Shift-select all three of them (or use Ctrl-select, if they're not sequentially located); then drag and drop them directly into the Washington DC library (see Figure 9.16).

#1 Open this **#3** Move clips here **#2** Select these

Figure 9.16
Moving library items.

Moving items among different libraries will not break links to them in your movies. This only occurs if you moved the locations of the original files on your PC. Library items, if you remember, are just links to the originals. When you move them to a different library, the links are updated.

The rest of this section will cover setting up a subtitle file for export, and then reimporting and applying it to the Washington DC video clips.

1. Go to the Washington DC library and import Washington D.C. videos Jewels#4–6. Rearrange all the Jewels clips so they're in order.

2. Place the Jewel clips (1–6) into the empty Timeline in order. Save this project as **MySubtitles**.

3. The next several instructions will ask you to place titles at distinct locations for precise amounts of time. You will not be using any of the title samples but will create them from scratch instead. As you did in the previous chapter, to add each text clip, select the Title library icon in the Library panel to initiate the text tools, and then double-click in the Preview panel where you want to insert the text. You can place your text in the lower-left corner, but it really doesn't matter where you put it. The subtitle format will place it correctly in the end. Select the Title library. Double-click in the lower portion of the Preview window.

4. In the Options panel > Edit tab, set the font to something common, like Arial. Set the font color to something that will contrast well in any scene, such as black or white, and then choose a small font size, like 12. Set the text justification to Align Left, the line spacing to the smallest setting of 60, and keep the rotation at 0.

5. Go to the Attribute tab. Make sure that Apply is *not* checked under the Animation radio button. Text filters are not carried over from previous text entries, so that setting is irrelevant.

6. Make sure your project is at the start and type your first text: **A French Queen's Diamond Earrings** (see Figure 9.17). Click in the Timeline to set the title and view it more easily.

   In the Timeline, stretch it to the right until it "snaps" to the end of the Jewels1 clip at 0:00:06:22. Preview the clip to see that all effects are turned off.

Don't worry about keeping the title within the title safe zone. Importing the subtitle file will place it correctly afterward.

Figure 9.17
First subtitle entry.

7. Type in your next subtitle entry: **Crown and Necklace Gifts from Napoleon**. Start: 0:00:11:00. Duration: 0:00:25:00. Use the Preview panel to set the start point (see Figure 9.18).

Figure 9.18
Clip start time.

Tip

One method to set start and duration values is by manually moving the Timeline clip. Grab the center of the clip (not the end) in the Timeline. As you move it, the timecode number you'll see is the time-code where it will start. To adjust the duration, click and drag the end of the clip. The timecode that appears will then be the duration (see Figure 9.19).

Figure 9.19
Clip duration.

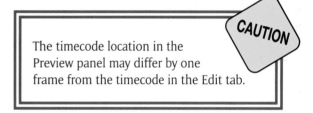

The timecode location in the Preview panel may differ by one frame from the timecode in the Edit tab.

8. Type in your next text: **37.8 Carat Chalk Emerald**. Start: 00:42:16. Duration: 00:11:00.

9. Type in your next text: **Diamonds are a Girl's Best Friend!** Start: 01:07:00. Duration: 00:11:24.

10. Type in your next text: **Mackey Emerald and Diamond Necklace**. Start: 01:32:00. Duration: 00:18:27 (the end of the Jewel5 clip).

11. Preview the project to check for errors.

12. Fit the project to the Timeline. In the Edit panel, click Save Subtitle File. Name it **Jewels_subtitles**. Choose English from the language drop-down list (though you can choose a different language to translate to *if* you have that language's font on your system). Since you only have one title track, you need not touch the Export: from the track number option at the bottom of the Save As dialog box. Save it to your lessons folder. Click Save.

There are two benefits to formatting subtitle text before you actually import it. First, it will apply the same formatting to all the text clips in the file so you won't have to do it manually one by one, after they're placed in the Timeline. Second, you can change the formatting to better reflect the background you may be using it for.

If you also have title track #2 displayed in the Timeline *and* you have a title in it, then the Save As dialog box will give you the choice of selecting which track to save (#1 or #2), but it will only save one of those tracks each time.

14. Preview the results. Notice the consistency of the formatting and onscreen placement. (See Figure 9.20.)

13. Delete all the titles in the Timeline. Rewind your project to the start. This will make room to import and place the new subtitles file. In the Edit panel, click Open Subtitle File. Locate the file you just saved. Before you click Open, you'll see that you have several formatting options right there that can then be applied to all the text blocks at once.

Change the font if you like, but realize you don't have the luxury of seeing an example of it before you do so. If you have Futura, change it to that. Change the font size to 18 and line leading to 100. Keep the font color white, and add a black glow shadow. Set Import: To Title Track Number 1 in the list at the very bottom. Click Open. Click OK to the alert box.

37.8 Carat Chalk Emerald

Figure 9.20
Finished subtitle.

CAUTION

Although you can import a subtitle file into any VideoStudio project, initial placement will be determined by the project you created it from, as it records the previous timecode placements. You can still reposition any of the titles in the timeline afterward, though.

15. If necessary, open the Title library again. Close the Options panel. Drag the very first subtitle into the Title library and drop it. By doing so, you now have a library item that is preformatted for future subtitles. You could have also added it to a custom library.

Drag this new Title library item back to the Timeline and drop it at the end of the last subtitle. Extend it to the end of your project. Notice that it's conveniently placed in the same location and is formatted the same as all the other subtitles. Change the text to say **Ka-Ching!** You may have to adjust the horizontal positioning of the text block.

Subtitles and video captions, as you've now seen, can be a chore to create. Although there are tools out there that specifically work on this feature, VSX5 has the basic tools to do it as well. With a little planning and practice, this tool can be very useful in giving your videos a more consistent, professional look. Not bad for a software application that costs less than $100!

Quick Quiz

1. What factors should you consider in creating titles? (See "Font Considerations.")

2. How many titles can you have at the same time in a single text track? (See "Creating Multiple Titles.")

3. What new feature in VSX5 provides an added level of title customization? (See "Using Titles in Overlay Tracks.")

4. What are subtitles used for? (See "Creating and Using Subtitles.")

Getting Your Monet on with the

Painting Creator

T HE PAINTING CREATOR, introduced in version 12, might possibly be the most unique feature in any video editing application that costs less than $100. The name Painting Creator doesn't even do the feature justice. The Painting Creator allows you to actually draw, write, and/or paint on actual video frames!

Painting on video frames is a common feature in the high-end world of video production. The term is referred to as *rotoscoping*. Rotoscoping is an animation technique in which animators trace over and add graphics to live-action film, frame by frame. The word came from a device called a *rotoscope*. Originally, pre-recorded live-action film images were projected onto a frosted glass panel, and then additional graphics were drawn by an animator onto the glass. These two images were then combined to create the final frames. This projection equipment was called a rotoscope. The process is still referred to as rotoscoping, but you can now apply this same process using the VSX5 software instead.

What Is the Painting Creator?

V SX5'S PAINTING CREATOR is a feature that allows you to record painting, drawing, and writing strokes as an animation or still, to use as an overlay effect, or as a substitute for a background graphic or video on any video track.

Figure 10.1
Launching the Painting Creator.

The Painting Creator contains an art studio full of drawing tools, including pencils, crayons, paintbrushes, airbrushes, markers, and more. Once you create a "painting," it will then be rendered out to a file that's added to your Media library, which you can then use in your video projects.

The Painting Creator does have some limitations. You can only use one frame as a reference on which to paint. In other words, you cannot paint on a video clip as it's playing. If an object is not moving, it's not an issue. This is very difficult, though, if you want to paint a mustache on someone walking across the room or flames coming out of a moving car. Something to consider.

On the plus side, though, you can animate any painting you create and overlay it onto any Timeline clip or use as a standalone background. The Painting Creator will actually record your painting strokes and play them back as an animation. This chapter will show you how it all works.

To get started, you'll need to open the Painting Creator. Go to the Tools menu at the top of your screen and choose Painting Creator, as shown in Figure 10.1.

The Painting Creator Window

This section will introduce you to the Painting Creator window (see Figure 10.2). (Remember that you can pause your mouse over any tool to see a pop-up description.) Understanding the Painting Creator tools, how and why they're grouped the way they are, and what they do will make this chapter much easier for you to get through. This section outlines each Painting Creator tool and its purpose. As before, feel free to click on each one and test it out. (Just don't click OK. This will create a painting file that we're not quite ready for yet.)

Figure 10.2
Painting Creator window.

A. **Canvas/Preview window:** This is where you will do your actual painting and drawing using the painting tools on the top of the Painting Creator window. A slider in the View controls (see "F" in Figure 10.2) will adjust the opacity level of the background. The background image can be of the current Timeline view or other choices.

B. **Art library:** (See Figure 10.3 for more detail.) This shows the paintings and animations you've created (1) in the Painting Creator. The tools at the top of the library allow for playback (2), deleting any item (3), and adjusting the clip's duration (4).

Number 5 denotes an item that can't be deleted (built-in samples). Number 6 specifies the item as an animation, as opposed to a still painting. Right-clicking on a library item will also display several of these tool choices for you.

Figure 10.3
Art library details.

C. Brush panel: This is your box of art supplies. They include, from the left, Paintbrush, Airbrush, Crayon, Charcoal, Chalk, Pencil, Marker, Oil Paint, Particle, Drop Water, and Bristle. When selecting an art tool from the Brush panel, both the tool and the gear in the lower-right corner of the thumbnail will become highlighted, with the gear turning blue. Select a brush and click on the gear to see a drop-down list of custom settings you can apply to the art tool. See Figure 10.4 for an example.

Figure 10.4
Art brush adjustments.

D. Brush Thickness adjuster: (See Figure 10.5 for more detail.) Use these interactive sliders to set the width (1) and height (2), and then view the size and shape of your brush (3). If you click and lock the small padlock (4) in the lower right, you will adjust both height and width at the same time, maintaining the aspect ratio as you resize it. The Oil Paint and Bristle brushes do not have the size locking ability.

Tip

A shortcut for resizing the brushes and maintaining the aspect ratio is to hold down the Shift+Ctrl+Alt keys while adjusting the brush thickness.

Click the Texture option square (3) to the immediate left of the color square to choose a texture to paint with (see Figure 10.7). Painting with textures will respond to any brush you select (dry or wet media). Combine a color and a texture to paint with a colored texture.

Figure 10.5
Brush Thickness adjuster.

E. **Color palette:** (See Figure 10.6 for more detail.) Click a color in the palette (1) to change your brush to that color to draw/paint with. The color you select will be displayed in the small square to the left (2). You can also click that same color square to select a color from the usual Color Pickers you've used before in VSX5.

Figure 10.7
Texture option selector.

Just to the right of the Color palette is the Eyedropper tool (number 4 in Figure 10.6). By default, it is unchecked. If you mouse over the Color palette, your cursor will *still* change to an eyedropper. In keeping with the eyedropper's color picking theme, this eyedropper indicates that you can choose a color from the palette to draw with.

Something different happens when you select the Eyedropper tool itself—a red check will appear next to it, indicating that it's been selected.

Figure 10.6
Color palette details.

When you select the Eyedropper tool, you can *also* choose a color from anything in the Painting Creator Preview window. Beware, though, that the color selected will be affected by the transparency setting of the background image. Click the Eyedropper tool again to turn off this additional color-picking feature.

Just to the right of the Eyedropper tool is the Eraser tool (5). Click this icon (a red check will appear again) to convert your cursor to an eraser. You can use the interactive Brush Thickness adjuster to change the eraser size. Be sure to click it again to turn it off when you're done, or you'll keep on erasing.

F. **View controls:** In this tab of controls (see Figure 10.8 for more detail) are from the left, the Clear Preview Window tool (1), Zoom In (2) and Zoom Out (3), Actual Size view (4), Background Image Option button (5), and the Background Image Transparency slider (6).

Figure 10.8
Painting canvas View controls.

One click of the Clear Preview Window tool will clear the entire canvas of your painting, much quicker and easier than using the eraser tool in many cases. Beware that this process *cannot* be undone, whereas the eraser function can be undone.

The Zoom tools work in preset increments to zoom into and out of your painting.

The Background Image Option dialog box (see Figure 10.9) includes options on what background you'll be using as a reference to rotoscope on. The first option, Refer to the Default Background Color, is set by choices explained in the "G" entry of this list. Current Timeline Image comes from whatever is being viewed in the Preview panel of the main VSX5 screen. The current Timeline frame will then be carried into the Painting Creator and used as the background image. It is only a reference, though, as you don't actually paint on the image itself. So, if want to use the Timeline as a reference image but don't see it when you're in the Painting Creator, this choice has not been set.

Customize Image allows you to reference a separate image, perhaps one that's not even included in your VSX5 project. Click the small Browse button (three dots) adjacent to the empty field to locate your image. Choosing this option will activate two other options at the bottom. The last choice, Auto Rotate Image According to EXIF Information, means it will rotate the photograph according to information stored inside the photo itself (metadata) that was created and added when the photo was taken.

Click to locate image

Figure 10.9
Background Image Option dialog box.

Prefs   Settings

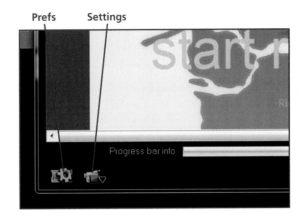

Progress bar info

Figure 10.10
Preferences and Settings icons.

G. **Preferences and Settings:** (See Figure 10.10 for more detail.) Click the left icon to access the Preferences dialog box (see Figure 10.11). Default Macro Duration sets the length of your Painting Creator animation, anywhere from 1 to 15 seconds. (You can still change the duration of any individual item in the Art library by right-clicking on its thumbnail in the library.)

To the right of Preferences is the Settings icon. Click this to set the default drawing mode to either Animation or Still mode. Still mode allows you to create a static painting. Animation mode will record your brush-strokes and create an animation out of them. Leave it in Animation mode because it's easy to change an animation into a still, but not the other way around.

Figure 10.11
Preferences dialog box.

If you possess (or can borrow) a pen-based, pressure-sensitive drawing tablet, I highly recommend using it with the Painting Creator, as well as many other apps with painting features such as Corel Painter and Adobe Photoshop.

A Wacom tablet will put you into a more suitable creative environment, where using the various brushes will feel more realistic. VSX5 will also recognize that you have the tablet and will display an additional settings icon in the bottom-left corner of the Painting Creator window (see Figure 10.12).

There, you can toggle to use basic Wacom tablet controls for brush size, brush transparency, or both, just for use in the Painting Creator. When any of these options are enabled, your tablet will reference these attributes you've already set in the tablet's preferences.

In other words, you can choose to use your Wacom settings in VSX5 or not through these settings.

Figure 10.12
Wacom tablet settings.

H. Start/Stop Recording: This button toggles the recording process on and off of whatever you paint or draw in the Preview window. It's unique in that it only records actual paint strokes, not the time it takes to change brushes, colors, and so on. This way you can take your time without feeling rushed to create your artwork.

Setup for Using the Painting Creator

AS DISCUSSED IN THE previous section, because the Painting Creator is a painting and drawing feature, it would be advantageous to use a drawing tablet with a pen to create your art, such as one from Wacom. So if you have one, by all means hook it up.

The next thing you need to do is place the playback head in the Timeline onto the frame you want to display as a reference in the Painting Creator Preview window (if, in fact, you want to reference the Timeline). The frame you select will be carried into the Painting Creator window and used as a reference for you to paint on. Any reference graphic is optional, though; you can just paint on a blank canvas, too.

The next few steps will set up your art studio for the painting process that comes after it.

1. In VSX5, open the Chapter 9 file and save it as **Chapter 10**. Make sure your custom library, Balloon Trip, is open. This will ensure that any paintings you create will be saved in that library automatically.

2. Temporarily, move the two Motion overlays (D05 and F02) underneath the main track's MAP image, over to the left. See Figure 10.13. (You only want the MAP image as a reference.)

3. Place the playback head anywhere along the main track's MAP.jpg image (anywhere between the 13 and 19 second marks). You should only see the MAP image in the main window's Preview panel.

Figure 10.13
Move the Motion overlay clips to the left.

Creating and Applying Painting Creations

NOW THAT YOU NOW know where all the Painting Creator tools are and what they do, you can really get down to business. So let's get you actually painting something and incorporating it into your video project!

The following steps will show you how to paint an animated path on the MAP image showing the route the balloon trip family took on their adventures.

1. Make sure the Timeline playback head is still somewhere over the MAP image. Open the Painting Creator application from the Tools menu. In the Brush panel, choose the Paintbrush (first brush on the left).

2. Lock the brush size aspect ratio by clicking the padlock on the Brush Thickness adjuster.

Tip

If you forget to lock the brush size aspect ratio and find that you accidentally created an odd-sized brush, simply lock the padlock and adjust the size again. It will automatically return the brush to an even horizontal/vertical size so that you can start over.

3. Size the brush to around 11. As you make an adjustment, the brush size will be displayed adjacent to the brush tip.

4. Choose a blue or green (or blue/green) brush color. This will contrast nicely on the MAP image.

5. Set the Background Transparency slider to about 1/3 from the left side. See Figure 10.14.

Figure 10.14
My brush settings.

6. Click the Start Recording button in the upper-right area. You don't need to start drawing right away. The Painting Creator only records your paint strokes, not the duration that the Start Recording button is active.

7. Draw a path similar to the one shown in Figure 10.15. If you make a mistake or want to start over, use Undo or click the Clear Preview Window icon (also Ctrl+N). You can redo your drawing as many times as you like without having to stop recording. It will only record the final drawing you make.

   This is the first part of your drawing. The next step will show you how to finish it, but do not click Stop Recording yet.

Tip

You do not have to start drawing just because the recording function is on. The Painting Creator does not record based on time, but rather just your brushstrokes themselves, so you can take your time to get it right. It will not record anything you undo, so you can undo and redo any stroke or clear the entire screen and restart. A stroke is considered a single line you lay down, not the entire painting. It will record anything you erase, though, as that is considered a paint stroke, so keep that in mind. You can also practice painting before doing any recording.

Figure 10.15
Recording your drawing.

8. Now you'll highlight the final destination. Change your brush size to about 20, and change the color to red.

9. Using the texture tool to the right of the Background Image Transparency slider, add a texture to your brush—something with a very tight pattern. It will show up better on a paint stroke.

10. Draw a circle around Vancouver that connects to the end of the path you just created. The texture you chose will be reflected in the paint stroke.

11. Click Stop Recording. Your painting is immediately added to the Art library on the right. However, it has not yet been added to your video gallery outside of the Painting Creator. Notice that the drawing shows only the paint strokes and does not include the background map. Remember that the background image used in the Preview window is only there as a reference. Because of this, many paintings can be reused on different backgrounds or as standalone paintings, if you like.

12. Right-click on your new Art library item (which is at the bottom of the list) and choose Change Duration. Change it to 6 seconds. (The default length is 3 seconds and the maximum length is 15 seconds.) Click OK.

13. Click the Play button above the Art library (and to the right of the Record button) to preview what you've created. After it's played, it will clear the Preview window so you can create another one if you like.

    It's still not ready to be included in your video gallery just yet, but this gives you a chance to see if you like what you made. If you don't like it, right-click on the item in the library and choose Remove Gallery Item, and then start over again. Remember that you can also use the Clear Preview Window tool before stopping the recording to try again, too.

14. Click OK. This will render the painting to a file compatible for use in your VSX5 Timeline. You will see a progress bar along the bottom of the window. The Painting Creator application will then close and save your painting to the video gallery or custom library, whichever you currently have open—in this case, your Balloon Trip library. Give the application a minute or so to save your file.

Tip

When in the Painting Creator, clicking OK while any gallery item is selected will also render that item to the currently open library or gallery.

15. Back in the main VSX5 library where the new Painter Creator movie is located, change the file name to **Map_Painting**.

CAUTION

Similar to other media elements, the name you apply to a Painting Creator file in your library is not kept when you put the clip into the Timeline. It will instead resort back to the original file name, but again, only in the Timeline.

16. From the Balloon Trip library, place your new painting clip in overlay track 1 directly beneath and in sync with the MAP image in the video track. It should already be the same length as the MAP image (6 seconds).

17. Move the two clips (MotionD05 and MotionF02), that you previously set aside, back to where they were, in line with the MAP and Map_Painting clips (see Figure 10.16).

Move clips back to the right   **Place Painting file here**

Figure 10.16
Timeline view with Painting inserted.

18. Preview this section of your project. Nice, huh? Shall we do another one? That was a rhetorical question, by the way.... Save your project.

19. Drop the DSC03700 image (the single hot air balloon) to the video track right before your *Star Wars* rolling credits. Remember the video track is the topmost Timeline track. Extend its length to 10 seconds. Ripple Edit should have also moved the item in overlay track 1 to the right.

20. Double-click the balloon image to open the Options panel. In the Photo panel, make sure that Resampling Option is set to Fit to Project Size. See Figure 10.17. This is a convenient situation where changing the aspect of the image doesn't make it look strange.

Double-click this image #1   **Choose Fit to Project Size #2**

Figure 10.17
Adding and resizing a Timeline image.

21. Place the playback head over this new balloon image, just as you did with the MAP image, and launch the Painting Creator application again.

22. Stick with the same Paintbrush tool, choose white as your color, and select a brush size of about 11.

23. Click the small gear in the Paintbrush's thumbnail to access the brush settings. Set the Soft Edge to around 75. You can only use the slider, so just get as close as you can. Click OK.

24. Click Start Recording and outline the balloon similar to what's shown in Figure 10.18. As before, your recording will play back in the order that you paint. Therefore, what I did was first outline the balloon. Then I outlined the stripes of the balloon, scribbled inside them, and wrote the words as a finale. If you make a mistake, use Undo. If you use the Erase mode (unlike undo or restart), be aware that it will record the process of erasing (unless you want that, of course).

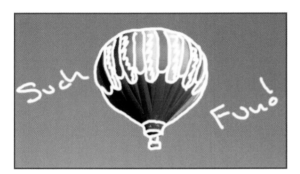

Figure 10.18
Balloon painting.

25. Click Stop Recording. Right-click on the new item in the Painting Creator library and change the duration to 10 seconds. Click Play to preview.

26. Click OK to render your new painting and save it to the same Balloon Trip library.

27. Back in the main VSX5 view, rename your new painting **Balloon_outline**.

28. Place your new clip under, and in-line with, DSC03700. Preview this section. Sweet!

29. Save your project.

Quick Quiz

1. What is Rotoscoping? (See the Chapter 10 Introduction.)

2. Name the two types of Painting Creator files you can make. (See "What Is the Painting Creator?")

3. Name at least five different brushes available to draw with. (See "The Painting Creator Window.")

4. Describe the process of creating and adding a Painting Creator file to your video library. (See "Creating and Applying Painting Creations.")

5. To prevent starting all over again, what should you do if you make an error when painting? (See "Creating and Applying Painting Creations.")

Screen Capturing for
e-Learning

VSX5 NOT ONLY INCLUDES the ability to record from numerous video devices, both analog and digital, to create videos and slideshows for a multitude of purposes, but it can now add another recording option. One of the several major new features in VSX5 is its ability to record actual computer screen activity. Screen recording is exactly what you might think it is. It's the process of recording everything you do on your computer, in this case, as a video.

There are many reasons you may want to record screen activity. The most important and logical reason I can think of is showing others how to accomplish a task through an actual demonstration or a how-to presentation. A task might include showing, step-by-step, a feature in an application, such as using Styles in Word, playing a game, or showing someone how to maneuver or navigate a webpage. In the process of recording a task, example activities might include tracking your mouse movement, opening and closing windows and menus, creating a graphic, moving an item from one place to another, and surfing the Internet.

There are several applications that specialize in screen recording, such as TechSmith's Camtasia or Captivate by Adobe Systems, and they are probably stronger in the specifics of screen recording. But none combines all the additional video capture, editing, and output features of VSX5, such as adding subtitles and outputting to a DVD. If you've already used one of these other applications, you'll find many of the tools and settings in the screen capture feature of VSX5 very familiar to you.

Most of these uses for the screen capture feature can be grouped under the heading of e-Learning.

Exploring the World of e-Learning

THE TERM E-LEARNING is a broad umbrella that includes anything created and displayed electronically (hence the "e" in e-Learning) for the purpose of learning and teaching. E-Learning is used at all levels of education from K-12, to higher education, to career development and skill certification. There are several major advantages of e-Learning. Although e-Learning can still be used in a classroom, one of its main benefits is that it can be accessed remotely, such as in the home or office, instead of a classroom.

Being able to learn something outside a classroom removes the logistical barriers of having to be in an exact location at an exact time to take a class. It can be thought of as anytime, anyplace learning. This can, in turn, greatly reduce the *cost* of learning. Anyone, anywhere on the globe with a computer and Internet connection can take a class or tutorial and can take it when it works best for them, any day, any time.

There are several subcategories of e-Learning, including classroom-based training (CBT), Internet-based training (IBT), and web-based training (WBT). Since VSX5 can create video and interactive content (including HTML5-based links you'll be learning in the next chapter), it can be used for all these delivery mechanisms.

Also, there are many e-Learning developers who may use several applications to create e-Learning projects, including apps to create graphics, animations, and advanced interactivity. Many corporate customers also employ Learning Management Systems (LMS) that will track users' information, course usage, and grading for such uses as certifications and both scholarly and career advancement.

Additional VSX5 features can be used in conjunction with screen recording to produce an e-Learning project, including voice narration, the track visibility option and subtitles for multilanguage courses, and of course outputting to a web-based video or to a DVD.

Using VSX5 for e-Learning

I N THIS CHAPTER, I'LL INTRODUCE you to this new screen recording feature. We'll cover an actual recording of the screen, with added narration, and then add titles in preparation of creating an actual online tutorial, all from within VSX5. Although, you've already learned how to create subtitles in Chapter 9, we'll repeat the process here so you can see another of the benefits of using them—in this case, creating separate title tracks for English and Spanish viewers. At the end of this chapter, I'll give you a taste of outputting your project to an actual video file. In future chapters, you'll learn how to output this and other VSX5 projects to video files, the web, and DVDs.

Since the only application I *know* we both have in common that we can record screen activity in is VideoStudio X5, that's what we'll use. We'll create a very short e-Learning piece that shows viewers how to create a new Media library in VSX5.

Let's start with setting up the screen capturing options.

Setting Up a Screen Capture

S CREEN CAPTURING, AS WITH most features in VSX5, is full-featured, yet much easier to accomplish than you might think, especially if you've done it before in other specialty screen recording applications. It requires first enabling the feature and setting parameters for what area of the computer screen to record (full or partial screen), which actual monitor to record (primary or secondary), audio (narration), and where to save your recording to (which media library). Although you can and will probably want to record

where your mouse moves when recording (so you can point things out), you won't want to record your mouse moving to the control panel to turn it on and off; therefore, convenient keyboard short-cuts are also available to start and stop recording.

The screen capturing feature in VSX5 can be accessed from either the Capture Step tab or the Edit Step tab. Since we'll be recording activity in the Edit Step, that's where we'll launch it from. Ready? Let's set up the screen recording feature.

Although not mandatory, if you have a headset with a recording option or a microphone, grab it for this lesson. The connection to your computer will most likely need to be of the "mini" variety. The mini connection usually entails two small stereo plugs: one that will fit into your computer's headphone jack (for listening to playback) and one that will fit into the recording jack (for, umm, recording).

Figure 11.1
Initial screen record access.

1. Launch VSX5 into a new project. If you have an external headset, hook it up now to capture better quality audio. It's not mandatory for this exercise, but it will help drastically improve your final quality.

3. Click the Screen Capture icon in the top row, center (see Figure 11.2).

CAUTION

You can wait to connect your headset until just before recording, but you'll probably need to close and reopen the Screen Capture window for it to be noticed by VSX5, so it's best to connect it now.

2. Make sure your Media library is open and selected. Don't worry about which gallery is selected in your media library for now. Click on the Record/Capture Option on the top of your Timeline (see Figure 11.1) to open the Record/Capture Options window.

Figure 11.2
Launching the Screen Capture feature.

4. When you click to open the Screen Capture icon, VSX5 itself will minimize, but everything else that you have open will remain as is, such as other apps and browsers (which are apps, of course...). VideoStudio doesn't think you want to record itself, so it hides, but in this case, you *do* want it visible! We'll get to that in a minute.

The Screen Capture control will display on top of everything and can be moved anywhere on your screen, in case it's hiding an important area, without a problem. It will always remain in the forefront of everything else, unless it's minimized to the taskbar at the bottom of your window. See Figure 11.3. You can also minimize or close any other windows so you'll only show those you'll be recording. But you don't have to—in fact, don't even bother. I'll cover this reason in a moment as well.

5. For now, go ahead and minimize all your open windows (see Figure 11.4), so you can more easily see the recording area according to the Screen Capture control panel settings. You should only see your desktop and the Screen Capture control panel. Notice that there is a thin border around the very outer edge of your screen (see Figure 11.5). This represents the default recording area for the screen capture, which is Fullscreen. Since VSX5 works best in Fullscreen view, I'll eventually return to this look, but for now, let's see what other options are available.

Figure 11.4
How to minimize windows.

Figure 11.3
The Screen Capture control panel.

Figure 11.5
The default Screen Capture Record area.

6. Below the drop-down that says Fullscreen (the screen area selector), click the small chain link to lock the aspect ratio of your screen recording size. Add new values for width (W) and height (H). Since the aspect ratio is locked, you only need to enter a value into one of the fields and then press Enter to set that first value. The other field will adjust accordingly. Make sure these values are, of course, smaller than your current values. I entered 1280 into the width, then I pressed Enter. The new window size on my screen is now 1280×800. See Figure 11.6. The Fullscreen heading above will change to say Custom.

Lock aspect ratio

New screen recording area

Change screen recording size

Figure 11.6
Custom Screen Capture Record area.

Tip

If you have the screen size aspect ratio link locked, you only have to enter one of the width and height values—either one. When you press Enter, the other value will be entered automatically.

7. Return the screen size to Fullscreen, by using the drop-down that now says Custom. Maximize some or all of the windows you had before to make them visible again.

Choosing Your Screen Capture Settings

Now, we'll review all the other possible screen capture settings and how they'll affect your recordings; then we'll set up your options for a specific e-Learning tutorial recording.

1. In the lower-left corner of the Screen Capture window, click Settings to expand the window to view and set the additional options available to you. See Figure 11.7.

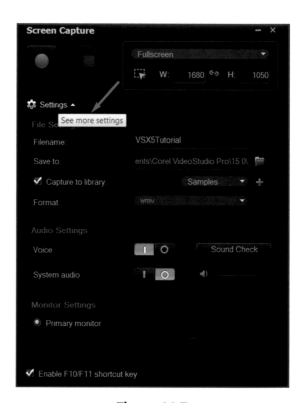

Figure 11.7
Expanding the Settings view.

2. Let's start from the top of the settings and work our way down. Under the File Settings region, enter a file name of **VSX5Tutorial**.

3. Set the recording to save to your VSX5 Saved Lessons folder.

4. Capture to Library should already be checked. If it is not, check it. Just to the right of the list that's currently labeled Samples, click the "+" to add a new gallery to your library. Call it VSX5 Tutorial. See Figure 11.8. Click OK. Leave the Format as wmv (it's the only choice anyway).

Figure 11.8
Setting a Capture Library gallery.

5. Under Audio Settings, a dark yellow button means the audio setting is selected and active. Make sure | is active next to voice and O is active next to system audio. You will be recording your voice, but you will *not* be recording audio coming from your computer.

6. Click Sound Check. The sound check window will open. If you have a headset connected, the Input Device field will say External Microphone. If you don't have one connected, it will say Internal Microphone. See Figure 11.9.

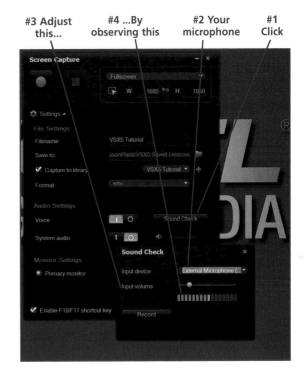

Figure 11.9
Audio settings.

7. Speak (normally) into your microphone to conduct a sound check. Adjust the Input volume, so that speaking only produces green bars. Try to avoid yellow and red bars that will indicate possible distortion when you replay your audio. Close the Sound Check window when you're happy with these settings.

CAUTION

If you're recording an application that also uses F10 & F11 as keyboard shortcuts, these same keys in VSX5 will take precedent. You will be unable to use those keys in the application you're recording or using.

8. Monitor Settings will only be highlighted if it sees that you have another monitor. If you are running multiple monitors, select whichever monitor (Primary or Secondary) contains all the main VSX5 windows.

9. Make sure Enable F10/F11 shortcut key is checked. After you click the Record button in the Screen Capture window, you will use F11 whenever you want to pause the recording and press F11 again to resume recording. You will use F10 when you're done recording.

10. The Screen recording tool has a great feature where you can choose which specific application/window to record and record only that window, even though you may have several other windows visible. To screen record only VSX5, click the screen size list at the top (it should say Fullscreen again) and select Untitled-Corel VideoStudio Pro. See Figure 11.10. The VSX5 window will then reappear and take up the entire screen. This will be what you'll record.

11. Make sure the playback head is at the start of your Timeline.

Figure 11.10
Setting which window to record.

Tip

A great Windows utility that I use all the time is one called Fences, by Stardock (www.stardock.com/products/fences/). This organizational utility will group all your Desktop folders into "fenced yards" that you can hide at will. When I conduct screen recordings for tutorials, all I do is press the Esc key, and everything on my entire Desktop will hide, so it won't show up in the recording. You can also specify any icon to be excluded from hiding. Pressing Esc again brings everything back into view.

Recording Your Screen

NOW, WE'RE FINALLY READY to record screen activity and narration. I've created a script for you to follow after you click Record. For the sake of time, we'll dispense with an introduction and conclusion and get right down to explaining to our "students" just how to create a new media folder in VSX5.

The script is structured so that it tells you exactly what to say, with what to do in parentheses. In other words, Say This, (Do This) at the same time. The script will be as follows:

> Start—
> This VideoStudio Pro X5 tutorial will show you how to create a new Media library. You can create as many as you need to organize your video project content. This is done in the Library Navigation panel near the top here (circle your mouse around the Navigation panel). The panel already includes a Samples gallery (point that out, too). To create a new custom gallery, click the + Add button at the top of the panel (Click + Add at the top of the panel).
>
> Create a name for your new gallery. In this case, I'll name it My New Gallery (name it My New Gallery). To add content to your new gallery, click Browse on the bottom here (Click Browse) and navigate to content to add to your gallery (add some video content from your lessons folders). And that's all there is to it.
> —End.

Tip

It is not mandatory to record narration at the same time as the video. You can also do it before or even afterward. You can turn off the recording of audio in the Screen capture window's settings area and instead record audio using your screen recording as a reference.

Simply place your finished screen recording into the Timeline, open the Record/Capture Options panel again, and use the Voice-over choice. Record your narration as you're watching the video portion. You can also do it all vice versa; record the voiceover, and then do the screen recording.

Are you ready? Now, follow these steps to create your screen recording. Remember that F11 will pause/restart your recording, and F10 will start/stop your recording. Take as much time as you like, and redo it if necessary. Nothing is permanent, and it can always be redone. All your recordings will be placed into the gallery you created. You can delete all the ones you don't like anytime directly from there before you place one into the Timeline.

1. Close the Settings drop-down in the Screen Capture window so all you see is the screen capture controls. Move the control panel so it won't be in the way of the VSX5 Navigation panel.

2. Click the big red record button in the top left of the control panel to start your recording. It will count down 3-2-1. Follow the script as written above. Don't worry about being exact; you're just learning this.

3. Once you're done, click F10 to stop the recording. Figure 11.11 shows what will appear next. Click OK to close the info box.

Figure 11.11
Screen capture is complete.

4. Close the Screen Capture control panel by clicking the X in its upper-right corner. Open your VSX5 Tutorial library gallery. Your screen recording should be in there!

5. Save your project as **My VSX5 Tutorial**.

Editing Your Screen Recording

THAT WASN'T SO HARD, was it? Now, it's just a matter of adding your recording to the Timeline, cutting out any unwanted parts, and incorporating any other project assets you would like to add. Let's add some subtitles in English for the hearing impaired and different subtitles for Spanish-speaking viewers.

1. Place the screen recording clip you want to use (if you created several) into the Timeline.

2. If there are parts of your video you would like to cut out, right-click on them in the Timeline and choose Multi-trim Video (see Figure 11.12). As you learned back in Chapter 4, use the mark-in and mark-out tools to save only those parts you want.

Tip

This is one case where it might be easier to mark the areas you *don't* want and then choose Invert Selection to save the parts you *do* want. See Figure 11.13.

3. If you recorded your audio separately from the video and find that you spoke too fast and your video is lagging behind your voiceover, you can extend any video frame for additional seconds so that the video catches up to your voiceover. To do this, place your playback on the frame you would like to stay on the screen for awhile. Go to Edit > Take a Snapshot. This will create a jpg image and put it in the currently selected gallery. See Figure 11.14. Do not move your playback head yet.

Figure 11.12
Multi-trim Video feature.

#2   #1 Playback head   #3 New still image

Figure 11.14
Take a Snapshot.

Figure 11.13
Invert Selection.

Tip

Place the still image into your recording where you're only talking and *not* doing any onscreen activity, because video activity will not show with a still image being displayed.

4. Right-click again on the video clip exactly where your playback is and choose Split Clip. This will create a slot where you can place your new snapshot image.

5. Drag and drop your still image into the slot between your two clips. Use the options panel to adjust its length until your video catches up with your audio. See Figure 11.15.

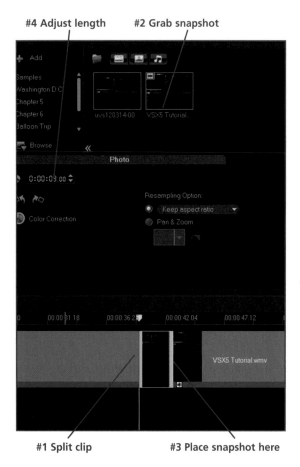

#4 Adjust length   **#2 Grab snapshot**

#1 Split clip   **#3 Place snapshot here**

Figure 11.15
Insert snapshot.

6. Now you'll add some subtitles in English. Subtitles will help those who are hearing impaired to also enjoy your tutorial. You will use the basic title feature. You will not be using any of the special animated titles included with VSX5. Following is a list of suggested titles I want you to add:

▶ Creating a new Media library

▶ You'll use the Library Navigation panel

▶ Click + Add button at the top

▶ Name your new gallery

▶ Click Browse to add content

▶ You're Done!

7. Place these in the Timeline where you actually voice it as well. Then you can start playing your video and stop where you mention you'll be teaching the viewers how to create a new Media library. At that point in the Timeline, click Title in the Navigation panel. Double-click to add the text near the bottom of the screen. Adjust the font so it will fit, but don't worry about the formatting beyond that. Exporting and importing the subtitle file will take care of all that.

8. Continue with all the rest of the titles. I made each title last for 5 seconds. Your Timeline might look like Figure 11.16.

9. Double-click on the first subtitle you created to open the Options panel.

10. Click Save Subtitle File. Name it **VSX5_Tutorial_English**. Click Save.

11. Shift-select all the titles in the title track and press Delete. Rewind your playback to the beginning.

Figure 11.16
Inserted subtitles.

12. Back in the Options panel, click Open
Subtitle file and highlight the subtitle
file you just created, but don't click Open
just yet.

13. In the bottom of the Open window, choose
Language > English, Font > Arial Black, Font
size > 18, Line leading > 100, Font color >
white and Glow shadow > black. Click Open.
Click OK to the warning box.

Creating a Multilanguage Project

NOW, YOU'LL CREATE a Spanish subti-
tled version. There are two ways you can
do this. You can create the final video with
the English subtitles and then replace the titles
with Spanish text and save it again. A better way,
though, is to have your project contain *both* the
English *and* Spanish subtitles, and then simply
hide one or the other and create a movie that way.
This way everything is contained in one project.
Let's do it the latter way.

1. Using the Track Manager, add the second
title track.

2. Starting with the first title in Title track 1,
copy and paste each one into Title track 2.
To do this, right-click on the title in track 1 and
choose Copy. Move your cursor, with the copy
attached to it, straight down to Title track 2
and left-click to drop it. See Figure 11.17.

#1 Right-click to copy

#2 Left-click to paste

Figure 11.17
Copying a title.

3. Now for the faster way. Shift-select the rest of the title tracks and then repeat step 2. See Figure 11.18.

4. Click the Enable title track icon on the far left of Title track 1 to temporarily hide this track so the two title tracks don't overlap. See Figure 11.19.

Figure 11.19
Hiding a track.

#1 Right-click to copy

#2 Left-click to paste

Figure 11.18
Copying/pasting multiple assets.

5. Replace the text in Title track 2 with the following Spanish phrases. The copied subtitles are already formatted correctly, but they might be off center after changing the text. Therefore, after changing the text to Spanish, use the Alignment tools in the Options window (the one with the arrows pointing in different directions). Click the bottom-center choice. You may have to lower the font size slightly in some of the Spanish titles to allow them to fit within the title safe area.

 ▶ Creación de una nueva biblioteca de medios

 ▶ Vamos a usar la biblioteca panel de navegación

 ▶ Haga clic en + Añadir en la parte superior

 ▶ El nombre de su nueva galería

 ▶ Haga clic en Examinar para agregar contenido

 ▶ ¡Ya está!

6. As you did before, double-click any one of the new Spanish titles. In the Options panel, choose Save Subtitle File. Save it as **MySpanishSubtitle**. Now you have both languages that perhaps can be used at another time.

7. Save your project.

Your Timeline might look like Figure 11.20. As you can see, you can easily create one project with two or more possible outcomes, just by enabling/disabling different tracks. We'll cover how to output these projects to video files, the web, and DVDs in Chapter 15.

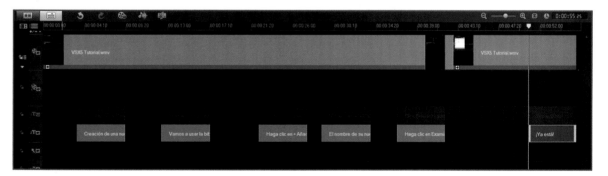

Figure 11.20
Two language title tracks.

Sharing Your First Movie

ALTHOUGH YOU'VE ALREADY created some quick video outputs and we'll be covering the processes of outputting your projects in all sorts of formats for various purposes starting in Chapter 15, it's time you learned more of the basics now, in case you want to test or show off your projects. Plus—it's just awesome to see all your hard work show up in movies. Let's take your short e-Learning piece and create a video out of it. It's easy and fast. Here we go.

1. Go to the Share tab. Click Create Video File. You have a lot of choices, that again, will be explained in detail later in the book. I really just want to show you how easy it is to create a simple video to play back on your computer right now.

2. Scroll down to WMV and choose WMV HD 720 30p. This stands for Windows Media Video (wmv), High-Definition (HD), 720 lines of resolution, 30 frames per second, and progressive scan (both fields simultaneously, as opposed to interlaced, which is alternating fields). Save it either to your saved lessons folder or to your desktop.

3. When it's finished rendering, locate and double-click it to launch it in your computer's default media player and BAM, you're well on your way to creating complete videos from capture to sharing!

Quick Quiz

1. What is the term that describes such electronic learning techniques as web-based training and computer-based training? (See "Exploring the World of e-Learning.")

2. When setting the screen size you want to record in the Screen Capture window, why would you enable the small chain link between the width and height entry fields? (See "Choosing Your Screen Capture Settings.")

3. What are at least two ways to add audio narration to a screen capture project? (See "Recording Your Screen.")

4. What is an easy way to extend a portion of a screen capture scene? (See "Editing Your Screen Recording.")

5. What is the best way to create a multi-language video out of one project? (See "Creating a Multilanguage Project.")

Web Authoring in

HTML5 and VSX5

HTML5 IS CONSIDERED the single biggest leap forward in web technology of the last generation. HTML5 is a language for structuring and presenting content for the World Wide Web and is a core technology of the Internet originally proposed by Opera Software (not Al Gore).

What Is HTML5?

HTML STANDS FOR HyperText Markup Language. HTML code, or elements, are the basic building blocks of webpages. HTML is written in the form of tags enclosed in angle brackets (e.g., <html>), within the web page content. HTML tags most commonly come in pairs like <h1> and </h1>. The first tag in a pair is the start tag, and the second tag is the end tag (they are also called opening tags and closing tags). In between these tags web designers can add text, tags, comments, and other types of text-based content.

The new HTML5 adds many new features. These include the new <video>, <audio>, and <canvas> elements, as well as the integration of Scalable Vector Graphics (SVG) content that replaces the use of generic <object> tags. These features are designed to make it easy to include and handle multimedia and graphical content on the web without having to resort to proprietary plugins and APIs. Can you see the appeal that it might have for VSX5 developers?

As a result, being able to create a video in the HTML5 format allows you, for the very first time in VSX5, to have a video that includes interactivity, in the form of embedded hyperlinks, where viewers can jump to another point in your video or even to an external website. This is huge. Previous to HTML5, this feature was only available through video developed in Adobe Flash. Flash, has recently taken heat for its incompatibility with new hardware and large resource requirements, not to mention requiring a dedicated up-to-date software component to run the Flash plug-in. But, similar to Flash, HTML5 will run in all compatible browsers and across multiple platforms.

Internal jump-to points in VSX5 are created by setting "chapter" markers along your Timeline. We have yet to discuss chapter markers, but they are simply markers you add to any point in the Timeline to designate such items as project guides, DVD menu chapters, and hyperlink jump-to points. We'll use the DVD menu example in Chapters 16 and 17 on creating DVDs.

Currently, the HTML5 video feature in VSX5 is compatible with those browsers supporting the HTML5 technology. At press time, these include Google Chrome 12, Internet Explorer 9, and Mozilla Firefox 7 (and, of course, any later versions than these). It is also supported in the Safari browser for iPhone, iPad, and iPod Touch devices.

VSX5 also supports the WebM video format that can be embedded into HTML5 webpages. WebM is dedicated to developing a high-quality, open video format for the web that is freely available to everyone (www.webmproject.org/). It assails to improve on the no-plug-in, cross-platform playback ability, but for video. While it remains to be seen if this standard will stick (and for how long), it is a feature also in VSX5's HTML capabilities.

Setting Up Your HTML5 Project

HTML5 PROJECTS IN VSX5 are special projects. You still cannot have videos with hyperlinks embedded on them. To get around this, you have to designate that links go onto separate graphics or titles in overlay tracks in your video project instead. HTML5 allows for separate layers on top of videos that will then allow for hyperlinks.

One big drawback of using HTML5 features inside a video clip is you cannot stop/pause the video upon playback to wait for the viewer to click a link. If the viewer doesn't click the link when it's available, it will pass by and it'll be too late, unless of course that link lasts the entire length of the video or you manually rewind the video and play it back again. Chapter markers can be used to set go-to points, but not to pause a video.

The other limitation is when constructing an HTML5 project. *No* video may go into any overlay track, only the background video tracks. It won't even let you if you try. Luckily, you can still layer videos, because an HTML5 project allows for up to three background tracks. You add these using the Track Manager.

When you start a special HTML5 project, a dialog box will appear (see Figure 12.1). This states that everything you place in the video track (in this case any or all of the three possible background tracks) will be rendered, or flattened, to one video file when exporting to HTML5. This warning is nothing to be alarmed about, because everything in a regular video gets flattened upon rendering anyway. What's different here is that anything in overlay layers will remain as separate assets.

Figure 12.1
HTML5 warning.

In VSX5, you can create an HTML5 project from scratch or use the HTML5 template that comes included with VSX5. We'll start with creating one using the template, as it contains all the placeholders and chapter markers to give you a quicker, easier idea on how this feature works. After that we'll cover another new feature that shows how you can import a multilayered graphic from PaintShop Pro and add hyperlinks to the separate objects in the separate layers.

Using an HTML5 Template

U SING AN HTML5 TEMPLATE in VSX5 will be very similar to using an Instant Project. In fact, the one that comes included is located in the same library and accessed from the Navigation panel. Just like an Instant Project, we'll be adding this multilayered template straight into the Timeline. Chapter markers have already been placed on the Timeline. We will add hyperlinks onto "go-to" arrows already placed in the template that will be used to jump to other parts of the video—in this case, the chapter marks. Let's begin.

Figure 12.2
New HTML5 project.

You've already learned how to replace template placeholders with your own videos and graphics, so we'll dispense with this extra step in this lesson and concentrate on just the HTML5 features.

1. Instead of File > New, choose File > New HTML5 Project. See Figure 12.2. The warning box I described will show up. Click OK to close it. The only difference you will notice at first is that the video track is now purposefully named Background Track #1 in the Timeline.

2. Select the Instant Project icon in the Navigation panel. You will see two headings, one called HTML5, the other called Custom. Custom will be empty. Select the HTML5 gallery. You will only see one template. Drag it to the Timeline. See Figure 12.3. Notice how the tracks are labeled on the left side of the Timeline. The first three tracks are background tracks. The next three tracks are overlay tracks, followed by the two title tracks.

3. This step is optional, but if you would like to add your own content, you will need to set up another custom gallery because your previous galleries have not carried over into your HTML5 project. Remember, to replace a placeholder with your own content, simply drag the new content over the placeholder in the Timeline while holding down the Ctrl key. To drop it in, let go of your mouse *before* you let go of the Ctrl key. Keep in mind that the replacement clip must be at least as long (in time) as the placeholder. Also remember that video clips can *only* go into the background tracks, not any of the overlay tracks.

Background tracks   **Overlay tracks**   **Place template in Timeline**

Figure 12.3
Adding the HTML5 template.

CAUTION

In HTML5 projects in VSX5, video clips may *only* go into the background Timeline tracks. The overlay tracks are reserved for still images and text.

Working with Chapter/Cue Points

Chapter points and cue points are markers set in the Timeline that are used as functional and managerial markers. Green chapter points are used to set chapters in DVDs, web addresses, and go-to points in hyperlinks. Blue cue points are used only as project references. These green chapter and blue cue points are represented by up-facing arrows in the top portion of your Timeline. Let's take a look at the go-to or chapter points that have already been added to this template.

1. Go to Settings > Chapter Point Manager. The Chapter Manager manages the chapter markers added along the Timeline. In this case, these chapter points represent the jump-to points (hyperlinks) in an HTML5 project. In the Timeline, these are displayed as inverted green arrows. See Figure 12.4. As you can see, in the Manager, you can add new go-to points, delete them, rename them, and go to them in the Timeline.

Chapter points   **Current chapter point**

Figure 12.4
Chapter Point Manager.

2. In the Manager, select the first one and name it Page 1. See Figure 12.5. Click OK.

Figure 12.5
Renaming a chapter point.

Figure 12.6
Renamed chapters.

3. Rename the second chapter point **Page 2**. Rename the next ones, **Scene 1, Scene 2, Scene 3,** and **Scene 4**. See Figure 12.6. Click Close when finished. Although you won't see any visual difference in the Timeline, the green chapter point indicators are now named for easier linking identification later.

4. Save your project as **My_HTML5_Template**. Notice that the file extension has changed to .VSH, standing for a VideoStudioHTML file.

5. You can, of course, move and delete chapter and cue points. You can also add them right into the Timeline, bypassing the Chapter and Cue Point Managers. When manually adjusting points, you will need to be very careful, as it's very easy to miss them and inadvertently add another one.

   In the Timeline, there is a chapter marker at the 19 sec mark (the third marker). Move it with your mouse to between slide 1 and slide 2.

You may have noticed that in the Chapter Point Manager you can convert a chapter point to a cue point. You also have access to the Cue Point Manager in the Settings menu, where you can do the opposite, too. So, what's the difference between a chapter point and a cue point? Cue points should only be used as reference points when managing a video project. They do not actually trigger anything. You may use them as notes for either yourself or other video production members. Chapter points specify disc (DVD) menu chapters and hyperlinks (go-to points). Chapter points are functional; cue points are only for project management. Chapter points are green. Cue points are blue.

6. Remove the third chapter point you just moved by dragging it up off the Timeline. It will disappear. Do the same thing if you also accidentally created a new point when you tried to move the point in step 4.

7. There is another way to add markers directly on the Timeline. Move the playback head to the 19 sec mark. Remember, you can home into the exact frame using the timecode field in the Preview panel. Click the Add/Remove Chapter Point icon (+/-) in the upper left of the Timeline (see Figure 12.7). This will add the chapter point back to where it was originally. Rename it back to **Scene 1**.

#2 Click here   #3 Choose this   #1 Go here

Figure 12.8
Switching to cue points.

Figure 12.7
Adding a chapter point.

8. Now you'll learn how to add a cue point. Move the playback head to 02:07.04. This is where the conclusion begins. You first need to switch over to the Cue point view. Open the Chapter/Cue menu (the really small down arrow next to the +/- icon) and select Cue Point (see Figure 12.8). All the chapter points will disappear.

9. The Add/Remove Chapter Point button has now changed to say Add/Remove Cue Point. Similar to what you did in step 7, add a cue point to the beginning of the conclusion. You should now have a blue cue point on the Timeline. See Figure 12.9.

Figure 12.9
Placing a cue point.

10. You *can* rename any cue or chapter point simply by double-clicking on it, but that is also the easiest way to mistakenly add another point you don't want. If you miss the point even by a little, you'll just add another one adjacent to it. Instead, use the Cue Point Manager. Use either the icon in the Timeline (again, the small arrow next to the +/- icon) or the Settings menu to open the Cue Point Manager. Rename the cue point to say Update Conclusion. Click OK, and then click Close to return to the Timeline.

11. In the Chapter/Cue menu, click Chapter Point to return to the Chapter Point view in the Timeline.

12. Save your project.

Adding/deleting chapter/cue points cannot be undone via undo/redo. There are at least four ways to delete a point:

▶ Using your mouse, grab a chapter point and simply drag it off the Timeline.

▶ Use the Chapter Point Manager to delete individual markers.

▶ Right-click in the Timeline strip where the points are and choose Remove All Chapter Points.

▶ Click the Add/Remove Chapter or Cue Point button in the Timeline.

CAUTION

You can *only* use the last method of deleting chapters and points if the playback head is *exactly* where the point is located.

Although chapters can be automatically created by scene breaks when exporting to DVD, chapter points allow you to enter breaks in between scenes and will then be carried over when you create a DVD.

Having said all this, VSX5 seems to blur the line between cue points and chapter points and lets the user use either one in many instances. Although chapter points are the only ones used to make DVD chapters, either chapter or cue points can be used for hyperlinks. For the sake of consistency, we'll only use chapter points for hyperlinks.

Adding Internal Links

Internal hyperlinks can be added very easily in VSX5. You'll use the chapter points you learned about in the last section to place them. Hyperlinks cannot be added to a video—only still graphics and titles (text). Remember that videos and graphics are rendered out as separate items when saving as an HTML5 video. Let's use the graphics and text in this project to let the viewers jump to the various chapter points in the Timeline. We'll start with the forward and back arrows.

1. Select the very first graphic in Overlay track 1 (the overlay track right below background track 3). As you do so, you'll see that the forward arrow in the Preview panel becomes highlighted. Right-click on it in the Timeline and choose Add Link. See Figure 12.10.

#1 Right-click   **#2 Choose Add Link...**

Figure 12.10
Setting up a hyperlink.

2. In the Add Link window, make sure the Select from cue/chapter point radio button is checked. Also make sure the Chapter Point list is visible.

3. In the list on the right, select the second choice, Page 2. See Figure 12.11. This will add a hyperlink onto the right arrow that will jump the viewer to the next page of content choices. Click OK.

Figure 12.11
Adding an internal hyperlink.

4. Using the same method as in step 3, add a hyperlink to the second graphic in Overlay track 1 (the back-facing arrow) that points to Page 1.

5. In the same overlay track, link the third arrow graphic to Scene 2. Link the next arrow to Scene 3 and the final arrow in Overlay track 1 to scene 4.

6. In overlay track 2 (not video track 2), all the arrows need to link backward (hence, they point backward). Link the first arrow to scene 1, the second arrow to scene 2, and the final back arrow to scene 3.

7. Let's now change all the titles that currently say VideoStudio, starting with Title track 1. Return the playback to the home position. In this first frame, you'll see two instances of VideoStudio. Change the top VideoStudio title to say **Scene 1** and then link it to Scene 1. Change the bottom VideoStudio title (in title track 2) to say **Scene 2** and link it to Scene 2. See Figure 12.12.

Figure 12.12
Hyperlinking text.

8. Change the text and links to titles on page 2 to **Scenes 3** and **4,** respectively.

9. In Title track 1, change the very last title to say simply, **The End**.

10. There are 4 titles left in Title track 1 that you haven't changed yet. Change them all to say **Index** and link them all to Page 1.

11. Save your project.

Tip

When you add a link to any asset in the Timeline, a small (again, *really* small) icon will show up on the lower left of it in the Timeline in the shape of a small world globe. That's how you can, at a glance, know which Timeline objects have links applied to them.

Outputting an HTML5 Movie

I N SOME PREVIOUS CHAPTERS and at the end of the last chapter, you learned the very basics of sharing a movie by outputting to a common video format. In this section, you'll output this HTML5 template to a video as well. Choices for sharing an HTML5 project are limited compared to regular VSX5 projects because they are designed for a limited playback mechanism—the HTML browser.

The process is still easy, but the files created are different. You can still save it in many of the available video formats, because it will strip out the HTML components and flatten the entire movie into one file. That's easy for VSX5 to do. Therefore, you can save HTML5 projects in regular video formats, but movies starting out as regular VSX5 projects cannot be converted into an HTML5 project unless you save the HTML project as a video first and reimport it into a regular VSX5 project. Let's output an HTML5 project as an HTML5 movie and play it back in an Internet browser.

Tip

Viewers of HTML5 movies containing embedded hyperlinks will only be able to click hyperlinks as long as the linked object (graphic or text) appears onscreen. Unfortunately, there is still no way to set a pause in the video (besides the viewer pausing the movie himself and waiting to click a link to proceed). Keep this in mind when creating your own HTML5 project.

1. Go to the Share tab.

2. Click Create Video File. Flip through the choices to see that most of the video file formats are still available for output here. Pause (but don't click) over Export as VSP Project. If selected, this will convert your HTML5 project with the .vsh file extension to one with the .vsp extension. If you like, you can then reopen the project in VSX5 and output the file to all the other options available in the Sharing step.

3. Click Create HTML5 File. Change the Folder path to your VSX5 Saved Lessons folder. Keep the Project folder name as is (it should already say My_HTML5_Template). You will need a separate folder for the output because this will create a lot of companion files. Change the Project Dimensions to HD (16:9).

4. Check the checkbox next to Flatten audio and background video. It's better to be safe than sorry when it comes to browser playback compatibilities.

5. Notice that quite a few files will be created (Note Total files: 24), not just one video file. See Figure 12.13 for the desired settings. Click OK. The project will take some time to finish, because it's also creating a WebM version.

Figure 12.13
Create HTML5 Files window.

6. When the project is finished rendering, locate and open the My_HTML5_Template folder in your saved lessons folder. It may have opened automatically for you.

CAUTION

Rendering out an HTML5 movie can take a *very* long time. This one you just did may have taken a couple hours or more. I can't explain why at this point. I just wanted you to be aware of the issue. It's not that your computer has stalled.

7. Double-click the file named Index. It will open your HTML5 project in your default Internet browser. Make sure it opens in one of the previously mentioned HTML5 supported browsers. It will not play right away. The movie will open surrounded by a playback control panel that is waiting for you to click Play. Click the full screen button on the lower right, and then the Play button. See Figure 12.14.

Play   Full Screen

Figure 12.14
Playing an HTML5 movie.

8. Click some of the links as they go by, remembering that the video will not wait for you to do so.

9. When you're done, return to the folder containing the HTML5 files you just rendered. Open some of the folders to see what was created. Items include javascript (js) and cascading style sheets (css), all of which are necessary to create a cross-platform, cross-browser HTML experience.

10. Close your HTML5 files folder and Internet browser.

In the next section, I'll teach you how to use a multilayered graphic coming from Corel's PaintShop Pro to add additional HTML5 hyperlinks that, this time, will link externally to other websites.

Creating an HTML5 Movie from Scratch

COREL'S PAINTSHOP PRO, like many image-editing applications, has the ability to utilize multiple layers to keep objects and effects separate from each other for editing and blending purposes. VSX5's use of tracks behaves similarly to layers in PaintShop Pro, but there are also differences. Whereas VSX5 layers work with motion effects, PaintShop Pro uses effects that affect still images only. PaintShop Pro also has a better ability to blend effects and colors.

But the feature I want to discuss here is the new VSX5 capability that takes advantage of multi-layered images from PaintShop Pro. VSX5 will let you import a PaintShop Pro image (in the .psp format) straight into a VSX5 gallery. The beauty of this is that you can drag and drop a multilayered PSP file straight into the Timeline and it will, like an Instant Project, add and fill in all the necessary additional tracks it needs to work. This can save a lot of time. You can use this feature for both regular and HTML5 projects. Let me show you what I mean.

1. Go to File > New HTML5 Project.

2. Select the Media Library at the top of the Navigation panel. Create a new gallery called PaintShop Pro. From your VSX5_LessonPlans open the Other folder, add the Butterflies file to the new gallery. This file is a multilayered file from PaintShop Pro. Each butterfly is on a separate layer.

3. Drag the single Butterfly gallery item into your Timeline so that it starts with the first layer on Background Track #3. See Figure 12.15. You want all the actual butterfly layers in overlay tracks so you can add links to them. Save your project as **Butterfly_HTML5**.

Figure 12.15
Adding a PSP graphic.

4. Deselect all the items in the Timeline by clicking anywhere in the Timeline except on Butterflies.psp.

5. Double-click each butterfly track and extend its length to 30 seconds. Fit your Timeline to view.

6. Now we'll animate a simple path for each butterfly (just to make clicking the hyperlinks on them a little more challenging), using the Attribute > Direction feature in the Options panel. For example, for the butterfly in Video track 2, I chose to enter from the upper left and exit to the lower right. See Figure 12.16.

Figure 12.16
Butterfly motion path.

7. As you learned in a previous chapter, the blue line in the Preview panel (in the Options > Attribute tab) indicates the duration the butterfly is stationary, while the length of each end indicates the length of the entrance and exit paths. Drag each blue line so it's longer than it is now, as shown in Figure 12.17. This will give you and the viewer a better chance to click each hyperlinked butterfly.

Figure 12.17
Adjusting motion path time length.

8. Repeat steps 6 & 7 for the other four butterflies. Remember to choose an animation path and the enter and exit values.

Adding External Hyperlinks

This time, let's add external hyperlinks that will open up an actual website, as opposed to internal hyperlinks going to another part of the same movie.

1. Right-click on the first butterfly in the Timeline (*overlay* track 1) and choose Add Link.

> External hyperlinks in VSX5 will automatically open up a new tab or window in your browser and go to a website, leaving your HTML5 movie still available in the other tab. This way, you won't have to use the back button.

2. In the Add Link window, make sure the Enter the URL Link: radio button is selected. http:// is already added to the link field. After it, add www.nationalgeographic.com/. See Figure 12.18. Click OK when done.

3. In no particular order, add the following links to the remaining four butterflies: www.en.wikipedia.org/wiki/Butterfly, www.kidsbutterfly.org/, www.butterflywebsite.com/, and www.thebutterflysite.com/.

4. Save your project.

5. As you did exporting your first HTML5 movie, go to the Share tab.

6. Click Create HTML5 File.

7. Change the folder path to your saved lessons folder. Leave the Project folder name as is. Change the project dimensions to HD (16:9) and check Flatten audio and background video. Click OK.

8. This time, the wait should be just a few minutes.

9. Open the Butterfly_HTML5 folder and double-click the Index file to open your latest HTML5 project in a browser.

#1 **#2**

Figure 12.18
Adding an external link.

10. Click on any of the butterflies going by. You will be sent to the website linked to that butterfly. The link will open in a new tab or window. To try a different link, return to the previous window/tab and click Play again. If the movie has played to the end, click Play again to restart it.

11. Close your Internet browser when done. Close VideoStudio X5.

Quick Quiz

1. What does HTML stand for? (See "What Is HTML5?")

2. What items in an HTML5 project cannot have hyperlinks attached to them? (See "Setting Up Your HTML5 Project.")

3. How do you initiate an HTML5 project in VSX5 that's different from a regular project? (See "Using an HTML5 Template.")

4. What are the differences between chapter points and cue points? (See "Working with Chapter/Cue Points.")

5. Why do you need a separate folder to output your HTML5 movie? (See "Outputting an HTML5 Movie.")

Stop-Motion Animation and Time-Lapse

Photography

THE TWO FEATURES COVERED in this chapter were brand new to VideoStudio Pro X4, again, adding amazing functionality and just plain fun for an application costing less than $100. You may or may not be familiar with the terms stop-motion animation and time-lapse photography, so I'll take some time to explain them before discussing how they're applied in VSX5.

What Is Time-Lapse Photography?

TIME-LAPSE PHOTOGRAPHY is the process of making something that normally moves and changes very slowly seem to occur much faster. This is done by taking a series of photos over a long period of time (e.g., hours, days, or longer) at intermittent intervals (e.g., every 1 min, 30 minutes, or once a day).

Stringing all these photos together in a timeline and playing them back at normal video speed makes whatever you shot over that long time period condense into just a few seconds or minutes. Think of the blooming of a flower that normally takes an entire day occurring in only a minute's time. You can set up a time-lapse system to record the snowfall from a blizzard accumulating in a few seconds what actually took a day or more. A common thing to shoot is a normal day from dawn to dusk and then the night's lights as they come on and the moon rises.

Time-lapse can be taken with either a regular photo camera or a video camera. Obviously, you want to use a digital camera, so the files are ready to use without any conversion needed. Many photo cameras have the ability to take a photo holding the shutter open for an extended period of time. This is commonly called time exposure photography and technically called *long-exposure photography*.

By holding the shutter open long enough for an object to move, you can create the effect of motion blur (see Figure 13.1). But this is not time-lapse, in that it only creates one image. Time-lapse creates multiple images, so each one is crisp and clear. Playing a sequence of images creates a sense of motion, but without the blur.

Figure 13.1
Motion blur example.

Some cameras have a built-in time-lapse shutter ability where you can set how often a picture is taken, how long the shutter stays open, and how many pictures you want to take. Those who don't have it can purchase an external "shutter controller" that will do this for you. It controls the shutter release on your camera. You should also incorporate a tripod to keep the camera still for the duration of your shoot.

Many digital video cameras also have a time-lapse ability through a feature called *interval recording*. In this case, in the camera's menu, you tell it how many frames you want to shoot each time and how many times you want to do the shoot. Sometimes, it'll just go until either the battery dies or you run out of storage space. Creating a video using a built-in time-lapse feature saves on storage space in your camera. You can still create a time-lapse video in VSX5 of a video captured at regular speed by just speeding up the clip in the Timeline. VSX5 will toss out unnecessary frames at that stage of the process instead. The downside to that is, if you want to shoot a time-lapse sequence and just shorten it afterward, you'll have to shoot for hours to get what you want. Not a very efficient use of storage space.

Creating a Time-Lapse Effect

Y OU'RE GOING TO CONCENTRATE on creating a time-lapse video from a series of photographs from a digital still camera. Included with your lesson files is a folder called Time-lapse. Inside it is a sequence of over 800 digital photos spanning the length of a day overlooking the city of Taipei, Taiwan. Can you imagine having to import all these photos into one of your project libraries?

You probably remember that you can import media straight into the Timeline, bypassing libraries, via the File > Insert Media File to Timeline command > (Insert video, digital media, and so on). VSX5 has an additional choice, called Insert Photo for Time-lapse/Strobe. The command in this process will also give you additional options, specifically geared toward time-lapse.

You might be wondering why you just can't import the photos to the Timeline using the normal File > Insert Media File to Timeline command > Insert Photo. You can, but the issue here is that each photo would be placed on the Timeline for a duration of 3 seconds (90 frames). Doing it this way would make your video 41 minutes long! Using the VSX5 Time-lapse feature makes each image last only one frame.

Now that you understand what time-lapse is and how it works, it's time to put this into practice. To create a Time-lapse effect in VSX5, follow these steps.

1. Open VSX5 as a new project. Save it as **MyTimeLapse**. Create a custom library called **Chapter 13** and open it. You'll use this library to save all the movies you'll create in this chapter.

2. Select File > Insert Media File to Timeline > Insert Photo for Time-lapse/Strobe. Locate and open the Time-lapse folder. Just in case there are other files in there you won't need, select JPG from the Files of Type drop-down list. JPG might be near the top of the list instead of in alphabetical order. There are over 800 photo images in this folder.

VSX5's Time-lapse feature can handle up to 10,000 images.

At press time, there was an issue with file name lengths when importing time-lapse images. If you get an error that states your files have too many characters, you have the same issue. You can use the batch processing feature in many image editing applications to shorten the files' names. VSX5 does not have a batch renaming function. I recommend just numbering them starting with 1.

To check whether the fix is available from Corel, open your Corel Guide via the orange circle in the upper-right corner of your screen. Then click the two gears in the upper right of the Corel Guide window and select Check for Updates.

3. Click anywhere in the images window, press Ctrl+A to select all the images, and then click Open. The Time-lapse/Strobe dialog box will appear. (See Figure 13.2.) You'll try this process with different settings so that you can see the differences in the video, but first let's learn about the options. I'll start at the bottom of the window and work up.

Figure 13.2
Time-lapse/Strobe dialog box.

▶ **Total Duration:** At the very bottom, above the OK button, is the total duration of your video, if all the images were used in the Timeline. There are 808 images in the Timeline. 808 divided by 30fps (frames per second and normal video playback speed) equals a video 26 seconds and 28 frames long, or just short of 27 seconds. Watch this number change as the choices above it are altered.

▶ **Frame Duration:** This allows you to set how long that each frame you keep will last on the Timeline.

▶ **Drop:** Displays how many frames you want to discard in between the frames you want to keep.

▶ **Keep field:** Displays how many frames in a row you would like to keep.

▶ **Preview:** You can click the Play button to preview any setting before adding it to the Timeline.

In conclusion, you can tell VSX5 which frames to keep, for how long, and which frames to delete. The limitation is that these settings apply to the entire sequence—you can't designate the display of nonsequential frames. You would have to do this manually in the Timeline, and it would play back weird anyway.

The top portion of the Time-lapse/Strobe window displays one example of what frames are saved when certain options are used.

4. Leave the options at Keep: 1 frame, Drop: 0 frames, and Frame Duration: 0:0:0:1 (1 frame). These are the most basic options and keep all the photos you took at one frame duration each. Click OK.

5. Fit the project in the Timeline window. (See Figure 13.3.) Your Timeline will show a series of many, many vertical lines. Remember there are 808 images in there. By clicking the plus (+) magnifying glass in the upper right of the Timeline, zoom in five times, and you'll finally start seeing individual frames. In the Preview panel, click the Enlarge icon (lower right corner) to play this back at full screen. Play the sequence to preview it. Press the Escape key when done to return to the regular view.

Figure 13.3
Timeline view of 808 images.

Now let's try some different options when you import the sequence of images. Select Undo or Ctrl+Z to empty the Timeline.

1. Repeat steps 2 and 3 to grab the same 808 images again and return to the Time-lapse/ Strobe dialog box.

2. This time, keep one frame and drop four frames. Notice the updated duration, and click OK.

3. Fit the project in the Timeline window and play it back. Notice that even at such a speedy playback, the motion is still pretty smooth. Try playing back at full screen, too. Undo and repeat to return to the Time-lapse/ Strobe dialog box again with the same 808 images.

Creating a Strobe Effect from a Time-Lapse Sequence

BY HOLDING FRAMES (duplicating them) for longer than one frame, you can create the impression of a strobe effect. A strobe effect (think of the 1970s disco scene) will appear to freeze motion with each flash of light, or frame, go out for a time, and then flash again with objects in new locations. This makes videos appear jumpy. The more you hold the frames (or actually duplicate them), and the more frames you drop in between, the jumpier the appearance.

The following steps will show you how to create a strobe video effect using the Time-lapse options.

1. You should have the Time-lapse/Strobe window open from the last section. This time, keep one frame, drop two frames, and increase the duration to four frames (see Figure 13.4). The video remains close to the original length but will now seem to jump from one frame to the next and hold a bit longer. Click OK. Enlarge the view and click Play. Watch the clouds and the cars on the bridge to notice the effect.

2. Undo. This will clear the Timeline again. Reimport the images. This time, increase the previous effect by repeating step one and keeping one frame, dropping four frames, and holding each kept frame for eight frames. Now the effect should be very evident. Click OK and preview this setting as well.

Figure 13.4
Detail of the Time-lapse/Strobe dialog box selections.

3. You cannot, in the current video format, add effects to this sequence of images in the Timeline because each image is treated as a separate clip. You'd be adding effects separately.

    The best thing to do is save it as a video clip and then bring it back into your Timeline to replace what is currently there. Make sure your Chapter 13 library is open. Go to the Share step and click Create Video File. Save the sequence as a WMV > WMV HD 720 30p to your lessons folder. After it's done rendering, it will be placed in your Chapter 13 library and will start playing in the Preview panel.

4. Click the Undo arrow in the Timeline's tool-bar again. If this doesn't empty the Timeline, click anywhere in the Timeline to activate it, press Ctrl+A, and press your Delete key. Bring your new MyTimeLapse.wmv clip from the library into the Timeline.

5. Go to Filter library. Drop the Bubble effect on to the Timeline clip. This effect actually reflects parts of your video into the bubbles. Double-click the Timeline clip to open the Options panel. In the Filter preset drop-down list, double-click the last choice on the second row (see Figure 13.5).

Figure 13.5
Choosing the Bubble effect preset.

6. Click Customize Filter. In the Basic tab on the lower left, adjust Density to 40 and Variation to 80. This will create more bubbles and increase the size variations from small to large. Click OK and preview your movie. It's even better in full-screen mode.

7. From the Filter library again, drop the Brightness & Contrast effect onto the video and choose the last preset in the second row. Preview your video. Save your video with both effects as **Mytime-lapse-effects** using the same WMV choice as last time. Preview it again. Pretty cool, huh?

Creating a Strobe Effect from an Existing Video

YOU CAN ALSO CREATE the same strobe effect using an existing video clip. It will do the same thing that it did with a time-lapse sequence, by dropping some frames and increasing the duration of others.

This technique would not make sense for the city scene we worked on earlier. It's only logical for shorter scenes. You wouldn't want to take a single all-day-long video shot of Taipei, only to drop frames and make it a time-lapse, would you? You would just use the Time-lapse feature instead. The original video would be 18 hours long and take up who knows how much storage space.

1. Clear your Timeline.

2. Open your My New Gallery gallery where the three videos from Kauai are located. If these videos are not in this gallery, please add them from the Videos > Kauai folder. Place all three videos in order (1,2,3) into your Timeline. Fit your project into the Timeline window. Deselect the three clips and reselect just the Kauai1.avi clip. Preview this clip before any adjustments are added.

3. Right-click on the Kauai1 clip in the Timeline and select Speed/Time-lapse. The Speed/Time-lapse dialog box will open (see Figure 13.6). You used this dialog earlier in Chapter 4, when you adjusted the speed of a video clip.

Figure 13.6
Speed/Time-lapse dialog box.

4. Let's alter Kauai1, but try to keep it as close to its original length as possible. The Original clip duration value, in the center of the window, indicates this clip is 52 seconds, 29 frames long, for a total of 1,589 frames. Notice there is not a Drop frames setting. In this case, the Speed setting will take care of this for you. Set the Frame frequency to 4, and click the Preview button at the bottom. A preview will display in the Preview panel in the main window.

Notice the strobe effect that's created. Remember that if you have a frame duration of two frames or more, this will happen because the video pauses, then moves, pauses, then moves, and so on, creating a staccato effect. The effect will only increase with higher frame frequencies.

Also, notice that the duration has remained the same. This happens because you kept the speed at 100%. The Speed setting determined what frames were dropped to maintain the desired speed. Click OK.

5. Right-click on the Kauai2 clip in the Timeline and select Speed/Time-lapse again. Click Preview to see the original. This time, set Frame frequency to 4 frames and the Speed to 200 (type it in, use the arrows, or use the slider) and preview. This really destroys the video and interferes with the audio, too. Not liking it? Return the Frame frequency to 0 frame and preview it. Still not the best, but it's better. Now you know you'll need to consider any audio in a clip when doing any time-lapse effect. Click OK.

6. Right-click on the Kauai3 clip in the Timeline and select Speed/Time-lapse. Click Preview to see the original. This clip just begs for anything to speed it up. Increase the Speed all the way up to 600 and preview it. Increase the Frame frequency to 8 and preview it again. Click OK. All the clips should now reflect their new, mostly shorter, durations.

7. Drop the video filter Fish Eye on to the Kauai3 clip and preview it. Sorry, I couldn't help doing that.

8. Save this project if you like, but we won't be using it again in the book.

In conclusion, you have learned that time-lapse photography and time-lapse video is a combination of increased playback speed and dropped frames. Adding frame durations of longer than one frame, along with higher speed and dropped frames, will create a strobe effect.

Where creating a time-lapse video from a series of photographs can have artistic, but also technical, even scientific purposes, creating one out of an existing video is really just for fun and creativity.

Let's now tackle another big newer feature in VSX5—stop-motion animation.

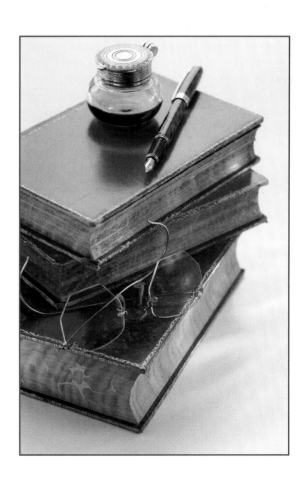

What Is Stop-Motion Animation?

Stop motion, ALSO REFERRED to as *stop action*, is the process of making an object appear to move, when it's normally unable to do so on its own—in other words animating an inanimate object. Examples can be a Transformer toy that transforms from a car to a robot (hint, hint). You know it doesn't do this on its own, but you could take photos of small, incremental position changes at each stage of its transformation. You would move it, take a picture, move it again, take another picture, and so on. If you string these photos together into a video, it would look as if the toy was "transforming" on its own, without any human intervention, assuming of course your hands don't appear in the video! Similar techniques can be applied to action hero figures as well as LEGOs and other objects.

Another example is Claymation. You might be familiar with the Wallace and Gromit cartoons and movies by the famous Claymation expert, Nick Park (www.wallaceandgromit.com). Claymation originates from the process of molding each character from clay.

Claymation is popular because of the ease with which you can create and pose unlimited characters and objects. Stop motion can be an extremely tedious process, especially for something so exacting as Claymation. You need to determine how many frames each position needs in order to make the animation look realistic, as well as how much to reshape an object so it doesn't look like it's moving too fast or too slow. The big plus side to this cool technique is its low cost; anyone can do it using even household objects. You can even practice stop motion animation by making a coin move across the table (hint, hint again).

Stop Motion in VSX5

CREATING STOP MOTION in VSX5 is a record/capture process; therefore, you'll be working in the VSX5 Capture step for this section. It will also be necessary for you to have a capture device, such as either a digital video camera or a webcam. Obviously, a DV camera would be easier to maneuver and position for the best shots, but in a pinch, a webcam can still work for you.

VSX5's Stop Motion animation feature works with any webcam supporting Microsoft's DirectShow media capture and playback architecture.

If you have a DV camera, connect it to your PC as described in Chapter 4 in the section, "Importing via the Capture Tab." You will not need a storage device (e.g., mini-disc or DV tape), because you'll be capturing directly to your PC. If you don't have an external device connected, but only have a webcam and it's either connected or built in, VSX5 will recognize it instead and turn it on automatically, using it by default for this feature. If you have both, you will be able to select which one you want to use via a drop-down list when you launch the stop-motion operation.

Remember that the idea of stop-motion animation is to create motion out of something where no motion is expected or naturally occurring. There are no demo clips included to work with here—you are on your own, but with my guidance, of course! You'll create two levels of stop motion. You will need your dining room table or a similar surface that has at least a 2x2-foot square area cleared so objects can move around without interference. Don't worry about background noise, because this process does not capture audio.

The first attempt will be an easy one using the Auto Capture technique and some coins moving around your table. For this, you'll need four quarters and a silver dollar, or five pennies and a nickel.

The second test will be using the manual capture feature, so you'll have more time to set up each scene. This allows you to use a more complex object to reposition, such as a Transformer toy (what I'll be using). You could also use a Rubik's Cube to show how to solve it (I won't be using one of those; I'm not that smart) or a jigsaw puzzle in the act of being completed (could take you awhile, so maybe a small puzzle).

Capturing Stop-Motion Automatically

These steps for the automatic technique may seem intimidating at first, but you can repeat them until you're happy with the results. I want you to learn this method because it will make the manual process seem SO much easier. This method is perfect if you're comfortable with repositioning your objects quickly.

1. Create a new project. There's no need to save your time-lapse project, unless you want to.

2. Go to the Capture step and select Stop Motion (see Figure 13.7). The Stop Motion window will open (see Figure 13.8).

Figure 13.7
Launching the Stop Motion feature.

Figure 13.8
The Stop Motion window.

Figure 13.9
Enable Auto Capture button.

3. At the top, name your project **Coin Duel**. If you're using just your webcam, it will turn on automatically and you should see yourself. (Eeek!) If you have a digital video camera connected, turn it to the Record position (VSX5 will take a moment to discover it) and VSX5 will ask if you want to use this device. If you click Yes, give it a minute or two, and its view will show up in the Stop Motion Preview window, replacing the webcam view. You may also choose your desired device from the drop-down list in the top-right corner of the Stop Motion window. My screenshot already shows my coin duel setup on my dining room table.

4. In the drop-down list adjacent to Save to Library, select Chapter 13. If you forgot to create this library, click the plus sign (+) to the right of this list to add a new library folder and name it **Chapter 13**.

5. Next to Auto Capture, select Enable Auto Capture (the "|" button on the left). See Figure 13.9.

6. Click the Set Time button to the right, as shown in Figure 13.10. In the Capture Settings dialog box, set Capture Frequency to 0:0:5 (5 seconds). Set the Total Capture Duration to 0:1:15 (1 min, 15 seconds). These settings will provide you with 15 shots, each taken 5 seconds apart. Click OK to close the Capture Settings window and return to the Stop Motion window.

Leave the Onion Skin slider where it is. This feature allows you to set a transparency of the previous shot, and at the same time, compare the previous shot to the shot you're about to take. (See Figure 13.11.) Think of the term *onion skin* as akin to using tracing paper that allows you to draw while seeing the previous image underneath, which you can use as a reference.

#2 **#1**

Figure 13.10
Stop Motion feature Capture Settings dialog box.

I would suggest grabbing a pencil and blank piece of paper to storyboard your 15 shots (see Figure 13.12). It need not be elaborate at all; it's just enough planning so you can quickly refer to it and create your moves in the set time. If you need more time, feel free to increase the capture frequency. You'll also need to increase the total capture time to compensate. Take the frame duration and multiply it by how many frames you want to arrive at the total frame duration (e.g., 5 seconds frame duration $\times$ 15 shots = 75 sec, or 1 minute, 15 seconds). It might be easier to attempt the settings listed here first, and then try yours afterward.

Figure 13.11
Onion Skin feature.

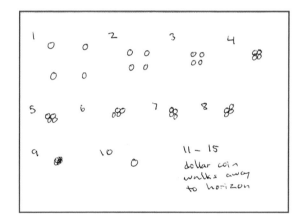

Figure 13.12
Simple storyboard.

7. Read through this step *completely* first before attempting.

After you click the red Record button (centered under the Preview window), the first frame will be captured immediately, so make sure it's positioned correctly. After that, you'll have 5 seconds to move the coins into their next position before the next shot is captured. Each captured shot will be instantly deposited into the tray at the bottom of the Stop Motion window. This can be a tough process, because one mistake will throw off your whole sequence; but try it anyway. You won't hurt anything by trying, and you can always start over.

Last frame　　　Captured frames

Figure 13.13
Completed captured frames.

Tip

You might consider extending the duration of your planned capture, adding an additional 10–15 frames (2–3 shutter clicks), to give you some room for error. You can always delete unwanted frames after the capture is complete.

When your coins are in the starting position (refer back to Figure 13.8), and you're mentally and physically prepared to reposition the coins after each shot, click the Record button. Keep repositioning after each shot, and be sure to get your hands out of the way. Watch for the new frame to appear in the tray and then reposition your coins again, until all 15 frames are captured into the tray.

The recording will stop automatically when the total set time has been reached. All the frames you captured will appear in the tray (see Figure 13.13).

Did you do it? If not, don't be discouraged. (I SO did not do it right the first time either, or the second time). If you're going to try again, select all the captured frames in the tray, right-click and choose Delete, and then repeat this step again. You won't be doing anything wrong by trying again.

8. If you want to keep what you've captured, click the Save button on the bottom right of the Stop Motion capture window. Click Exit to leave the Stop Motion window and return to the Capture step window. You will see your new capture movie in the Capture library with a file extension of .UISX (the Ulead Image Sequence capture file format).

9. Return to the Edit step. Your animation will be visible in the Chapter 13 library (assuming that library was open beforehand). Add the .UISX file to the Timeline, and then fit the project to the Timeline window. Right-click on the Timeline clip to access the context menu (see Figure 13.14). Items to note:

A. You can no longer adjust the Speed/Time-lapse of this clip in its current format.

B. You can edit the clip by right-clicking on it in the Timeline and choosing Edit in Stop Motion from the context menu. You may want to do this to delete unwanted frames or add additional ones to the end.

C. Because this is an image sequence in a video container, as opposed to an actual movie clip, you can still split the animation back into its separate images.

Figure 13.14
UISX Options menu.

10. I think this coin animation goes a little too fast. We can't adjust the speed in the Timeline, so do we need to start all over? Nope. Right-click on the clip and choose Edit in Stop Motion. Click OK in the warning box.

11. Adjust the Image Duration to 10 frames At the bottom of the screen, click Save, and then Exit. The Timeline clip will double in length and, when previewed, will play at half speed.

12. Try adding video effects for additional flair. Try FX Ripple or Kaleidoscope or Light or RotoSketch.

13. Go to the Share step. Create Video File > WMV > WMV HD 720 30p. Name it **MyStopMotion1**. As an option, when it's finished rendering, replace the clip currently in the Timeline with the new movie you just made and that is now in your library. Afterward, if you right-click on the clip in the Timeline, you'll see that the normal video options appear, as well as in the Options panel.

Capturing Stop-Motion Manually

I'm about to make the previous section a whole lot easier for you by letting you snap Stop Motion frames when *you're* ready, not when the timer says so. You have to promise, though, that you'll find a much more complex item to maneuver. I would like you to find an object that will look cool animating forward as well as backward. I used a Transformer robot toy. What? You think I'm kidding?

1. Return to the Stop Motion window (via the Capture step). Choose either your webcam or your digital video camera to use again.

2. Set up your object for the first frame. Name your animation **MyStopMotion2**. Set your image duration to 10 frames. Click the Disable Auto Capture button (see Figure 13.15). Now you will not need to hurry up and position your objects between frames; you can take your time.

Told you I had a Transformer!   Disable Auto-Capture

Figure 13.15
Disabling the Auto Capture option.

3. When you're ready for the first shot, click the red Record button. It will snap only one frame. Keep doing this through one sequence of building *or* breaking down your object. Either build it *or* break it down, but don't go both ways; you won't need to. You'll see what I mean shortly.

4. When you're finished, click Save, and then Exit. You can just click Exit, too, and it'll ask if you want to save the animation.

Tip

You'll notice that after the first frame is shot, the Preview window dims somewhat. This occurs because the Onion Skin feature switches on. If you want to compare the previous frame without the Onion Skin feature, you can either move the slider all the way to the left, or just click the previous (or any) frame in the tray, and it will turn off temporarily. Click the Record button just once to return to capture mode and turn Onion Skin back on. Click Record again to take the next shot.

5. Return to the Edit step and make sure your new stop-motion animation is in your library. It should be titled MyStopMotion2.uisx. Clear your Timeline and place your new clip into it. Fit the project in the Timeline window. Drop the same clip again at the end of the first one. You should have two of the same MyStopMotion2.uisx clips in a row. Fit your project in the Timeline window.

6. Select the second clip in the Timeline. In the Options panel, select Reverse Video. Rewind and preview your project. Your object (and my Transformer) will now build up and break down in one sequence. Save it as a .WMV video as before, if you desire.

I put examples of my time-lapse and stop motion animations in the Lessons folder in a folder titled Examples. It's nothing professional; I just used the same tools and instructions I've covered in this chapter. In case you were wondering, for this last sequence, I used the Transformer called Cliffjumper.

So, there you go. Along with the Painting Creator, the Time-lapse and Stop Motion features are probably the coolest and most fun features you'll find in VSX5. Hopefully, this chapter has taken the fear out of attempting these features on your own. As with all software, you can't break anything by trying. You can either undo steps or delete entire processes and start over. If you feel you were overwhelmed by this chapter, go through it again. I guarantee that feeling will pass.

Can you distinguish the difference between time-lapse photography and stop-motion animation? Time-lapse captures real objects and places going through their processes. Normally lasting hours or days, this process shortens them to minutes or seconds, so you can see what occurs much more quickly, saving time and storage space.

Stop-motion animation creates motion from inanimate objects by manually adjusting them to create a sense of motion or activity. This can be for entertainment (Claymation), simulation (my Transformer animation), or for training purposes (product assembly).

The next chapter will cover other advanced features. Although they may seem simpler and perhaps less creative in nature, they are no less important; in fact, they're perhaps even more important for purposes of efficiency and group collaboration.

Quick Quiz

1. Describe time-lapse photography. (See "What Is Time-Lapse Photography?")

2. In time-lapse, what is the result of increasing frame durations? (See "Creating a Strobe Effect from a Time-Lapse Sequence.")

3. Describe Stop Motion animation. (See "What Is Stop-Motion Animation?")

4. What is the Onion Skin feature used for? (See "Capturing Stop-Motion Automatically.")

5. What was the name of the Transformer toy I used for the Stop Motion example? (See "Capturing Stop-Motion Manually.")

Advanced
Features

THIS CHAPTER ON ADVANCED features brings you close to the end of learning all there is to know about capturing and editing your videos in VideoStudio Pro X5. VSX5 has many extra features that, if it weren't for this book, you might not even bother to explore. While they're not necessary for creating a quality video production for the beginner to intermediate videographer, they can make finishing and sharing your projects quicker and easier.

Here are some of the features I'll cover in this chapter:

▶ Creating **custom mask frames** will add further customization to overlays.

▶ Making your own **screensaver** will allow you to advance your creativity beyond videos.

▶ **Batch conversion** takes out the monotony of file maintenance and reduces the time of processing multiple files individually.

- Creating a **Smart Package** will organize your projects in a way that makes it easier to share with colleagues, so that they, too, can work on them.

- **Smart Proxy Manager** makes working with large HD video files a breeze by avoiding the sluggish performance normally associated with editing and previewing such memory hogging files.

- The **Movie Template Manager** will help you create reusable settings when sharing your movies.

Although titled "Advanced Features," the topics covered in this chapter are all very easy to use. Let's try them out.

Creating a Custom Mask Frame

BACK IN CHAPTER 7, in the section "Applying a Mask Effect," I made mention of the ability to import and apply your own custom masks created in image editing software. Here are the steps for creating a custom mask frame in Corel's Painter application. I used Painter because of the abstract painting effect I could easily create, and I really enjoy using it. You could also consider Microsoft Paint, Corel PaintShop Pro, or Adobe's Photoshop.

1. Open up Painter or one of the other apps I mentioned above. Open a new canvas/file/window and size it as follows: Width = 800, Height = 500, and 300 pixels per inch.

2. Use the paint bucket to fill the canvas with black.

3. Select a paintbrush. Use a Gouache or Felt Pen to make a solid mask. Use something like a Real Bristle or Impressionist brush to make a variable patterned fill. Select white as your brush color.

4. You can paint your mask shape something similar to what's shown in Figure 14.1. Remember that your video will show completely through anything that you paint white. It will not show at all anywhere that is black. It will also show through anywhere there's a shade of grey, but only to a certain degree. The closer the color is to white, the more of your video will show. The opposite is true where the color is closer to black. This is how masks work. The more white, the more you see.

Figure 14.1
Custom mask created in Corel Painter.

#2   #1

Figure 14.2
Change to Overlay Track 2.

5. Save the file as **Mymask.BMP** to your saved lessons folder. If you can't save as a BMP, a good backup format is PNG. If you like, I've saved this example, called VSX5_Mask, in the Other folder inside your VSX5_Lesson Plans folder.

6. Open your VSX5 Chapter 10 project and save it as **Chapter 14**.

7. Toward the end of your project, directly under your second Painting Creator file, add the intro family.jpg image (from your Balloon Trip library) to Overlay Track 2. Make the length match that of the clips above it.

8. In the Preview panel, make the image smaller and tuck it down to the lower-left corner (see Figure 14.2).

9. Double-click the intro family.jpg image in the Timeline. In the Attribute panel, click Mask & Chroma Key.

10. Check Apply Overlay Options and then Mask Frame from the Type drop-down list.

11. To the right of the Mask library, click the plus sign (+).

12. Import your BMP mask image. Click OK in the Convert dialog box.

13. Your new mask frame is now in the Mask Frame list and is automatically applied to your overlay clip (see Figure 14.3).

And that is how custom mask frames are done!

Applied here

Imported here

Figure 14.3
Adding a custom mask frame.

Saving Time with Batch Conversion

BATCH CONVERSION IS A great time-saver and available in many applications that work with images, videos, or any other large collections of files. It accomplishes what the name implies: the Batch Convert feature allows you to quickly and easily convert a large number of video files to another video file format, instead of doing it one by one.

The Batch Convert feature also lets you convert VSX5 projects into finished video files. This is the same as going through the Share step, but it will do it to multiple projects and apply the same settings all at once. The options provided to you here are the same ones available when you export a movie through the Share step.

1. Go to the File menu and select Batch Convert (see Figure 14.4). This will take you directly to the Batch Convert dialog box.

Figure 14.4
Accessing the Batch Convert feature.

2. Click the Add button in the upper-right corner. In the Open Video File dialog, click the Files of Type drop-down list to view all the file types that can be converted. Notice that they are all video or animation file formats. Keep the All Formats option selected. Locate and select the five videos in the Lake Tahoe folder of your Lessons video folder. Click Open.

3. In the Batch Convert dialog box, click the Browse button (the icon with the 3 dots) to the right of the Save in Folder field (see Figure 14.5). Create a new folder called **Converted** within your Lessons folder. Click OK.

Figure 14.5
Saving your files.

4. Choose MPEG-4 Files from the Save as type drop-down list. Click the Options button to set the video save options. Since you won't actually be using the converted files, you don't need to add them to a VSX5 library. Keep the Save to Library box unchecked.

5. Next, click the General tab, and choose Video Only from the Data Track drop-down list. Select Frame Size > Standard > 720×480. Change the Frame Rate to 29.970, the same rate as the source videos. Review the other choices but leave them unchanged. For the correct settings, see Figure 14.6. Click OK to close only the Video Save Options dialog box.

Figure 14.6
Video Save Options dialog box.

Figure 14.7
Task Report dialog box.

6. Click Convert. After the rendering has completed, the Task Report dialog box should indicate that all the files were successfully converted (see Figure 14.7). Click OK to close the Task Report dialog. Compare the file sizes from the original .AVI ones to the new MPEG ones. Tahoe1 should have been reduced from 66.7 MB down to 2.38 MB. Feel free to play both movies and notice, not surprisingly, that there are trade-offs in quality.

Let's do a batch conversion with a couple of the chapter projects you've created. This technique is great if you have a bunch of projects that all need to be shared at the same settings, perhaps for a website, wedding videos, or a corporate marketing campaign.

1. Return to File > Batch Convert. In the Batch Convert dialog, add the following projects: Chapter 8, Chapter 10, Chapter 14. (You should have these saved in your VSX5 Saved Lessons folder.) Click Open.

2. In the Batch Convert dialog box, this time choose QuickTime Movie Files from the Save as type drop-down list.

3. Click the Options button, and in the General tab, choose a standard frame size of 720×480. Keep all other choices at their defaults. Click OK and click Convert. Your files should still be saved to the Converted folder you made earlier. When finished, play one of the files to preview it.

Creating a Smart Package

REMEMBER WHEN I discussed the project file that VSX5 creates and how it only contains pointers to the media files it uses and instructions on how to use them? Also, remember that if any of the media files are moved on your PC that the library files would then show up as broken links and you then have to reestablish the links manually?

This becomes a major issue when working in a collaborative environment, whether it be a multimedia team at work, an outside advertising agency, or even just transferring your project to a different computer (e.g., from work to home). If you're missing just one file, then the project screeches to a halt until that file is found and returned to its proper location, creating time and cost delays. This is where the Smart Package feature can help.

Creating a Smart Package is a very simple task, but it's a huge time and stress saver. Instead of just saving the project, Smart Package saves the project and all the associated files that go with it into a single folder. A Smart Package will ensure that there are no missing files or broken links. A nice bonus is that it doesn't move any of your original files but instead makes copies of them so that the original ones stay where you have them.

You can even "zip" (or compress) the package if you like, making it even smaller. This newer feature in VSX5 provides the ability to save either uncompressed files or compressed files to save space. Compressed files are saved in the ubiquitous Corel WinZip format. Another benefit is that the compressed package is reduced to one file, instead of

a folder of multiple files. You'll try both in this section in order to see the differences.

The following steps will guide you through this career-saving feature of using Smart Packages to gather your files and save them in a convenient folder or single file.

1. In your Chapter 14 project, select File > Smart Package (see Figure 14.8). VSX5 might ask you to save your project again.

Figure 14.8
Opening the Smart Package feature.

2. In the Smart Package dialog box (see Figure 14.9), make sure the Folder radio button is chosen. Create a location for your folder. (I created a folder called MySmartPackages in VSX5 Saved Lessons.) Insert the name **Chapter14Pkg** in both the Project folder name and the Project file name fields.

Figure 14.9
The Smart Package dialog box.

3. In the lower portion, you'll see information displayed about your Smart Package, including the number of files it will gather and the resulting size of the folder. Click OK to create the Smart Package. You will receive a confirmation of its success.

In VSX5, create a new project. Under File > Open Project, locate and open the Chapter14pkg.vsp file in the folder you just created. The project opens completely and without any broken links. You can now hand this entire folder off to someone else and be assured that all the files involved in your project will be included and will open correctly.

Outside of VSX5, open the folder that contains your Smart Package. All your project files are also now in there, copied from wherever they are on your PC. Talk about convenience!

Now I'll show you how to use and compare the WinZip option.

1. Return to VSX5 and select File > Smart Package. In the Smart Package dialog box, select the Zip file radio button instead of Folder. Insert the name **Chapter14PkgZip** in both the Project Folder Name and the Project File Name fields. Click OK.

2. In the Zip Project Package window that displays, click the Change Compression button. Legacy Compression will ensure that anyone with the WinZip application will be able to open the file, even very old versions. If you know that others involved in your project have a more recent version of WinZip, choose the Best Method option. That way, you'll be assured of maximum file size savings. If you're familiar with the individual compression choices, feel free to choose the last choice and then choose your desired compression method from the list. I chose the Best Method option for my project.

3. If you'll be transferring your files via email or a small capacity thumb drive, you may opt to split the file sizes into smaller chunks by using the Split Zip File option. When you've chosen your desired options, click OK to create your zipped Smart Package.

It's possible that you may not see any file size savings. Digital videos, JPGs, and MP3s are already compressed files.

The Smart Proxy Manager

HIGH-DEFINITION (HD) files can be four times larger (or more) than their standard-definition counterparts. Working with large HD files can bring your PC to a slow crawl when scrolling the Timeline and previewing HD clips, especially when filters and overlay layers are involved.

The main purpose of the Smart Proxy feature in VSX5 is to improve your editing experience when working with these large, high-resolution (or even large standard-resolution) files. When you edit and preview files above a certain size, Smart Proxy will kick in and use substitute files that are lower in resolution and file size.

This will make scrolling the Timeline faster and previewing clips smoother. This feature is especially useful when working with a less than optimal video editing computer and when using HDV, AVCHD, and Blu-ray video clips. When your project is shared, VideoStudio will resort back to and render your project using the original larger, higher quality files.

Follow along with these steps to learn how to take advantage of the Smart Proxy feature.

1. Open a new, blank project.

2. Go to Settings > Smart Proxy Manager > and check Enable Smart Proxy (see Figure 14.10). You can also do this in the next step; this is just a shortcut you should know about.

Figure 14.10
Enabling the Smart Proxy feature.

3. Go to Settings > Smart Proxy Manager > Settings. This is the same window you'll see if you go to Settings > Preferences > Performance. Because of step 2, Enable Smart Proxy will already be checked.

4. Since the largest files that are included in the lessons are 720×480, you need to lower the minimum file size limit that Smart Proxy will work on so Smart Proxy will kick in when it detects files larger than that. In the Video Size drop-down list, select 352×240. This is the smallest size that Smart Proxy will work with. Uncheck Auto Generate Proxy Template. Click OK.

5. Open your Balloon Trip library; then Shift-select the six original HD video clips and only the video clips (clips Balloon-2 through Balloon-7). Skip the Painting Creator movies and the ones you created from the project.

6. Follow this step quickly with step 7. Place all the selected video files in one step, into the main video track of the Timeline.

7. Quickly open Settings > Smart Proxy Manager > Smart Proxy Queue Manager. This dialog box shows you the progress of VSX5 creating those smaller sized proxy files to work with in the Timeline (see Figure 14.11). Let it complete its job. When the Queue Manager is finished, the list should be empty, and your files are now listed in the Smart Proxy File Manager. Click OK to close the Queue Manager.

Tip

The Queue Manager does not have to remain open for this process to continue. I just want you to observe the process.

SmartProxy will not automatically create proxy files if the videos are already on the Timeline. Be sure to enable SmartProxy before you add your video content to the Timeline.

Figure 14.11
Smart Proxy Queue Manager.

8. In the main Video library, right-click on Balloon2.mpg and choose Properties. Note the file size. In this case, it's almost 23 MB. Click OK.

9. Go to Settings > Smart Proxy Manager > Smart Proxy File Manager (see Figure 14.12). This dialog box shows the results of the Smart Proxy process. These are the file sizes of the clips currently in the Timeline. Which ones do you think will respond better during editing and previewing? Until you delete them from this list, the smart proxies will remain and will continue to be used when added to the Timeline.

Figure 14.12
Smart Proxy Manager dialog box.

Using the Movie Template Manager

MOVIE TEMPLATES IN VSX5 are presets used to create multiple final movies for the same purpose, a template for creating a movie a certain way, size, format, and so on. Currently, the Share step > Create Video File list only contains choices for particular file formats, screen sizes, and destinations. What if you're always creating files for your website that you want to have a consistent look and feel from video to video?

Wouldn't it be nice to choose a template that would use all the appropriate option settings with just one click instead of going through and setting all your required options each and every time? That's what the Template Manager allows you to do. Let's have you create one.

10. To delete any of the proxies, click the check-box to the left of any of them and then click Delete selected proxy files in the lower left. Click Exit when finished.

1. Go to Settings > Make Movie Templates Manager and click New.

2. Choose QuickTime Movie Files from the File Format list. Name your template **For My Website**. Click OK.

3. In the Template Options window that shows up next, notice that you can create files of a specific size. This is helpful for sites designed for users with limited bandwidth, companies that set file size limits, or those who may not have the capabilities of using a streaming server. Leave it unchecked.

4. In the General tab, choose a frame size of Standard > 320×240.

5. In the Compression tab, choose Video under the Compression drop-down list. Click OK. Close the Make Movie Template Manager window.

6. Open your Chapter 14 project without saving the current one. Go to the Share step. Click on Create Video File. At the bottom of the list is your newly created For My Website option (see Figure 14.13). Notice that QuickTime is already selected as the file type. Name your file **MyWebsiteMovie** and click Save. Locate the new file and notice the difference in size.

Figure 14.13
New video file template.

60P/50P Editing

THE LAST ADVANCED FEATURE is also new in VSX5. It involves the ability to capture higher frame rates from advanced cameras. If you have a video camera that captures at rates of 50 or 60 frames per second (fps), you can set your preferences to accept these rates. Simply go to Settings > Enable 60P/50P editing. If you don't set this ability and you attempt to edit a 50 or 60 fps file, your video will be truncated.

Quick Quiz

1. What colors are used to create a custom mask frame? (See "Creating a Custom Mask Frame.")

2. What's the main benefit of using the Batch Convert feature? (See "Saving Time with Batch Conversion.")

3. What's the main benefit of saving your project as a Smart Package? (See "Creating a Smart Package.")

4. When is using the Smart Proxy Manager helpful? (See "The Smart Proxy Manager.")

5. How does the Movie Template Manager make outputting your movie easier? (See "Using the Movie Template Manager.")

Sharing Your
Videos

AS I MENTIONED AT THE START of the last chapter, you've learned just about all you can learn about creating awesome videos in VSX5, but that won't do you much good until you learn how to share them with the world. You've touched on it with some basic .wmv videos and others in recent chapters, but there's so much more! You know that there are three steps in VideoStudio: Capture, Edit, and Share. It's time to delve into the Share step with fervor. The Share step will give you opportunities to send your videos to all corners of the digital universe—including video and audio files, regular movies and DVDs, standard definition and high definition—and to export to something as big as your TV or as small as your video iPod. You can create movies for YouTube, Vimeo, Flickr, Facebook, and even make 3D movies!

The advantage of the way VSX5 organizes the Share step for video neophytes and intermediate hobbyists is that it lets you choose the destination or file type first, rather than a particular file format. You only need to know where you want your video to play or what category of file you want, such as video or sound, regular file or DVD, standard or HD, for Facebook or YouTube or your iPhone. From there, you select the appropriate options to set dimensions and frame speed, interlaced or progressive, and so on.

After these choices are made, VSX5 will select the details, such as video and audio compression, on its own. You can still choose your own details if you like through the options and custom settings, but you don't have to.

Finishing Your Movie

THE FIRST THING YOU NEED to do is make some final adjustments to the Balloon Trip project to make it complete and ready for prime time use. Many of the current scene changes are rather abrupt, so you'll need to create some smoother transitions and perhaps some pauses so the viewer can grasp a scene before it changes to the next one. This will also help you review some of the things you've learned so far.

1. Open the Chapter 15 project and save it as **Final_movie**.

2. Make sure that Ripple Editing is enabled on all your tracks. All the little padlocks should be locked.

3. Extend both the first black color chip in the background video track and the first text clip in the title track to 6 seconds.

4. Double-click the text clip you just extended to bring it up in the Preview panel. The first block of text should be selected (Our Summer Balloon Trip). Go to the Attribute tab in the Options panel.

5. Select the Double-T icon adjacent to the animation drop-down list. In the Pop-Up Animation dialog box, choose Intermediate in the Pause list. See Figure 15.1. Click OK.

Figure 15.1
Creating a title pause duration.

6. Repeat step 5 with the lower block of text in the same clip. This will ensure that the entire text clip will animate on entry, and then pause for effect, before moving to the next scene.

7. Also, add an intermediate pause duration to the text under the pickup truck video clip.

8. Above the ending Star Wars credits, add a black color chip to the main video track right before the other black color chip. Set it to only a 1-second duration. Because Ripple Editing is set, this will move the ending credits forward 1 second, creating a short pause before the credits roll.

Preview the part of the project just before the appearance of the pickup truck. See how it ends abruptly and jumps right to the truck clip? Let me show you how you can fix this.

1. Select the MAP image in the background video track (not the overlay track). In the Preview panel, click the End button to move the playback head to the end of the MAP clip. This also happens to be the same frame where the other three clips in the overlay tracks under it end.

2. Click Project to view all the clips at this particular time. Open your Balloon Trip library. Go to Edit > Take a Snapshot. (See Figure 15.2.) This will save a BMP of that frame and deposit it in your Balloon Trip library. If you don't see it at first, make sure all the file types are set to be visible at the top of your gallery (video, graphics, audio). (VSX5 will save it as some weird, unrelated name again. Don't bother changing it.)

Figure 15.2
Saving a snapshot frame.

3. From the library, drag the BMP file into the main video track right before the Balloon-2 video. Leave the clip at its default duration of 3 seconds. Drop a crossfade transition between the snapshot and Balloon-2 (see Figure 15.3). This will again move all other clips directly below it forward, creating a 3-second pause between the map and the next video clips.

4. Save your project. You are now ready to create a video file.

#2   #3   #1

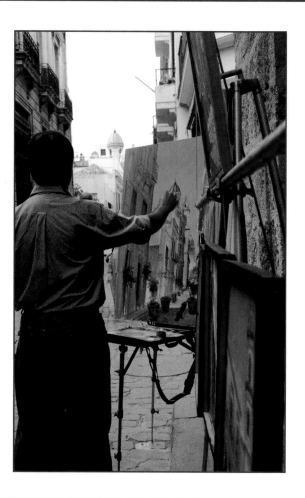

Figure 15.3
Using a snapshot to create a pause.

Creating a Video File

T HE FIRST EXPORT OPTION in the Share step, Create Video File, outputs single, all-in-one video files for multiple destinations in your choice of file formats. You first choose the file type, and then such items as the dimensions and frame rate, video or slideshow, or mobile device type.

Go to the Share step and click Create Video File. As I go through the following list, feel free to expand each Create Video File selection by pausing your cursor over it and viewing the fly-out list to the right of each choice to see the more specific choices available. (See Figure 15.4.)

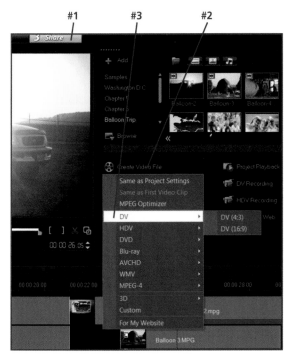

Figure 15.4
Viewing Create Video File options.

▶ **Same as Project Settings:** This is a great choice if you want to create a movie with the same dimensions as your project settings. This takes all the guesswork out of trying to determine these settings manually. Your project will be saved as either an MPEG or AVI file, depending on the choice you set in Settings > Project Properties.

▶ **Same as First Video Clip:** Ensures that all other clips in your Timeline conform to the first clip you used. This will only work, though, if you have a video clip as the first clip in your Timeline. It will not work for this project because it has a color chip as the first clip.

▶ **MPEG Optimizer:** Analyzes and finds the best MPEG settings or the Optimal project settings profile to use and maintains the quality of your project. As an additional feature, you can now specify the target file size of your output to comply with file size limitations for your desired output. The MPEG Optimizer automatically detects changes in your project and renders out only the edited portions for faster rendering times. MPEG Optimizer also works for HD MPEGs that use the AVCHD codec (Blu-ray, AVCHD, etc.) and come out as M2t or mts files. It will render your movie once and only once. If, though, you rendered your video and *then* rendered it again with the MPEG Optimizer, it would rerender the same items again. You can also set a maximum file size. I'll expand on this in the section "Using the MPEG Optimizer" later in the chapter.

▶ **DV:** Creates standard definition AVI movies in either standard (4:3) or widescreen views (16:9).

(4:3) for standard and (16:9) for widescreen refers to the aspect ratio of your movie screen. For example, in standard, for every 4 inches across, there are 3 inches of height. For widescreen, there are 16 inches of width for every 9 inches of height.

▶ **HDV:** Creates high-definition MPEG movies at different fields (720, 1080), interlaced (i) or progressive (p), and for TVs or PCs. Again, choose your options, and VSX5 will do the rest.

▶ **DVD:** Creates single-file movies in the DVD standard MPEG-2 format, but it won't send you through the disc editing and burning process. This allows you to create movies with DVD settings ahead of time. Combine them later with other MPEG-2 movies to create a longer DVD in your Timeline, and the project settings will already be done. You can then use the Create Disc option to add menus and chapters.

▶ **Blu-ray:** Creates movies in the MPEG Transport Stream (.m2t) format and a higher compressed setting than web formats.

▶ **AVCHD:** This is still the most popular output today for homemade HD videos. They can be burned to a regular DVD or copied back to an AVCHD camcorder.

▶ **WMV:** This is the preferred file format for playback on your PCs, but it creates larger files due to less compression.

▶ **MPEG-4:** This is the best choice when you need the smallest file possible for things like iPods, iPhones, PSPs, Android devices, and so on. There are even a couple choices that will keep the resolution at HD (H.264) for you.

▶ **3D:** This is a newer feature in VSX5, and a darn cool one at that. It will create two kinds of 3D content. The first can be viewed with those paper glasses of old (with one red lens and one cyan lens), which are also the glasses most commonly used to view printed 3D images. The other type of 3D is the kind used in the new 3D HD TVs. The 3D feature here will save movies for DVDs (MPEG-2), Blu-ray, AVCHD, and WMV (see Figure 15.5). (See the section "Exporting to 3D" later in this chapter, where you'll get to make both file types.)

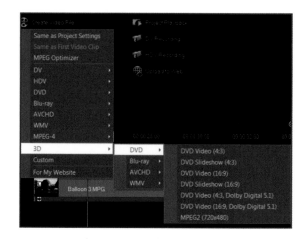

Figure 15.5
3D DVD choices.

▶ **Custom:** Allows you to create video files not found in the main list (see Figure 15.6). These include AVI, 3GPP (for 3G phones), AutoDesk animation files, QuickTime, and others. After making a choice, use the Options button to narrow your settings.

Figure 15.6
Custom output choices.

Figure 15.7
File size comparisons.

Let's try out some of these options to practice the various ways of creating single video files for playback on various digital devices.

1. Under Create Video File, select Same as Project Settings and save your movie into a new folder called **Final_movies** in your VSX5 Saved Lessons folder. Name the file **Same_Settings_Movie**. Click Save.

2. Save your movie again as WMV > WMV HD 720 30p. Name it **Wmv_Movie**.

3. Create another one using MPEG-4 > MPEG-4 HD. Name it **MPEG4-HD_Movie**.

4. Create another one using MPEG-4 > iPod MPEG-4. Name it **iPod_Movie**.

5. Preview all the movie types for quality differences and compare all the file sizes (see Figure 15.7). Although the HD file is the biggest, the WMV one is close behind. MPEG4-HD is still highly compressed while keeping it in HD quality, so it's still a larger file size, but the Web > YouTube HD has a lower resolution (1280×720) and bit rate as well as different audio settings. It's the HD file type that YouTube uses for its HD files. The iPod one is the smallest. The WMV movie is larger than the Same_Settings movie; while Same_Settings also uses MPEG compression (Project Properties), it also throws away more data than WMV.

Tip

It's impossible to cover all the recommendations here for each situation in which you might need to create a video file. There are just too many possibilities. I recommend Googling a situation such as, "Videos for the web," to learn more.

Don't be afraid to ask your friends who may have video experience, too. Try the Corel User to User Web Board on Corel VideoStudio (see Appendix B). That and your own experience will get you where you need to be. Take each accomplishment as a learning experience, and don't be afraid to experiment with different selections. After all, they're only a bunch of bits that you can delete if it doesn't work, and then you can try something different.

Creating a Video File of a Portion of the Project

IF YOU HAVE A LARGE PROJECT and want to share just a portion of it, you can. You may want to do this to have someone else examine just a portion of it for recommendations, to create a preview trailer, or to split the video into multiple parts to email them more easily.

1. Move your Timeline to the end of HD-Travel_Start. This is done most easily by selecting the clip in the Timeline and clicking the End button in the Preview panel. Select Project so that all tracks will be previewed and saved.

2. In the Preview panel, set a Mark-Out point. This sets a preview range (see Figure 15.8).

Figure 15.8
Setting a preview range.

3. Go to Share > Create Video File, and choose any setting.

4. Click Options. Make sure that the Preview Range option is selected. Also, make sure that Perform Smart Render is checked. This changes-only rendering takes advantage of all previously rendered clips by using them again, avoiding rerendering the same data and speeding up the process. Click OK.

5. Name the video portion **Preview_Movie** and click Save. Play your new movie to preview.

Using the MPEG Optimizer

SINCE THIS PROJECT'S SETTINGS already have your movie set in the MPEG format (you'll make sure), you can now use the MPEG Optimizer to speed up the rendering process. The Optimizer uses Smart Render. Smart Render only spends time rendering what has not been rendered before. In large DVD projects, this can save a huge amount of time, because DVDs are rendered in the MPEG-2 format, the exact format that the Optimizer uses.

When you use Create Video File, you also have the option to use Smart Render, even when your project template is set to AVI, not MPEG. So what is the benefit of using the MPEG Optimizer if it also uses Smart Render? The answer is, for when you create DVDs. When you burn the DVD in the final step, it allows you to choose an optimal profile, see what needs to be reencoded, specify specific file size, and view all the necessary details regarding the file type (res, bit rate, audio settings, etc). Once complete, your MPEG file will be completely compliant and not need any rerendering when burning your disc. A newer feature in the Optimizer is that you can set a maximum file size, and it will compress your project to that size. Just remember there might be a trade-off in quality.

Smart Render creates the compliant file, but you don't have the option to see all the details, choose the optimal profile, or set the file size.

For this section, we need to make some adjustments to our project to fully take advantage of the MPEG Optimizer. For ease, we'll create a quick new project that will make the features of the Optimizer more obvious. Any MPEGs to be optimized need to be on standalone layers on the Timeline; they cannot have overlays on them.

1. Create a new project and save the previous one.

2. Add Balloon-4 video to the video track.

3. Go to the Share step > Create Video File > MPEG Optimizer. Make sure the top radio button, Optimal project settings profile, is selected. Your view should look like Figure 15.9. Because the entire Timeline is made up of MPEG clips, the Optimizer's bars are both 100% green, indicating that the entire Timeline is already optimized and need not be rendered going forward unless changes are made to it. If you chose to output the file from the MPEG Optimizer with just the balloon video, it would effectively just copy the file to the location you chose and name it however you named it. Click Cancel to return to the main window.

4. Add Balloon-7 after Balloon-4. Notice that the Timeline indicates it is a WMV, not an MPEG file. Return to the MPEG Optimizer window described in step 3. It now indicates which MPEG part of the Timeline can be optimized and which cannot. Only 44.73% of your project will be optimized. A similar effect will occur if the WMV clip is overlaid on top of the MPEG clip. Only that portion of the MPEG that is standalone will be optimized. Try it, if you like. Remember that the MPEG will only need to be rendered once, even when outputting a DVD.

5. Click the Customized Converted Result File Size radio button. This allows you to create a file size targeted to comply with any bandwidth or server size limitations you may have. You can then set a desired file size in the Size Under field, using the minimum and maximum numbers to the right as a guide. Notice that the size of the project can be set anywhere between 9 and 26 MB. Set it to 15 MB, as in Figure 15.10.

Figure 15.9
MPEG Optimizer with only MPEG clips.

Figure 15.10
Customized converted result file size.

6. Click Accept. Name the file **MPEG_Optimized** and click Save. The file will be rendered as it would when creating any other movie, but the size will be very close to 15 MB.

7. To test the Optimizer, go to Create Video File > MPEG-4 > MPEG-4 HD. Name it **iPod MPEG**. The render should fly quickly through the MPEG and slow down for the rest of the project's rendering.

8. Return to the Final_Movie project without saving this one.

Creating a Sound File

IF YOU WANT TO SAVE JUST the audio from your project, you can. This is especially helpful if, after you split the audio off a video, you want to use the same sound with another movie. Or perhaps you want to convert the audio of a captured live performance and burn it to an audio CD. You can save the audio portion in the MP4A OOG, WAV, or WMA format.

1. Select Create Sound File in the Share step.

2. Name your file and choose which audio format you want. (Formats are explained near the end of Chapter 6 in the section called "Exporting Audio-Only Files.") Under Options, in the Files of Type drop-down list, click on the Compression tab to choose the compression you would like.

3. Click Save and preview your new audio file. Notice that it saved the music and the audio from one of the video clips near the end.

The Create Sound File feature will save audio from both audio tracks as well as any audio you have in the video tracks. Keep this in mind when choosing what you want to save. If you wish to not save the video's audio, right-click on it in the Timeline and choose Split Audio to place the audio in a separate audio track (provided you have one available). You can then delete it from the audio track. You can also mute the video track. The best option, though, is to use the Disable tracks feature (click the left end of a track to disable) to temporarily hide tracks from playback and output. That way you won't need to actually edit any of your Timeline clips.

Creating a Disc

THE CREATE DISC OPTION (DVD) goes much further than the single file created using the DVD option under Create Video File. Create Disc will launch VSX5's DVD authoring application, which will guide you through the steps of adding a menu(s) to access different chapters (scenes) and add a theme with an opening screen and a music track, all very similar to what you get when you rent a DVD title from the store or online (without the never-ending previews). None of the additions you make in the Create Disc feature will add to your Timeline project's content. It keeps them all separate.

Because of the full turnkey (all inclusive) process that this feature provides, I've devoted not one but two separate chapters that follow this one: one chapter discusses creating a standard-definition DVD, and the other discusses creating HD DVDs.

Exporting to a Mobile Device

MOBILE DEVICES COMPATIBLE with VSX5 include PSPs, Androids, many tablet devices, as well as Windows-based mobile devices, smart phones, and Pocket PCs. It will also accept other devices that use the same file formats created by these choices. You'll first need to create the video file, and then choose it from the video library. You cannot use projects currently in your Timeline.

> **CAUTION**
>
> Apple iProducts may not show in this window because Apple is very restrictive in where its devices are displayed, preferring iTunes. If the device shows up as an accessible drive on your PC, then it should also show up in this window.

1. Hook up your mobile device of choice to your computer, usually via a USB connection, like you would when you sync it.

2. In the Share step, choose Export to Mobile Device and select your device (or similar) and file size desired from the list. See Figure 15.11. Even if your device isn't in the list, all the files are MPEG-4 anyway, so that's the easy part. When choosing a dimension and frame rate, remember that the larger dimensions and higher frame rates will increase your file size.

   You may need to experiment with files for devices that aren't in the list, so once you figure it out, be sure to make a note of it.

3. Name your file at the top. Select your device in the window and click OK.

Figure 15.11
Mounted external devices.

Project Playback

PROJECT PLAYBACK CLEARS your screen and displays the whole project or a selected segment against a black background. You can use this feature to output to a video tape if you have a VGA to TV converter, camcorder, or a video recorder connected to your computer. Project Playback will allow you to manually control the output device when recording, too. Although I don't expect you to have the necessary recording equipment, I can at least show you what this playback screen looks like.

1. Create a preview area on your Timeline by adjusting the Mark-In and Mark-Out points in the Preview panel. An orange line will then appear in your Timeline. (Refer back to Figure 15.8.)

2. In the Share step, select Project Playback.

3. In the window that pops up, and if you have a preview area set up in your Timeline, you'll have the option to view the short section *or* the entire project in full screen. Select Preview Range and click Finish. A portion of your movie will now play without any background distractions or playback controls.

   Either wait until it's done playing or press Esc or the spacebar to stop playback and return to the main view.

4. If you desire, repeat step 3 viewing the Entire project.

DV and HDV Recordings

THESE CHOICES WILL CREATE movies and control your connected DV camcorder to send your projects out to DV tape, hard disk drive (HDD), or mini-disk camcorders. Use the DV option for standard-resolution recordings and use HDV for HD recordings. You must first create a video that your camera will accept. You will need an AVI video for the DV format and an MPEG for the HDV format. Luckily, we already have several of these. You'll be able to follow along, depending on the equipment you have.

1. Make sure your Balloon Trip library is open so the movies you create will be deposited there.

2. With your Final_Movie open, go to Share > Create Video File > DV > DV (16:9). This will save an AVI file. Name your movie **DV_export** and save to your Final_movies folder.

3. Connect your DV camcorder to your PC.

4. When your movie is done rendering, highlight the new DV_export clip in the library. Open the Share step and click DV Recording.

5. In the DV Recording – Preview Window (see Figure 15.12), click Play to preview the movie you just made. Click Next.

Figure 15.12
DV Recording – Preview Window.

6. Using the controls on your camcorder, move the tape to where you want to start recording on it, and then click the Record button in the Record window. (See Figure 15.13.) When your recording is done, click the Stop button.

Stop   Record

Figure 15.13
DV Recording – Record window.

7. Click Finish when your recording is done. Your tape-based camcorder will now have this movie recorded to it.

8. Return to the Share step and select HDV Recording. Choose either of the two options. Notice that this file will be saved as an MPEG instead. If you have an HD camcorder, follow the same steps in this section to send an HDV movie out to your HD camcorder.

Uploading to the Web

UPLOADING VIDEOS TO SOCIAL sites on the web has become almost as common today as making a phone call. Let me update that: as common today as making a cell phone call. Everyone with a smart phone is pointing at something and recording anything that moves. Uploading these short movies to sites like YouTube, Facebook, Vimeo, and Flickr is easy (almost too easy!). These sites have to make it easy so that anyone can do it, and, of course, they do.

In VSX5, you can first edit your movie (more social site folks really should be doing this!) and then upload it to either of these four sites without even leaving VideoStudio. Corel has agreements with all of them that integrate the VideoStudio workflow into the social sites' upload features.

It's okay if you don't have accounts with these sites; you'll have the choice to create an account or, if you have an account, you just log in and proceed. Let's try one by uploading the Final_movie file to YouTube. (Don't worry; I'll tell you where the upload actually occurs so you can stop if you like.)

1. With your Final_movie still open, choose Share > Upload to Web > YouTube > MPEG-4 HD (16:9). See Figure 15.14.

Figure 15.14
Choosing the YouTube Upload option.

2. Name it **MyYouTube_movie** and click Save. After the movie is rendered the Step 1 – Log in to YouTube window will pop up. See Figure 15.15.

3. In the Log in to YouTube window, enter your YouTube account info at the top or, to create a new account, click the Join YouTube link at the bottom.

    Joining YouTube will launch your Internet browser and open YouTube's Create Account page. Follow the instructions there to upload your movie (you'll need to locate your movie on your hard drive rather than in VideoStudio). Otherwise, in the Step –1 window, enter your username and password and click Next.

4. Check to agree to the terms and click Next again.

Figure 15.15
YouTube log-in window.

5. In the next screen, name your video, and add a description and search tags (search criteria might include family, Balloon, vacation, and so forth). Choose a category you want it to be listed in and a private or public choice. Private means your video will not be searchable and can only be accessed by those with the Internet address (URL) that you'll give to them via email or another means. Click Next.

6. (This is the step where uploading begins and is completely optional.) Confirm your choices and click the Upload Video button. This process could take a long time. Make sure your Internet connection is strong and reliable. Any break in your connection could derail the upload, causing you to start over again. Once your video is uploaded, the window will confirm its success. You can then click Finish.

7. All the other choices (Vimeo, Facebook, and Flickr) are similar to YouTube. The prompt windows will look different, but they will still guide you through the same process.

Exporting to 3D

PROBABLY THE COOLEST NEW feature that came out in version X4 of VideoStudio is the ability to create and export 3D movies. There is even a feature to upload these movies straight to your YouTube account (Upload to Web > YouTube 3D). VSX5 provides two methods for making 3D content, one of which you can view easily with glasses you probably already have laying around. The other method can be sent to the new 3D HD TVs. Let me first explain these two 3D options; then you'll create both of them so that you can see the differences.

Anaglyph is the rather old-fashioned, but still popular, method that is viewed through the paper glasses: the ones with one red lens and one cyan-colored lens. You probably already have a couple (or 50) of these paper glasses laying around. Anaglyph 3D is actually making a resurgence, as is everything in 3D, with the increased popularity of sharing photos and videos on the Internet.

There is a rather large limitation in how VSX5 renders out a 3D anaglyph movie. It doesn't do the 3D uniformly, but only at the top of the movie, gradually decreasing to zero change at the bottom. You'll see what I mean a bit later in this section. I'm not sure if or when this will be resolved.

The second 3D option in VSX5 is the side-by-side method. This is being popularized in the new 3D HD TVs. First VSX5 splits your movie into two movies displayed side-by-side, where each side is displayed in alternate half-frames. When this signal is sent to a 3D TV, the TV stretches both sides to fill the screen, but it still displays them in half frames. Your special (and expensive) polarizing 3D glasses are then responsible for letting you see one half-frame in one lens and the other half-frame in the other at just the right times without causing you to go into a seizure. This will produce the 3D effect without offsetting the images, meaning you can still view the TV without the glasses and it will look normal.

3D movies in the theater use mostly the Real3D cinema technique. It uses a different polarizing method that allows for 3D viewing at any angle and without needed batteries in the glasses. This technique is starting its move to 3D TVs now.

To create a 3D anaglyph movie, follow these steps.

1. With your Final_Movie still open, go to the Share step > Create Video File > 3D > AVCHD > AVCHD (1440×1080). Name it **MyAnaglyph_movie** and click Options.

2. Because of your 3D movie selection in step 1, the 3D Simulator box at the bottom should already be checked. Below that you'll see the two 3D methods previously discussed. Choose Anaglyph.

3. The Depth value sets the amount of 3D effect you want. Crank it to the highest number, 99. See Figure 15.16.

4. Click OK and save your anaglyph movie to your Final_movies folder. After it's done, don your fancy paper or plastic 3D glasses and have a look at it while it plays. Notice how the depth is graduated from the bottom to the top? It makes the video "lean" backward. Hopefully, Corel can improve on that soon because, otherwise, it's an awesome feature.

5. Redo the preceding steps, but this time, choose Side-by-Side in the Options window. Your resulting movie should look like Figure 15.17.

Figure 15.17
Side-by-side 3D results.

Figure 15.16
Anaglyph 3D options.

Quick Quiz

1. In the MPEG Optimizer, how is the time savings achieved? (See "Using the MPEG Optimizer.")

2. When saving as a sound file, what audio is saved other than what's in the audio tracks? (See "Creating a Sound File.")

3. When using Project Playback, how is your movie displayed on your computer? (See "Project Playback.")

4. What four social sharing sites can you upload directly to from within VSX5? (See "Uploading to the Web.")

5. What are the two methods in VSX5 for creating 3D movies, and what are the differences in how the movies are made? (See "Exporting to 3D.")

Creating a

Standard DVD

IT'S TIME TO GET YOUR pyromania on, because you'll be learning how to use VSX5 to burn DVDs. Okay, so this type of *burn* doesn't actually involve fire or even anything flammable; it's the common term that describes computers using a laser to engrave data onto a disc. DVDs hold so much data that they are the easiest way to save, store, and share longer movies. Just ask Netflix, Redbox, and Blockbuster!

Okay, so USB flash drives have caught up in capacity to DVDs, but so far, you can't use them to run movies on your laptops or TVs. Stay tuned, though.

Creating Hollywood-style DVDs in VSX5 is easier than you think. DVD choices run the gamut, including standard definition (SD) DVDs, AVCHD (currently the most popular consumer HD recording format), Blu-ray, and BD-J (Blu-ray Disc Java). All HD-formatted DVDs will be covered in the next chapter, including AVCHD and various Blu-ray DVDs.

Selecting Create Disc in VSX5 initiates the DVD options window (more like a separate mini-application), where you'll be guided through the entire process of assembling your clips/movies and adding chapters, menu items, a theme, and then burning your DVD. The DVD options are similar to VideoStudio's DV-to-DVD Wizard that I'll cover in the final chapter. With all that you'll learn in this chapter, Chapter 17 on HD DVDs will feel like a breeze for you.

For this chapter, you'll need a couple of blank DVDs (not CDs) and a DVD player on your PC that can also *burn* DVDs.

Tip

Not all PC DVD players have the capability to burn new DVDs. The easiest way to find out is to look at the DVD tray door on your PC for a phrase such as RW (read & write), Compact Disc-Re-Writable, or DVD Multi-recorder. If any of these phrases, or something similar, is inscribed on the tray door, you'll be able to burn DVDs in addition to playing them.

Multi-recorder will ensure that you can create both standard and at least AVCHD discs, but not necessarily Blu-ray; check your manual. Many PCs will also burn AVCHD without the multipurpose statement. Again, check your PC documentation to make sure.

What Are Your DVD Options?

WHAT KIND OF DVDs can you make, and what kind of blank DVDs can you use to make discs? You'll learn a little bit about DVDs first.

The average DVD SL (single-layer) storage capacity is 4.70 GB (gigabytes). These are the most typical in an electronics store. You can also purchase dual-layer (DL) DVDs. These can record two layers on the same side (at different depths), upping the capacity to 8.5–8.7 BG (single-sided, double-layer) or 9.40 GB (double-sided, single-layer). A dual-layer Blu-ray disc can store up to 50 GB. (A Blu-ray laser is much narrower in focus, so it can squeeze more data into a smaller space.) Blu-ray discs can record both standard and HD (including Blu-ray) content.

Blu-ray DVDs require your computer to have the special ability to record in these formats. Although Blu-ray recorders are showing up in PC desktops and laptops, dual-layer recording has rarely surfaced so far, not because it's new, but mainly because these discs are way more expensive and slower to burn than single-layer Blu-ray discs. DVD movies are created in the VOB (Video OBject) format to encompass extras such as audio, menus, and chapters.

Any of the blank DVDs you can get at locations like Best Buy, Target, and Office Depot are ones you can use to burn movies in VSX5, as long as they are single-layer. These include DVD+R/–R (write once, read many) and DVD+RW/–RW (write many, read many, reusable) and Blu-ray. Don't worry about the differences between + and –. The + format is a newer and competing format to the – format. Although there are technical differences, you likely won't notice them. You can still purchase both formats in stores. DVD recorders and players will work with both. Blank DVDs are inexpensive these days; you can purchase packs of 100 for $15–30 depending on the brand. (That's 15–30 cents each!)

Here, you'll create a DVD movie and burn it to disc using the Balloon Trip and the Tahoe movies. There are three main parts to making your DVD: Add Media, Menu & Preview, and Output. The VSX5 DVD options window will guide you every step of the way. Here we go!

Adding DVD Media

THE FIRST THING YOU NEED to do for your DVD is gather the movies you want to include. You're not limited to just the Balloon movie currently in the Timeline; you can import multiple previously rendered movies, video clips, and VSX5 project files during the DVD assembly process. Your content doesn't even need to be the same format or dimensions, although differing dimensions will produce letterboxing frames around them, which is what you're about to do. Other content can come from mobile devices and compatible CD/DVD content.

The next chapter on AVCHD and Blu-ray movies will contain content that is all widescreen. (All HD content is created in widescreen, but not all widescreen content is HD.) This chapter, though, will incorporate both standard dimension and widescreen content. I want you to see the effects on each kind of dimension when rendered together so you can plan appropriately later.

This section will guide you through the first step in the DVD-making process.

1. Open your Final_Movie project. Go to Settings > Project Properties. Click Edit, and then go to the General tab. Make sure Display Aspect Ratio at the bottom is set to 16:9. Since the movie this time includes both standard and widescreen movies, you want to go with the largest common denominator. Click OK twice to lock in the project properties.

2. Click on the Share tab and select Create Disc > DVD. This choice allows you to create a disc adding both standard and/or HD content but will only create a standard def disc from it. Since you have chosen DVD instead of any of the HD choices lower in the list, all the content (standard and HD) will be converted to a standard definition in the end. This, combined with the previous setting, will create a standard definition DVD that has a 16:9 aspect ratio.

3. In the Add Media window, notice that the entire Balloon movie is represented as a single thumbnail, similar to the Storyboard view in the main screen (see Figure 16.1). While in the process of creating a DVD, you can no longer edit the original movies; you can only edit their order. That's why this thumbnail view is much more appropriate. Click on the thumbnail's title in the Timeline and rename your untitled movie to **Balloon Trip**.

   Expand the Advanced Editing section and make sure the Create Menu option is checked. (It should be by default.) You will then be prompted in the next Menu & Preview section for your menu options.

Add content choices   **Click here**   **Preview window**

Check this   **Rename movie**

Figure 16.1
The Add Media window.

4. Mouse over the four Add Media choices at the top left. The first option allows you to add all the video choices that VSX5 is able to convert into MPEG-2 DVD files. Click on it to view the Open Video File dialog box (see Figure 16.2). Your only choices will be compatible video files.

5. Navigate to VSX5_LessonPlans > Videos > Lake_Tahoe and add all five Tahoe videos by selecting them and clicking Open. All the Tahoe videos should be added to the Timeline in order. If they're not in order, you can easily rearrange them manually.

   The Balloon Trip movie is a widescreen clip, and the Tahoe movies are standard screen size.

   The small filmstrip icon in the lower-left corner of each of the video thumbnails indicates the files are movies, as opposed to still graphics. See Figure 16.3.

Figure 16.2
Compatible media files.

Additional movies added

Figure 16.3
Adding additional media.

The other three choices under Add Media include existing VideoStudio projects (VSP files), digital media from DVDs (DVD/DVD-VR, AVCHD, BDMV), and Import from Mobile Device. Files will be copied from these locations into the Timeline.

The last choice, Import from Mobile Device, opens a window similar to exporting to an external device. Instead, however, it displays compatible content on these devices where you can select files you want to use. (Go ahead and click Import from Mobile Device to see what happens.) Click Cancel when finished.

The term DVD-VR (Video Recording) may be new to you. It's yet *another* format for DVDs that encompasses all DVDs you can import content from. It encompasses DVD-R, DVD-RW, and DVD-RAM formats. DVD-RAM is (you guessed it) *another* DVD format that is supposed to provide better data integrity, data retention, and damage protection. We'll see who wins, but at least VSX5 supports these additional formats.

6. Below the Add Media icons, click Add/Edit Chapter. This option allows you to add scene breaks just like what you see in Hollywood DVDs. You can add chapters in two ways: either automatically through the naturally occurring scene breaks in your movies, or manually anywhere along the Timeline you choose. Let's try it manually first.

A couple of the Lake Tahoe clips are not separated correctly by their scene breaks. In the Add/Edit Chapter window, under the Currently selected clip list, choose Tahoe4 (see Figure 16.4). Move the playback head to timecode 04:15. Click Add Chapter, and a new clip will be added to the Add/Edit Chapter Timeline. (The Add Chapter button is beneath the Currently selected clip drop-down list.)

Figure 16.4
Adding chapters manually.

7. Back under the Currently selected clip list, choose Balloon Trip. Then click Auto Add Chapters. The Auto Add Chapters dialog box will appear.

8. In the Auto Add Chapters dialog, make sure the default setting is Insert Scenes as Chapters. (If it isn't, select it.) Click OK. As a result, a whole slew of vertical red dashes will be added along the Preview panel's Timeline, and another slew of new clips will appear in the Timeline below it. (See Figure 16.5.) Each Timeline clip represents where scenes will change in the movie.

Figure 16.5
Chapters automatically added to the Timeline.

Although this can be a useful feature, it has added a lot of chapters that are too short to be practical. Click Remove All Chapters to remove all the chapters from the Balloon trip movie. Then click OK to close the Add/Edit Chapter window.

9. If your blank DVD's capacity differs from the horizontal bar at the bottom of this window indicating the capacity of a normal single-sided blank DVD (DVD 4.7G), you can choose a different capacity from the drop-down on this bar. The bar next to that shows the current length of your movie (green) compared to the total capacity of the DVD. This will adjust depending on the DVD capacity.

Click Next to move to the second step in the DVD process: Menu & Preview.

DVD Menu & Preview

STEP 2 IN THE DVD process is where you'll select an entertaining theme that you can fully customize. This adds a sense of uniqueness to your DVD that no one else will have and that will make you the envy of friends, family members, and colleagues. Items you can consider adding include a decorative, themed introductory screen where your chapters will be listed.

You can add themes for school, vacations, or something professional for business use. These themes can be edited with your own background image, video, and background music. Other features include adding additional intro pages for notes or a story line, perhaps introducing the cast of characters in your video. You can also add decorations from a collection of clip art included with VSX5.

Tip

You can go back and forth through all three steps in the DVD options window without losing any of your changes, including titles and decorations. You can even close the DVD options window. It will save the work of your current project automatically and will even open the same project when you again choose Create Disc in the Share step. If, though, you choose Create > Disc with a *different* VSX5 project open, then the previous one will be *overwritten*.

Use the following steps to add entertaining DVD themes and learn about the choices you have in customizing them.

1. From the previous section, you should now be in step 2, Menu & Preview. On the left is the graphical list of possible themes for your DVD. Choose All from the list at the top. Next, choose the theme displayed in Figure 16.6 just so you can follow along with these steps.

Figure 16.6
Choosing a DVD theme.

What about the SmartScene gallery items? SmartScene menus don't behave any differently in functionality. Features in the Edit tab are even identical. So why the "SmartScene" moniker? In all the other gallery menus, if the screen contains three text buttons, after creating the disc, it will *only* generate one menu page. When the user clicks on the text button, the button jumps to that scene. No surprise, right?

In a SmartScene, though, if the screen contains three text buttons, after creating the disc, it will *also* generate three separate menu pages. When a user hovers over the text button, the scene will automatically jump to and display the corresponding menu page for preview (*auto-activation*). It won't just play a few seconds of video in the thumbnail window. In other words, it will jump to the corresponding menu page and begin playback of that scene, including audio, from the beginning.

Beware, though, that SmartScenes will consume significantly more memory compared to regular text menus.

2. In the Preview screen, you'll see the familiar frame of the title-safe zone (in this case, it's yellow). Double-click the text that starts with PRJ_ just above the Balloon Trip clip, and name it something corny like **My Summer Vacation**. That will encompass both the Balloon and Tahoe trips (yes, I know the Tahoe trip was in the winter). Click outside from it to set the text, but don't resize or reposition it. If you accidentally resize an object, right-click on it and choose Reset Selected Objects.

3. You should have three titles under the main My Summer Vacation title (Balloon Trip, Tahoe1, and Tahoe2). You can change these names as you did with the main title, or you can keep them as is. The arrows on the bottom of the Main Menu will advance you through the rest of the menus, but they won't work until you preview the movie, which you'll do soon.

4. The billboard screen in the main menu is black because the Balloon Trip movie starts off with a black color chip. Let's fix this. Click the Back button to return to the Add Media menu (step 1). Go to 0:00:2.29 in the Preview window. Right-click on the first thumbnail in the Timeline and choose Change Thumbnail. The thumbnail view of the first clip should now match what you see in the Preview window. Click Next to advance to the Menu and Preview step. You should no longer see a black background in the billboard's screen.

Figure 16.7
Changing a thumbnail.

294

5. The theme you selected added another menu page to incorporate the additional chapters you added in the Add Media step, specifically in the Tahoe4 clip.

   Just above the Playback controls, open the list adjacent to Currently Displayed Menu and choose Tahoe4. This is the second page of chapter links.

   Notice that the theme doesn't match the first page. There is a difference between the Main Menu and all the submenus after it. You can have a separate theme for the Main Menu and one for the rest of the submenus. (I'm not sure why you would want to, but that's just me.) Select the same theme as the Main Menu from the Gallery tab.

6. Still in the Tahoe4 menu, change the Tahoe4 title to **Lake Tahoe**. Then change the subtitles to **Tahoe3** and **Tahoe4**.

The little icon of the house in the lower left will take the viewer back to the Main Menu screen. You can try it when previewing your movie.

---

7. Click the Edit tab next to the Gallery tab. This is where you can swap out the background music, graphics, the video for this menu screen or all the menu screens in the introduction.

   Click the small screen icon on the left, just below where it says Background Image/Video, to open the list of background customization options. See Figure 16.8. Notice the three options for each choice. You can change the background for this menu only. All Main Menus means all the intro menus that don't include additional ones you may have added, such as note menus. All Menus includes the

first two choices. The last part of the list lets you reset the background to the original theme. Although this is a nice option, you don't need it for this project. Don't make any changes at this time.

This Background Image/Video list is more helpful if you have multiple menus and submenus, which you don't in this case. Most of your DVDs probably won't either, but the options are available if you need them.

Figure 16.8
Options for setting a custom background.

8. Click the Customize icon in the left area, a little past halfway down. This allows for several unique choices. Click Motion Filter, and select the one near the end that has stars on it. If you pause your mouse over it, it will identify itself with the label Star. Feel free to choose a different Menu In and Menu Out option.

9. At the bottom of the window is a series of different frame options for the clips in the menus. Scroll to near the end, and choose the filmstrip frame. See Figure 16.8. When you're done, click OK.

Figure 16.9
Choosing options in the Customize Menu window.

SmartScene Menu gallery items are limited to customizations of the button styles. You cannot customize the video thumbnail frames or the layout.

10. Back in the Edit tab of the Menu & Preview window, return to Main Menu using the Currently Displayed Menu list. Click the Add Decoration icon in the lower right. This opens a collection included with VSX5 of fun embellishments you can place anywhere onscreen and resize. Scroll down and open D32. Position it in the upper-left corner and enlarge it a little by grabbing the lower-right corner. (The cursor will display as a double-ended arrow.) This embellishment will help decorate the balloon movie thumbnail.

11. Reposition the My Summer Vacation title to the right so that it's in full view out of the way of the balloon decoration. See Figure 16.10.

Figure 16.10
Adding a decoration.

Tip

Again, if you accidentally resize/reshape an object (that is, a title or button) and want to reset it, right-click on the item in the Preview panel and choose Reset Selected Objects.

Decorations are in the PNG (Portable Network Graphic) format, which is a common format for Internet and print graphics. It allows for millions of colors (as opposed to a GIF, which is limited to 256 colors) and background transparency. PNG is also an open format (unlike GIF again), not requiring a license or royalties.

Figure 16.11
Creating a note page.

12. Apply the same customizations that you did to the Tahoe4 menu in steps 7 and 8.

13. Still in the main menu, click the Add Note Menu icon at the bottom. This adds another menu with the same theme after Tahoe4, where you can now add text in the billboard screen. Double-click on the small Enter Text Here field and type the following text: **I hope you enjoy** (press Enter key) **the home video of** (press Enter) **our Summer and** (press Enter) **Winter vacations!**

    Click outside the text to set the entry. Click Font Settings on the far left to choose a nice, decorative font. (Remember, don't use a font with really thin lines.) Reposition and resize the text block to the center of the screen. This will also increase the font size.

    Change the title to **Summer Vacation**. Your Preview panel should look similar to Figure 16.11.

14. Click the large Preview icon at the bottom of the window. This window allows you to use familiar remote control buttons to test the running and interactivity of your movie before burning to disc. It starts playing automatically, so click the titles or the thumbnail clips to play each scene. Because of the widescreen dimension of the Balloon movie, there is some letterboxing (black bordering) going on at the top and bottom, but the other standard dimension clips fill the full screen perfectly.

15. Click Back (not Close) to leave the Preview panel. Click Next to go to step 3, Output.

DVD Output

YOU'RE ALMOST THERE. In the Output step, you will set the final burn options, and the process begins. It's also the step where, if you screw up, you waste a bunch of blank DVDs, but such is the life of a videographer. Chalk it up to experience. I'll do my best to minimize any mistakes for you.

Be sure to grab at least two blank DVDs.

The Output step lets you set a bunch of options, but the most important one is the number of DVD copies. The Normalize Audio option is pretty important too, because it evens out the audio variations between movie clips. Be sure that the window is expanded to show all the options. If there is a double down-facing arrow on the right, click it to expand the options (see Figure 16.12). The options are explained here:

Click to expand options

Figure 16.12
DVD options.

▶ **Label:** Enables you to enter the name of the DVD.

▶ **Drive:** Select the disc burner to use to create your disc, just in case you have more than one.

▶ **Copies:** Choose the number of DVDs you want to burn from the same project.

▶ **Disc Type:** Displays the output disc format in your disc drive. It will say Empty until you insert a disc.

▶ **Create to Disc:** Allows you to directly burn your project onto a disc. This sounds like a "duh" choice, but it's optional in case you just want to do one or both of the next two options.

▶ **Create DVD Folders:** This is only enabled when the video file to be created is a DVD-Video. The files created are in preparation for burning the video file to a DVD. This also allows the user to view the finished DVD file on the computer using DVD-Video player software.

▶ **Create Disc Image:** Select this option if you plan to burn the video file several times. By selecting this option, you won't have to generate the file the next time you want to burn it.

▶ **Normalize Audio:** Different video clips may have different audio recording levels. To eliminate the varying levels when combined with other video clips, use Normalize to evaluate and adjust the audio to ensure a balanced level throughout.

The following steps will walk you through the DVD burning process.

1. Insert your blank DVD into your computer's DVD drive.

2. Enter a Label name of **Summer Vacation**.

3. Set Copies to 2.

4. Create to disc should already be selected. Keep the Recording format in the list to the right at DVD-Video.

5. Check Create DVD folders. Navigate to and select your folder Final_movies.

6. Uncheck Create disc image if it's not already unchecked. (It will be unchecked by default.) This is not necessary for this project.

7. Check Normalize audio since you have audio from both the Balloon Trip movie and the Lake Tahoe movies.

8. Click the Burn icon in the lower right to start the DVD burning process. Click OK to the warning box. See Figure 16.13.

Figure 16.13
The DVD Output window.

The DVD rendering process can take from minutes to several hours depending on the length.

Creating DVD Disc Labels

THE LAST MAJOR NEW FEATURE in VSX5 we'll cover in this book is its ability to create DVD and Audio Disc labels to place on your DVDs and CDs. The Disc label feature allows you to create and print labels, case covers, and DVD case inserts. Although you can add your own images, text, and icons to complete your layout, you can also just create a disc based on the current project you're working on. You can create your

labels either before you create your DVD or afterward. The following explains the process of setting up and printing disc labels.

1. After burning your discs from the previous section, return to the Add Media section of the Create Disc window. Click to select the last Tahoe clip in the bottom tray (Tahoe5). This will be the image we'll use as our disc label.

2. Click the Print disc label based on the current project icon. See Figure 16.14. This will take you to the Disc Label set up window. See Figure 16.15.

Figure 16.14
The Print disc label icon.

Figure 16.15
The Print Disc window.

3. Let's start by describing the features in this window. There are three tabs in the upper left:

   ▶ The General tab allows you to select a disc label or disc cover templates to start with. You can then customize the overall design of the disc label, disc cover, insert, or booklet. The actual dimensions of your media or label in relation to the selected paper size are displayed to serve as your guide.

   ▶ The Image tab allows you to adjust the properties of your images.

   ▶ The Text tab allows you to format and adjust the properties of your text.

4. The disc label creation options along the top of the window allow you to do the following tasks.

   ▶ Click Files to see that it lets you either Load and Edit an existing disc label or Save your current disc label project. See Figure 16.16.

Figure 16.16
Saving disc labels.

▶ To the right of Files, Add Image selects an image to add on to the label.

▶ Add Text adds a text object to the label.

▶ Add Icon adds an icon to the label that describes the type of DVD. Click it to preview the choices.

▶ Click Playlist to open the Add/Edit Playlist Information window to add information such as album title, artist name, and date. See Figure 16.17.

Figure 16.17
The Print Disc Playlist window.

▶ Click the gear in the far upper right to try out the two options there. Show/Hide Disc will toggle the bottom to resize the image so it covers the entire red ring that represents the disc.

5. Under the General tab, if your printer is connected and turned on, it should show up in the list. You also might see additional choices such as printing to PDF etc., depending on what is set up in your computer's printing control panel. Choose the printer you want to use.

6. Under the Media type drop-down, select the first choice, CD label, to start with. Afterward, you'll also use this list to print booklets and jewel case inserts.

7. Use the Paper size list to select what your labels will print on. It is recommended that you purchase self-adhesive labels specific for disc labels, like those from Avery.

8. In the Background section in the lower left, choose either a texture and/or color only if your label is not being covered by an image, such as the one we're currently making.

9. As you can see in the Preview window, the Tahoe picture does not completely cover the disc, so let's fix that. In the Preview window, click once on the Tahoe image to highlight it. Use the yellow points on the center top and center bottom to resize the image so it covers the entire red ring that represents the disc.

10. Step 9 automatically put you into the Image tab. Feel free to try any of the adjustments to see what happens or leave it as it was.

11. At the top of the Disc window, click the Add Text icon to go into the Text tab. A text insertion point will appear on the disc in the Preview window. Under Text options, select a creative font and a font size of 24 for now. Leave the font color at black.

12. Deselect the Shadow options. Under the Wrap text section, choose the second choice.

13. Click the Other Options gear in the far upper right and deselect Show/Hide Grid.

14. Double-click in the upper-left area to set a new location for your text insertion point. Type Family Vacation. Click once outside the text to set it. Use the yellow handles to resize it and the pink handle on the right to position it on your label.

15. One cool positioning feature is to just click anywhere inside the text box and drag to position it. It will adjust both its curvature and orientation depending on where you put it. Your label might look something like Figure 16.18.

16. When you're happy with the design and layout of your disc label, return to the General tab and choose how many copies you want in the Output options section. Insert your label paper into your printer and click the Print button in the lower right.

17. Continue by creating other labels and inserts if you like and/or click Close when you're done.

Figure 16.18
A possible disc look.

Creating and Copying a Disc Image File

A DISC IMAGE FILE IS A single file that captures the entire contents and file structure of a disc you already have. Creating a disc image file on your computer allows you to archive the source disc contents for backup or future burning.

In many cases, such as a wedding video, you might want to create another disc later. Once you close your project and quit VideoStudio, VSX5 will need to go through the entire rendering process again if you want to burn another disc. If you first use VSX5 to create a disc image and store it on your computer, you can then use the VSX5 Copying a

Disc File Image feature to save you from having to rerender the project. In this case, you will only need to burn the disc, which takes less time. Make sure you have sufficient space on your computer to store the disc image file. Here is how to use this feature.

Creating a Disc Image

1. In the Final_movie project, go to Share > Create Disc > whichever disc version you want (DV, AVCHD, etc.). I chose DVD.

2. Click Next until you arrive at the 3-Output step. Uncheck Create to disc and check Create disc image.

3. Rename your output file **FinalMovieDiscImage** and save it to your Saved Lesson Folders. See Figure 16.19.

4. Click the Burn icon in the lower right to create the disc image. Click OK to any warnings that pop up. After the disc image has been created, click Close to return to the Timeline view. Proceed to the next section.

Copying a Disc Image

Now that you have saved your DVD movie in a local format instead of on a disc, you can reuse it again and again to burn as many discs as you want. Another upside is that you no longer have to render all the menus. The output to DVD process will now only involve copying the ISO disc image onto your DVD.

1. With the same project open in VSX5, go to Tools > Burn from Disc image (ISO). See Figure 16.20.

Figure 16.19
Select to create a disc image.

Figure 16.20
Go to Burn from Disc image.

2. Insert a blank DVD into your PC's disc burner drive.

3. In the Burn from Disc image window, click the folder icon adjacent to the Source disc image file field at the top. Locate and select the disc image you created in the previous section.

4. Click the double downward-facing arrow just to the right of the Copy icon. Choose your write speed and number of DVDs you would like to burn. See Figure 16.21.

Figure 16.21
Burn from Disc image window.

5. When ready, click the Copy icon. Your disc will be created in a much shorter time than usual.

Quick Quiz

1. What is the capacity of most single-layer DVDs? (See "What Are Your DVD Options?")

2. What's the difference between a DVD +/−R and a DVD +/− RW? (See "What Are Your DVD Options?")

3. Name five things you can edit/customize on a DVD menu. (See "DVD Menu & Preview.")

4. What's the difference between SmartScenes and regular DVD scenes? (See "DVD Menu & Preview.")

5. What is Normalize Audio used for? (See "DVD Output.")

Creating an

HD DVD

THESE DAYS, IF YOU DON'T have a high-definition (HD) video camcorder, you're close to being in the minority, since even digital still cameras take HD video. Luckily for you, prices are lower than they've ever been. You can actually purchase pocket-sized HD camcorders for less than $150, which is amazing! Sure, they may not contain *all* the bells and whistles (okay, *any*) of the more expensive ones, but for ease of use and convenience, you can't beat them. They're also perfect starter camcorders for any video enthusiast and include easy upload capabilities.

Still in the budget arena, slightly larger hand-held camcorders can be found in the $250–$500 range. Extra features will include much larger zoom capabilities (pocket sizes may have up to 2X zoom), presets for different conditions (lighting, speed, and so on), still camera functions, and varying recording speeds and qualities. More expensive camcorders will bring you additional features such as a built-in light, image stabilization, and better shooting in low-light conditions. (See Appendix B for a camcorder buying guide from CNET.)

The HD format consists of Blu-ray (Blu-ray Disc, or BD) and AVCHD (Advanced Video Coding High Definition). BD camcorders, of which there are few at this point, start at about $600. Their discs are pricey, too; blank BD discs currently run about $1–1.50 each, which is about 3 to 5 times more than SD discs. To the average videographer, the quality differences between Blu-ray and AVCHD may not warrant the jump forward. AVCHD provides a huge leap compared to the quality of SD, but the leap from AVCHD to Blu-ray is not so drastic. It makes much more sense for Hollywood to use BD over regular HD-DVD because it enhances their already higher quality video. So when you go to buy your next camcorder, choose HD over SD— the better quality is worth the slightly higher price.

HD content takes up more storage and disc space than SD because of its higher bitrates and resolution. The higher the quality setting, the higher the bitrate and the better the captured data. AVCHD captures at a higher bitrate than SD, and BD captures at a higher bitrate than both SD and AVCHD. Many camcorders enable tweaking of bitrates. For example, your camcorder may have different quality settings for HD that allow for more recording in the same storage space. This is accomplished by changing the bitrate of your camcorder. The higher the quality setting, the higher the bitrate.

Now that you've read Chapter 16 and know how to create an SD DVD, it's a good time to learn the differences in creating AVCHD, Blu-ray, and Blu-ray-J discs.

Video data rate, generically known as *bitrate*, is the number of bits processed per unit of time. In digital multimedia, bitrate often refers to the number of bits used per unit of playback time in audio or video after data compression. The higher the bitrate, the larger the final output, but also the better the quality.

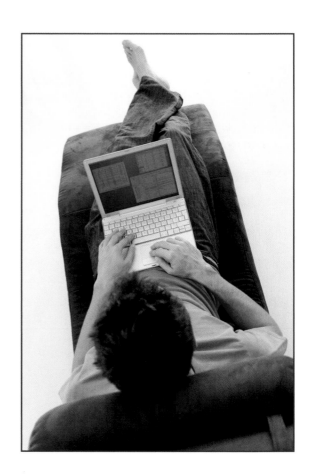

AVCHD Explained

MOST HD CONSUMER camcorders shoot in the much higher quality AVCHD format. Look for the AVCHD logo on your HD camcorder. This format can swallow up to 15 MB of storage per second of shooting, depending on the quality setting. The highest setting can fill a 30 GB camcorder drive in a little more than 30 minutes, but lower-quality settings can make it last up to an hour or more.

AVCHD uses a form of the video compression standard H.264, also known as a *codec* (compression/ decompression). One of the great features of AVCHD in the HD realm is that AVCHD videos can be burned to regular blank DVDs, but they will not play back on regular DVD players. You'll again need a Blu-ray player for playback. You will, of course, need an HDTV or PC with HD viewing to notice the increased playback quality. The differences between SD and AVCHD are quality and storage requirements. Blu-ray, though, is quite a bit different from both SD and AVCHD.

AVCHD may take up extra storage space over SD, but the vastly improved quality is worth it, especially since HD camcorders come with such large internal drives and available detachable memory sticks to handle the larger files.

Blu-ray Explained

AS OF 2008, ALL HOLLYWOOD HD videos are shot in a high enough resolution (up to 4K) that they can then be converted to Blu-ray for distribution. They then either produce Blu-ray DVDs and/or down-sample them for SD DVDs for those with only standard DVD players. Personal Blu-ray use has increased as well. Many of you probably own or have access to BD DVD playback capabilities with BD DVD players or Sony PlayStation systems, but my guess is that few of you have the capability to create your own BD discs or have a BD camcorder at this point. Next year, who knows?

> The nice thing about Blu-ray players is that they will play all DVD formats, standard and HD.

> Both LPCM (linear pulse-code modulation) and Dolby Digital are methods for encoding audio information digitally. LPCM is an uncompressed audio format designed for Blu-ray (and HD DVD) players that can supply up to 8 channel, 24 bit, 96 KHz audio. More technically, LPCM is used for the lossless encoding of audio data in the Compact disc Red Book standard (informally also known as Audio CD), introduced in 1982. Dolby Digital also includes many sound formats, with the highest quality being compressed to 5.1 channel, 16 bit, 48 KHz audio. I've heard it described this way: Dolby Digital allows you to hear rainfall all around you. LPCM allows you to hear every single raindrop hit the ground.

Creating BD discs requires a special BD burner; a regular DVD disc burner will not do. You will also need a special digital video recorder that records in the BD format, so you'll have BD content to assemble and output for a BD disc. Although a BD burner can take any file and record it to a BD disc, unless it was recorded in the Blu-ray format, it will not be of Blu-ray quality.

BD doesn't just have a higher disc capacity; it also has a much higher data rate, which results in much higher video and audio quality. It still takes twice the storage space of SD movies, though. Blu-ray supports Dolby Digital, DTS, and LPCM audio formats. Just like DVDs and CDs, Blu-ray discs also have read-only and read/write discs.

The disc burning and reading mechanism in a BD recorder/player uses a blue (closer to violet actually) laser that's in a narrower wavelength, allowing it to burn and read more data in a tighter space (up to 10 times more and up to 50 GB on dual-layer discs). SD discs rely on a red laser. Standard recorders, burners, and players are not compatible with BD content; they can't read it. The upside, though, is that most BD devices are compatible with both AVCHD and SD video.

BD files are actually smaller than AVCHD files due to better encoding and the laser burning process that's involved. BD uses m2ts as a container (file extension) that holds video and audio, each encoded with its own codec. For example, Blu-ray files in the m2ts format contain either mpeg2 or h.264 video and DDAC3 audio or LPCM audio. The BD format is also known as *BDAV* and *BDMV*. BDAV is simply a BD movie on disc, whereas BDMV is a BD movie with the familiar Hollywood-style menus and scene breaks.

This chapter concentrates on creating these HD videos, both in AVCHD and BD. It also covers features that distinguish HD from SD. If you're unfamiliar with creating an SD disc in VSX5, be sure to read Chapter 16 first. Grab a couple more blank standard DVDs. If you have a BD burner and BD player, get yourself a couple of blank BD discs, too. You'll only be using the Balloon Trip movie in these next sections.

If you have your own AVCHD or Blu-ray content, you are welcome to use it here. Just be sure to capture/import into a VSX5 library first.

Creating an AVCHD Disc

CREATING AN HD DISC using AVCHD in VSX5 is identical to creating a disc in SD, so you won't have trouble catching on. The features of AVCHD, however, are different from SD in terms of the content, the theme templates available, the editing capabilities, and, of course, the higher-quality results. Let me show you what these differences are and where they reside.

1. Open your Final_movie project.

2. Go to Share > Create Disc > AVCHD to launch the DVD Options window.

3. Click Next to go to the Menu & Preview step. This is where most of the differences are when it comes to AVCHD content. The Gallery tab has fewer theme choices. Click the first theme choice in the second row.

4. Change the title and subtitles to **My Summer Vacation** and **Balloon Trip, Tahoe1,** and **Tahoe2**, respectively (see Figure 17.1). These titles might actually already be made for you since it auto-saved the last disc info from your SD disc-making projects.

Figure 17.1
Choosing an AVCHD theme template from the Gallery tab.

5. Click the Edit tab. Here you will notice the limited editing choices. Although you can add a video as a background (i.e., behind the marquee), AVCHD menu choices in VSX5 are basically limited to still images only because of the narrow capabilities of the themes. There are no multiple video windows displaying chapter clips. That's just the way it is. All other options are the same as for an SD DVD.

6. Click the Preview icon at the bottom. Notice that there is no longer letterboxing of the video. The Balloon Trip video is widescreen, and so is AVCHD, so it fills the entire screen. Click Back.

7. Click Next to go to the Output step. As you'll see, Create to Disc is checked by default again, but there are no recording format choices to the right of Create Disc. Also, there is no choice to create a disc image. Other than that, options are the same as with a standard DVD.

8. Click the Burn icon in the lower left to burn your AVCHD DVD. When it's done, your DVD tray will spit out your finished product. Pop it back in to view the movie, or go play it on your TV.

Choosing a Blu-ray File Type

YOU'RE PROBABLY SAYING to yourself, "Uh, what? There are different Blu-ray file types? Is there never just one standard for anything?" I know, I feel your pain. Yes, there are several Blu-ray file types. This list covers the ones that are used in VSX5.

▶ **BDMV (Blu-ray Disc Movie):** This has three separate "profiles." I know... pain. These profiles support different features and require different hardware. The reason for multiple profiles was the lack of a finished specification at the time the first players were designed. VSX5 supports the most common 1.0 Profile, as do most BD players.

Tip

I ran into a BD disc incompatibility on my own BD player. I started running into errors in which the disc would just freeze after the previews and wouldn't play the actual movie.

After going to the support site of my BD player brand, I downloaded a Firmware update onto my computer. I then transferred the file to a thumb drive. Next, I inserted the thumb drive into the USB slot on my BD player and followed the online instructions to update the player's software. Problem solved.

1. **Profile 1.0:** The original profile supported on Blu-ray players prior to November 1, 2007. No secondary video decoder is included for Picture in Picture (PiP) support, and there is no Internet connectivity.

2. **Profile 1.1:** This adds PiP support via secondary video and audio decoders. It requires that a second program be present in the BDAV video stream. Also mandated is 256 MB of internal (persistent) storage.

3. **Profile 2.0:** The highest profile in the Blu-ray specifications increases internal storage to no less than 1 GB and adds an Internet connection for downloading content in conjunction with BDMV programming.

▶ **BD-J (Blu-ray's Java implementation):** These discs include interactive menus. BD-J is the name given to the Java-based software that will be included on BD-ROM discs and all BD players. BD-ROM stands for Blu-ray read-only memory, which are all playback-only BD discs. BD-J allows for BD menus and many other features.

▶ **BD-J Calendar:** A capability in BD-J discs, Calendar View automatically sorts still and video content by recorded date. This feature is not available in VSX5.

Creating a Blu-ray Disc

THERE ARE NOT A LOT OF differences in creating Blu-ray discs over SD or AVCHD discs in VSX5. In fact, the differences are so few that I'll just describe them to you. You should first complete the Share step with your Final_Movie file so you can follow along.

▶ In Menu & Preview (step 2), the Gallery theme choices are the same as for an AVCHD movie.

▶ In the Edit tab (see Figure 17.2), the custom choices are exactly like those for a standard DVD, except, under Moving Path in the lower left, there are Menu effects, but no Motion effects.

No Motion effects

Figure 17.2
Menu effects, but no Motion effects, in the Edit tab.

▶ Under Customize, the only custom layout choices are those for the navigation buttons. There are none for frames or overall layout placement. See Figure 17.3.

▶ In Output (step 3), there is no Save as a Disc image option.

Only custom navigation buttons

Figure 17.3
Custom navigation buttons only.

Creating a Blu-ray-J Disc

BLU-RAY-J (BD-J) DISCS have increased interactivity over other DVD implementations. In Hollywood DVDs, this allows them to be far more sophisticated than bonus content provided by standard DVDs, including network access, PiP, and access to expanded local storage. Collectively, these features (other than Internet access) are referred to as Bonus View, and the addition of Internet access is called BD Live.

The part of the feature that's available in VSX5's BD-J implementation is that all menus are branched out but remain within the main menu. I'll show you what I mean. You can join in on this section.

1. With your Final_Movie, go to Share > Create Disc > BD-J.

2. Click Add/Edit Chapters.

3. Click Auto Add Chapters. The Insert Scenes as Chapters option should already be selected. If not, select it and click OK. After the chapters have been added, click OK again.

4. Click Next. There are only three theme choices. Choose the top-right one.

5. Under the Preview window, you have three icons, all representing different stages in menu display. Click each one, from left to right, to see how the menus will be shown to the viewer. (See Figure 17.4.) These views are triggered by the left/right arrow keys on a remote control. Menus that are vertical will be controlled by the remote's up and down arrows.

Figure 17.4
BD-J menus and submenus.

6. Missing from this screen is the ability to add a Note screen. That's because all menu features are displayed in one screen, with no room for note screens. Click the Edit tab. Here, you'll notice other missing items but an addition of button sounds. Click the icon under the word *Button*. You have two button sound choices in VSX5, but you can access more from this window. Choose Select a Button Sound for All Menus (see Figure 17.5).

Figure 17.5
Choosing a different menu button sound.

Notice the file type choices in the Files of Type drop-down. Click to highlight each one, and click the Play button at the bottom to preview them. See Figure 17.6. Choose either one and click Open.

Figure 17.6
Button sound choices.

7. Click Next. If you have a blank BD disc, go ahead and burn a disc to see the results.

Quick Quiz

1. What is the most common format for the recording and playback of consumer-level HD content? (See "AVCHD Explained.")

2. What is the difference between BDAV and BDMV? (See "Blu-ray Explained.")

3. What is the difference between the menu options in a BD movie as opposed to a BD-J movie? (See "Creating a Blu-ray-J Disc.")

4. What is the only DVD format in VSX5 that doesn't allow you to add a Note page to a menu? (See "Creating a Blu-ray-J Disc.")

The DV-to-DVD
Wizard

N OW THAT YOU'VE REACHED the final chapter (congratulations, btw!), I want to show you an application inside VSX5 that's a great shortcut for creating DVDs. It's called the DV-to-DVD Wizard. The Wizard, accessible under the Tools menu, is a separate mini-application for working *only* with content from tape-based DV camcorders, VCRs or TVs. It is not designed for importing from existing files. It is also *only* used for creating DVDs, not slideshows, audio CDs, or uploads to a social site.

If you would like to create items other than DVDs with your tape-based camcorder content, you'll instead use the Capture Video and DV Quick Scan features under the Capture step in the main work area. You can achieve the same results with the Capture tab, but the Wizard produces the results more quickly and easily if you desire to go straight from tape/VCR/TV to DVD.

Deciding When to Use the DV-to-DVD Wizard

YOUR USE OF THE DV-to-DVD Wizard (aka the Wizard) should be based on the considerations of your available time, your level of experience, and the DVD's level of required editing. Also, consider whether the project warrants burning straight to a DVD from the particular sources mentioned earlier, without the requirements of editing individual clips, adding special effects, and adding further audio. Although the Wizard does not contain these editing tools, it does have an extensive list of DVD menu features.

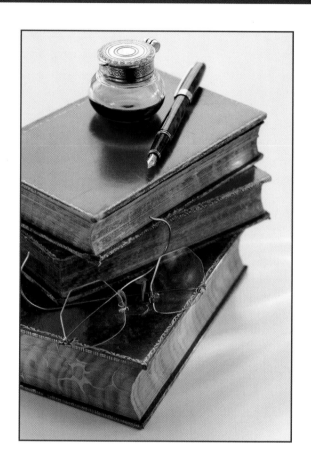

A DV camcorder is considered any source that requires a FireWire (IEEE 1394) connection to your computer that allows real-time capture (or even faster) from your source. It usually is best suited for mini-DV tapes where VSX5 will actually control the device. You'll read more about this as the chapter progresses.

Because this chapter involves capturing from a source I couldn't include in the lesson plans (a digital tape camcorder), if you have your own similar setup and content, please use it to follow along, or just read along for the *sheer* pleasure of it.

Gather your DV-tape camcorder loaded with a tape you want to convert to a DVD, your FireWire cable, and at least one blank regular DVD.

Connecting Your Video Source

CAPTURING STRAIGHT FROM a DV camcorder is quite easy. You will need an IEEE 1394, commonly called FireWire, cable to go from the camcorder directly to your computer. (USB, USB 2.0, and eSATA will not work.) I should stress this again because it bears repeating: if either your digital tape camcorder or your PC does not have a FireWire connection, you will *not* be able to use the DV-to-DVD Wizard.

DV camcorders usually require a mini-FireWire 4-pin connection. A desktop PC will most likely be equipped with the larger 6-pin IEEE connection. A laptop will have either the regular 6-pin or the mini-FireWire connection. No other hardware is necessary. Connect the 4-pin end of the FireWire cable to the appropriate port on your DV camcorder, called either the DV out or i.Link port. Connect the 6-pin end to the FireWire port on your PC. Many newer laptops contain the mini 4-pin FireWire connection instead of the larger 6-pin.

You can purchase several types of FireWire cables, as shown in Figure 18.1: ones with the larger 6-pin on both ends (second from the left), ones with the smaller 4-pin on both ends (second from the right), or ones with a 6-pin on one end and a 4-pin on the other. There is also a 9-pin FireWire connection (far right), but you shouldn't need that in these projects. So that you can differentiate, a more common USB cable is on the far left for reference.

Figure 18.1
Types of FireWire cables, also known as IEEE 1394 cables.

Capturing from a VCR or TV is a different story. VCRs and TVs produce analog signals that need to be converted to digital ones first. They require different cables and an analog-to-digital converter. Converters tend to be expensive, costing up to several hundred dollars. Output sources include RCA or S-video. The converter can be a card installed in your desktop computer or a separate standalone device that sits in the middle of the path between the camcorder and your computer.

Alternatively, some folks use a DV camcorder rated to have pass-through capabilities; that is, the camcorder itself is the "in-between" that connects to the analog device via RCA or S-Video connectors (see Figures 18.2 and 18.3) at one end, then into the camcorder's AV-In jack. The camcorder is then connected, in Play mode, via its mini-FireWire port to your computer. The analog source plays, its signal passes through the camcorder where the analog signal is converted to digital, and then that signal is captured on your computer into an application like the DV-to-DVD Wizard. Again, your camcorder must have this pass-through feature.

Figure 18.3
S-Video cable.

Something you should know is that VSX5 cannot control the playback of a TV or VCR. You'll need to control these from the devices themselves and click Capture at the right time, or you'll need to trim off the parts you won't want later. VSX5's capturing tools and the Wizard, on the other hand, *will* allow you to control the operation of your tape-based DV camcorder.

For the sake of simplicity and commonality, this chapter only discusses capturing from a tape DV camcorder.

Load the tape that you want to capture content from into your camcorder. Connect it via the FireWire cable to your PC, and turn your camcorder on and have it switched to Play mode.

Figure 18.2
RCA cable.

Scanning Your Content

NOW THAT YOU HAVE your hardware connected and you're ready to scan/ capture, it's time to prepare the software and begin the process of getting your content into the Wizard for your DVD.

Figure 18.4
Launching the DV-to-DVD Wizard.

I've discussed this previously, but it bears repeating. Scanning your content in the DV-to-DVD Wizard is different from actually capturing it. By quickly just scanning the scenes first, you can then decide which individual scenes you want to capture. After you decide which scenes you want, Capture records the full scenes into memory to output to your DVD. Therefore, capturing in the Wizard is actually a two-step process.

2. In the Wizard's first screen, if your camcorder is connected properly, powered on, and in Play mode, the Start Scan icon at the bottom left will be blinking; you might already see a frame from your camcorder's tape in the Wizard Preview panel. (See Figure 18.5.)

1. In VSX5, with your Final_movie still open, click on the Tools menu and select DV-to-DVD Wizard from the drop-down list. See Figure 18.4.

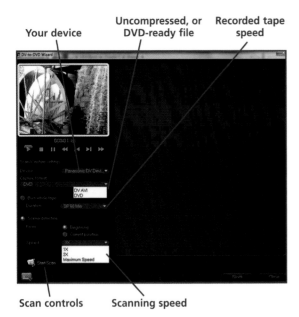

Your device — **Uncompressed, or DVD-ready file** — **Recorded tape speed**

Scan controls — **Scanning speed**

Figure 18.5
DV-to-DVD Wizard capture screen.

Tip

If the Start Scan icon is not blinking, make sure the cable is firmly connected, your camera is on and in Play mode, and you're using a FireWire connection (not USB). Try switching off and restarting your DV camcorder. If still not successful, then make sure your camcorder was manufactured in this century.

3. Your device name should be displayed below the Preview panel (again, see Figure 18.5). Under Capture format, choose either DV AVI to save uncompressed files, or choose DVD to convert to MPEG-2, thereby converting to DVD-ready files now, instead of later. I chose DV AVI. The process will work either way.

4. Choose either of the following options:

   ▶ Burn whole tape (ignore the settings under the Duration drop-down because VideoStudio will determine this setting based on the information on your DV tape).

   ▶ Scene detection, and From Beginning or Current position radio button. If Current position is selected, use the controls under the Preview panel to move your tape's position to where you want to start capturing. If you set it to From Beginning, VSX5 will move the playback of your camcorder to the start of your tape for you when you begin the scan process.

5. In the Speed drop-down list, if you want to watch the scanning process, choose 1X. If not, choose Maximum Speed. Refer back to Figure 18.5.

6. Click Start Scan. Continue until you've scanned all the scenes you might want to put onto your DVD. It's often preferable to just scan straight through, because you can delete unwanted scenes easily afterward, as you'll see in the next section.

7. After you've scanned your desired content, click Stop Scan (formally Start Scan). You should see something similar to Figure 18.6. There will be a thumbnail picture for each scene scanned. Thumbnails will be separated by when you started and stopped/paused recording your original footage. You're now ready to separate unwanted scenes.

Occasional first frames might be pixilated or blurry as you or your camera get situated when starting to record.

Figure 18.6
After scanning.

Choosing Which Content to Use

REMAINING IN THIS same screen (one of only two screens in the Wizard), you'll now select which scenes you just scanned that you want to actually capture and save to use for your DVD.

1. From the thumbnail collection that the scan process just created (on the right side; refer back to Figure 18.6), select any scene you want to preview and click the Play Selected Scene icon (see Figure 18.7). Your camera will then rewind to the start of that scene and play it again. See also the following tip.

Tip

Do not use the Playback controls under the Preview panel when previewing scanned scenes. These control the tape in your camcorder from where it last stopped and have nothing to do with playing the content you've already scanned.

Figure 18.7
Preview a scene.

Figure 18.8
Marked and unmarked scenes.

Although you can Shift-select a series of scenes and Ctrl-select a discontinuous set of scenes for other purposes, when previewing, you can only select one scene at a time to preview.

2. All scanned scenes are selected for your DVD by default and are represented by checkmarks in the lower-right corner of each thumbnail. Shift or Ctrl-select all scenes you do *not* want to include in your DVD. Then click Unmark Scene in the lower center of the window, as in Figure 18.8. You can also re-mark unmarked scenes by clicking Mark Scene.

3. Once you've selected all the scenes you want to save, click the Options icon in the lower-left corner of the Wizard window (refer to Figure 18.8 again) and select Save DV Quick Scan Digest. Save your file to your Chapter 18 lesson folder (make sure you create one first). This will create the Edit Decision List (EDL) discussed in earlier chapters. Using this Digest, the Wizard will know where to locate, on your tape, the scenes you want to capture. Again, the Wizard has yet to actually record the scenes; it has only scanned them for information.

4. To test step 3, close the Wizard, via the Close button in the far lower-right corner. Turn off your camera.

5. Quit and relaunch VSX5. Launch the Wizard. Using the same Options menu in the lower left, use the Open DV Quick Scan digest option to reopen the file you just saved. All your scenes should display. Click the Next button adjacent to the Close button. If you get an error message, click OK. This happened because your camera needs to be on so the digest can access the clips when it's ready to capture and burn them to a DVD. Turn your camera back on. Click No to the dialog box that shows up next, asking to delete the current scenes.

6. When the camera is ready, click Next again. You will be taken to the next window to add/edit a menu to your production and begin the burning process. Keep your camera connected and in the on/play position.

Formatting Your DVD

WELCOME TO THE SECOND of only two main screens in the DV-to-DVD Wizard. This work area will let you format the content you've just captured for final DVD output. Formatting will include adjusting such items as video settings and adding a theme with a menu so you can navigate the DVD when it plays on your TV or computer (see Figure 18.9).

Name your movie   Choose theme   Put DVD in drive

Edit titles   Add dates to scenes

Figure 18.9
Video formatting window in the DV-to-DVD Wizard.

1. Choose your theme from the Theme Template tray near the top. Choose your video quality from High, Standard, or Compact from the Video quality section (see Figure 18.10).

Figure 18.10
Selecting the DVD video quality.

2. If desired, choose your Video date information (see Figure 18.11). This is asking if you would like the date each clip was taken displayed as a caption on each scene, and for how long. Deselect Add as title, if you do not want to display date/time info on your video clips. I usually find it intrusive and annoying, but for certain situations it could be useful.

Figure 18.11
Adding a date caption.

CAUTION

There is an issue with adding the date information as described in step 2. The date information is currently not an option. Checking it or not will still create a DVD with the video date as your title. Entering a volume name will not make a difference either. Corel has mentioned a fix for this in a future release. Please keep that in mind.

3. Click Edit Title just above the theme templates selections to open the Edit Template Title dialog box for editing your DVD titles/menu (see Figure 18.12).

Figure 18.12
Click to access the Edit DVD title area.

4. As shown in Figure 18.13, note the Begin and End tabs at the top of this screen. In the Edit Template Title dialog, you can edit a text title at both the beginning and the end of your movie. Format the Begin and End text titles any way you wish. Click OK when you're done.

Figure 18.13
Menu formatting in the Edit Template
Title options for your DVD.

Figure 18.14
Advanced formatting options in the
DV-to-DVD Wizard.

5. You can also add chapters by scene breaks, recording date, or specific time segments. Remember that adding chapters will also create individual scenes on the DVD that can be accessed by the DVD menus. To the right of the Recording Format drop-down list, click the Advanced button. The Advanced Settings dialog box will open.

6. In the Advanced Settings dialog, and using Figure 18.14 as a guide, make sure that Auto add chapter is checked, and in this instance, select the by scene radio button. Keep everything else the same, including the Perform non-square pixel rendering option checked, and then click OK.

Here is some information regarding the Perform non-square pixel rendering option in the Advanced Settings dialog box and which you'll probably encounter elsewhere in VSX5. Pixels in the graphics world are square. A 100-pixel vertical line is the same length as a 100-pixel horizontal line on a graphics monitor. Pixels in the video world are *not* square, but rectangular. (Go figure.) If you render rectangular video pixels as square, your video will be squished from the sides and look unnatural. Perform non-square pixel rendering is checked by default and should be kept that way.

Burning Your DVD

THE FINAL STEP IN THE DV-to-DVD Wizard is to burn the actual DVD. This process is identical to the previous tasks you've learned on creating DVDs, but the feature here is included in the same window where you just formatted your DVD. These steps are included below.

1. If you haven't already, insert a blank DVD.

2. Back in the main screen, click the Burn icon in the lower right, as shown in Figure 18.15. There will be two blue progress bars to watch. The first one will show the total disc burning process. The second blue bar shows the progress of capturing each clip (see Figure 18.16). Once your DVD is finished, the tray will pop out and the dialog box shown in Figure 18.17 will appear.

Figure 18.15
Click to burn your DVD.

Figure 18.16
DVD burning progress bars.

Figure 18.17
Your DVD is done!

> **CAUTION**
>
> You can only create one DVD at a time in the Wizard. Each additional copy will need to go through the rendering process again, instead of just the disc burning process.

So, there you have it: VideoStudio X5's absolute quickest way to capture from a DV camcorder and burn to a DVD. It uses only two main screens and a couple minor ones. The most complicated part is getting your hardware set up.

Quick Quiz

1. What is the most common cable necessary to connect a digital video device to your computer? (See "Connecting Your Video Source.")

2. What setting do you need to have your DV camcorder set to for the Wizard to capture your movies? (See "Connecting Your Video Source.")

3. Why do you want to keep your video source constantly connected throughout the DV-to-DVD Wizard process? (See "Choosing Which Content to Use.")

4. Besides individual movie clips, what's an alternative to creating individual scenes on a DVD? (See "Formatting Your DVD.")

5. Why should you leave the Perform Non-Square Pixel Rendering option selected? (See "Formatting Your DVD.")

Appendix A: VSX5 Keyboard Shortcuts

THIS APPENDIX MIGHT BE useful for you to print out and keep handy. It covers all the shortcuts in VSX5 for tools and features that you can access using the keyboard instead of navigating to them with the mouse.

Menu Command Shortcuts

Keyboard Shortcut	Result
Ctrl+N	Create a new project.
Ctrl+O	Open a project.
Ctrl+S	Save a project.
Alt+Enter	Go to Project Properties.
F6	Go to Preferences.
Ctrl+Z	Undo.
Ctrl+Y	Redo.
Ctrl+C	Copy.
Ctrl+V	Paste.
Del	Delete.
F1	Go to Help.

Step Panel Shortcuts

Keyboard Shortcut	Result
Alt+C	Go to Capture step.
Alt+E	Go to Edit step.
Alt+F	Go to Effects library.
Alt+O	Go to Media library.
Alt+T	Go to Title library.
Alt+S	Go to Share step.
Up ↑	Go to the previous step.
Down ↓	Go to the next step.

Navigation Panel Shortcuts

Keyboard Shortcut	Result
F3	Set Mark-In.
F4	Set Mark-Out.
Ctrl+P	Play/Pause.
Space	Play/Pause.
Shift+Play button	Play the currently selected clip.
Home	Return to the starting segment or cue.
Ctrl+H	Go Home.
End	Move to the end segment or cue.
Ctrl+E	Go to End.
B	Return to previous frame.
F	Proceed to next frame.
Ctrl+R	Repeat.
Ctrl+L	Adjust system volume.
Ctrl+I	Split video.
Tab	Toggle between trim handles and Scrubber.
Enter	Press Tab or Enter to switch to the right trim handle if the left trim handle is active.
Left arrow	Use the left arrow key to move to the previous frame if you pressed Tab or Enter to make the trim handles or Scrubber tool active.
Right arrow	Use the right arrow key to move to the next frame if you pressed Tab or Enter to make the trim handles or Scrubber tool active.

Keyboard Shortcut	Result
Esc	Press Esc to deactivate the trim handles or Scrubber tool if you pressed Tab or Enter to activate and toggle between them.

Timeline Shortcuts

Keyboard Shortcut	Result
Ctrl+A	Selects all clips on the Timeline. Selects all characters in the onscreen Edit mode (single title).
Ctrl+X	Cuts selected characters in the onscreen Edit mode (single title).
Shift-click	Selects multiple clips in the same track. (To select multiple clips in the Library, Shift-click or Ctrl-click the clips.)
Left arrow	Select the previous clip on the Timeline.
Right arrow	Select the next clip on the Timeline.
+ / −	Zoom in/out.
Ctrl+Right arrow	Scroll forward.
Ctrl+Left arrow	Scroll backward.
Ctrl+Up/Page Up	Scroll up.
Ctrl+Down/Page Down	Scroll down.
Home	Move to the start of the Timeline.
End	Move to the end of the Timeline.
Ctrl+H	Return to the previous segment.
Ctrl+E	Go to the next segment.

Multi-Trim Video Shortcuts

Keyboard Shortcut	Result
Del	Delete.
F3	Set Mark-In.
F4	Set Mark-Out.
F5	Go backward in the clip.
F6	Go forward in the clip.
Esc	Cancel.

Layout Settings Shortcuts

Keyboard Shortcut	Result
F7	Switch to default.
Ctrl+1	Switch to Custom #1.
Ctrl+2	Switch to Custom #2.
Ctrl+3	Switch to Custom #3.
Alt+1	Save to Custom #1.
Alt+2	Save to Custom #2.
Alt+3	Save to Custom #3.

Other Shortcuts

Action	Result
Esc	Stops the capturing, recording, and rendering processes, or closes a dialog box without making changes. If you switched to a full-screen preview, press Esc to return to the Corel VideoStudio Pro workspace.
Double-click a transition in the Transition library	Automatically inserts a transition into the first empty transition slot between two clips. Repeating this process inserts a transition into the next empty transition slot.

Appendix B: Exploring Useful Websites

I'VE COME ACROSS SOME very useful websites in my videography research while writing this book. I hope you can take advantage of the knowledge these contain, just as I have. Some sites will contain content more current than others.

VideoStudio

Corel's VideoStudio Pro X5 website:
www.corel.com/corel/product/index.jsp?pid=prod4760101

Corel's VideoStudio Pro X5 Ultimate website:
www.corel.com/corel/product/index.jsp?pid=
prod4760101&cid=catalog50008&segid=6700256

**Corel User to User Web Board
(http://forum.corel.com/EN/):** A forum to ask questions and get answers. You must create a free account to ask questions, but the response time is usually very quick.

Corel User to User Web Board on Corel VideoStudio:
http://forum.corel.com/EN/viewforum.php?f=1&sid=
b2eb71cd9a3df0e5a7fdb26c5d3e28d8

Corel's VideoStudio Pro Tutorials on YouTube:
www.youtube.com/watch?v=ISsjhNLCjUY&feature=
results_main&playnext=1&list=PLDE7D821DA243DE74

Creating a custom mask frame:
www.youtube.com/watch?v=MqTtHeZhLN8

Corel video on Vimeo: http://vimeo.com/corelvideo

VideoStudio video tutorials you can purchase:
http://videostudiotutorials.com/

Custom VSX4-compatible music: www.smartsound.com/

NewBlue FX: www.newbluefx.com/

Videomaker magazine with buying guides and videography tips: www.videomaker.com

Mercalli Video Effects: www.prodad.com/

Corel's PaintShop Photo Pro

Corel's website on PaintShop Photo Pro: www.corel.com/
servlet/Satellite/us/en/Product/1184951547051#tabview=
tab0

Corel's PaintShop Photo Pro YouTube Tutorial Channel:
www.youtube.com/PaintShopPhotoPro#p/c/
66BE117109B1AEA2

General Videography Knowledge and Tools

CNET is an excellent source for technical knowledge, product reviews, and comparison shopping: www.cnet.com/

Camcorder buying guides: http://reviews.cnet.com/
camcorder-buying-guide/
www.pcworld.com/article/125646/how_to_buy_a_
digital_camcorder.html
www.camcorderinfo.com/content/Beginers-
Camcorder-Buying-Guide.htm
www.smart-review.com/camcorderbuyingguide.html
www.macworld.com/article/1139834/hdcamcorders.html

Reference website for MPEG: www.mpeg.org/

Dolby Laboratories: www.dolby.com/

JPEG Committee: www.jpeg.org/

How to convert MPEG files to other video files:
www.rersoft.com/mpg-video-file/

How to convert iPod audio files into other file formats:
http://docs.info.apple.com/article.html?artnum=93123

Wallace and Gromit Claymation:
www.wallaceandgromit.com/

Article on Side-by-Side 3D: www.best-3dtvs.com/
what-is-side-by-side-3d

Online encyclopedia: www.wikipedia.org/

WebM: www.webmproject.org

Video Utilities

Google Translate: www.translate.google.com

Hide your desktop utility:
www.stardock.com/products/fences/

Index